METROPOLITAN COMMUNITIES

METROPOLITAN COMMUNITIES

NEW FORMS OF URBAN SUB-COMMUNITIES
EDITED BY JOSEPH BENSMAN AND ARTHUR J. VIDICH

A NEW YORK TIMES BOOK

NEW VIEWPOINTS
A Division of Franklin Watts, Inc.
New York
1975

Library of Congress Cataloging in Publication Data

Bensman, Joseph, comp.
  Metropolitan communities.

  "A New York times book."
  Essays selected from the New York times.
  Bibliography: p.
  1. Cities and towns—United States—Addresses,
essays, lectures. 2. Suburbs—United States—
Addresses, essays, lectures. 3. United States—Social
conditions—1960– —Addresses, essays, lectures.
I. Vidich, Arthur J., joint comp. II. New York times.
III. Title.
HT334.U5B44   301.36'2'0973   74-11393
ISBN 0-531-05572-8

*The publishers are grateful to the contributors
herein for permission to reprint their articles.*

CONTENTS

INTRODUCTION

The dominant tradition in the study of the community has focused upon the decline or the eclipse of the community. Classical sociologists tended to conceptualize in many different ways two basic polar types of communities. These conceptualizations included community versus society, folk versus urban communities, *Gemeinschaft* versus *Gesellschaft*, mechanical versus organic societies and sacred versus secular societies. In doing so they usually focused on the deep sense of emotional commitment of person-to-person and the strong sense of identity that existed in the isolated small rural community as compared with the rationality, impersonality, isolation and anomie—i.e., normlessness—of the urban society. Moreover, they pointed to the decline of older forms of emotional expression as the isolated, spatially distinct ecological community was overpowered by large-scale urbanism, industrialization, mass institutions and centralized bureaucracies. To a large extent, this over-all focus reflects an underlying reality: rural society has been deeply penetrated by the institutions of urban, industrial society. However, this has not meant that the community has disappeared.

To the contrary, because of a basic reconstitution of social structure supporting and constraining personal and social life in urban society, the forms of community have radically changed. The historic folk societies developed their central characteristics because they were spatially isolated from other societies and because they were small. Their separation from other societies and the resultant density of internal personal relations allowed them to develop distinctive cultures which supported and reinforced the individual, even as he was submerged in and by this community culture.

What is important here is that the spatial isolation of the community allowed for the development of distinctive communities and created cultural, organizational, ceremonial and ritual limits on the behavior of the community members. Those limits provided cultural and objective bases for their activities. Thus, individuals were not plagued by the problem of choice because little choice was allowed, and conflicts in value were limited because the primitive community tended to have an overarching hierarchy of values. As a result, a person was permitted few choices, and so had few opportunities to be an "individual" making a choice. He could not experience himself as having a strong sense of his own individuality and subjectivity.

The growth of the metropolis, the gigantic city, destroyed the territorial limitations placed upon individuals. They were exposed to vast varieties of stimuli, of values, of choices and of cultures, so that in fact few external limits were placed on them. In theory, the absence of such limits might (as was conjectured in classical theories) cause a sense of normlessness, anxiety, alienation and indecision, and could lead some individuals to the point of suicide or other forms of extreme pathology. At the same time, for others who were strong enough to profit from the variety of values, cultures and choices offered by the city, the absence of limits could lead to a sense of freedom, liberation and opportunity.

Despite the negative theories of urbanism, and despite the fact that cities and their residents have many problems, it is clear that cities and urban areas have survived and continue to grow. At least up to now, the existence of urban problems and pathologies has not constituted a limit on urban growth. We suggest in this volume that the reason why cities have flourished, even though they provide little sense of spatial limits and order for the human personality, is that within the urban area city dwellers have constructed communities which serve the personal and psychological functions once supplied by the isolated rural community.

But these new urban communities are voluntary in nature, based on a choice of dwelling within the framework of selected values, institutions and cultures rather than on residential space per se. Here the locality where one lives is less an accident of birth than an individual choice. Thus selection of place of residence is based on the known characteristics—ethnic, class, cultural or social—of a neighborhood. Of course, income patterns of residential segregation and the sense of being accepted or excluded by a neighborhood are elements in that choice, but this means that the choices that others make in part determine the choice that an individual makes. However, those who make such choices create their own neighborhoods and by their selection of activities in the city-at-large, and by their patterns of consumption and preference, create an almost infinite variety of communities.

In the following essays, selected from *The New York Times,* we have attempted to present some of the major types of communities that are characteristic of contemporary American society. In selecting the essays we have been guided by a desire to emphasize the specific and concrete social and cultural content of these communities.

As background to our discussions of the community, we describe the major trends which have accounted for the urbanism and suburbanization of the United States, and we point to the forms these trends have taken since World War II. We have specifically related the trends to the demographic and economic factors that have contributed to the decline of the rural community and the dominance of urbanization and suburbanization.

In our presentation of the urban community in Parts two and three, we have attempted to describe the traditional forms of urban communities. These include class and ethnic communities, both as separate phenomena and as they are, and have been, interrelated in American history. Particular attention is focused on the increasing urbanization of the black and Spanish-speaking populations of the metropolis, and in Part four we examine how these groups affect older immigrant groups now into their second, third and subsequent generations in America and in the city.

Not only are crime, ethnic tension and conflict generic problems of the process of urbanization, but responses to them represent new bases for community organization and reorganization. Thus we point to the re-creation of ethnic communities, both at a neighborhood level and at larger institutional and organizational levels. The politicization of ethnic and class communities *in a direct and open form* is a recent trend in American urban life. We present these issues in Part five.

The newer politicization of the community has been aided and abetted by the creation of administrative communities which are a product of philanthropic activity, Federal and municipal legislation and a new activism on the part of ethnics, youth and the new and old middle classes.

The urban environment, simply because of its total size and the size of its institutional components, permits the development of both total communities and institutional communities whose particular culture and preferred or required behavioral style become the basis of a characteristic way of life. The dominance of a neighborhood by one institution can create a counter-community whose *raison d'être* may well be its opposition to an organization, institution, another group or the government.

Beyond this, individuals in their pursuit of a single value or a cluster of values may organize activities, institutions and ways of life that, in their inclusiveness and commitment, become communities. Thus a single value, voluntarily accepted, may provide a fabric and texture of life that permit almost any variety and range of the total human experience. These newer forms of community need not, as we have indicated, be based on spatial isolation: they can be based, in addition to adherence to common values, on availability of transportation, communication and effectiveness of organization. All these newer community forms are presented in Part five.

The materials covered in our discussion of the community have some limitations of which the reader should be aware. We have not attempted to cover occupational or professional communities simply because they ought to be treated separately. Our treatment of upper-class communities does not, we feel, provide sufficient information as to the economic basis of class or to its political consequence. Again, such a task is worthy of separate treatment, whose outlines we have suggested in our book *The New American Society* (Quadrangle, 1971). Finally, in our treatment of administrative communities, we have not presented in detail the legal and legislative history of the laws and administrative policies that have made such communities possible.

At the same time, we feel that only in journalistic descriptions of the urban community is it possible to see in detail the variety, the specificity, the novelty and the turbulence of urban life. Journalists as field observers are able to capture the vitality of the city, and to record new directions in community development in advance of most social science. They are able to present their material without the abstraction that all too frequently impedes recognition of the underlying social reality.

Because these are *New York Times* articles, there is inevitably some bias of selection in favor of trends in the New York scene. Wherever possible, however, we have endeavored to indicate the universality of those trends in the development of the American community. Moreover, we do believe that urbanization is a long-term, worldwide and universal development in which problems similar to those now best illustrated in the largest urban areas become characteristic of the entire urban world. We have indicated these general problems and trends in our introductions that precede each of the five parts.

PART ONE

OVER-ALL TRENDS

Urbanism, the growth of the city, is one of the oldest phenomena in human history. Certainly the Jewish prophets and Plato protested the growth of urbanism and urban vices in a world that was primarily local and rural. But the process of urbanism has continued throughout history despite a five hundred year interruption during the middle ages. Since the end of the middle ages the rate of urbanization has increased almost to the point where it is now difficult to mention rural society in the industrial nations as a significant fact. We live in an urban world in which agriculture in its most developed segments is almost as industrialized as non-agricultural industries. Less than 5 percent of the total labor force is engaged in the production of agricultural commodities and a significant part of this 5 percent is living in rural poverty. The percentage of the population that live in rural areas is now about 26 percent and many of these commute to work in industrial and urban settings. Gigantic urban complexes, central cities and their satellite cities and suburbs which often merge indistinguishably into each other contain almost three-quarters of the total population of the United States. Thus, despite the cries of overcrowding by the ecologists, 7 percent of the total land area contains 70 percent of the population, while the vast share of American land is relatively unpopulated. Rural and small town areas in America decline and stagnate.

The population concentration in urban areas is a product of a continuous scientific and technical revolution in agriculture which reduces the size of the labor force necessary to farm profitably. Moreover, because of the capital requirements necessary for industrialized agriculture, agriculture is profitable only to organized large scale commercial production units. In part, federal agricultural policy has encouraged such growth. The most dramatic technological changes demonstrating this process occurred after World War II with the large scale use of the Rust mechanical cotton picking machine and the recent application of mechanical tobacco picking devices which have displaced large numbers of black agricultural workers in the southern and border states. This displacement of black labor has intensified the migration of blacks to northern, southern and western cities. In previous decades, migration to the cities was more a product of the pull of new industrialization in the cities than the push of the industrialization of agriculture. Both northern and southern cities are faced with the problem of absorbing displaced agricultural populations whose migration to the city was not based primarily on the demand for additional unskilled and semi-skilled workers in the urban labor force.

In addition, agriculture and agricultural areas have been developed as nonprofit making gentlemanly farming hobbies frequently linked to tax exemptions (for the very rich) and as leisure time escapes for the middle classes and youth. For the rest, rural poverty and dependency becomes a major area for government supported poverty and welfare programs.

Through the first half of the 19th century, the growth of the city was concentrated in the central city. Suburbs have always been the residential area of the rich and the upper middle classes who sought to escape the noise, dirt and contamination brought to the city by its very congestion and by the stigma of the new immigrant working classes who did the basic work of the city. As the population of cities increased, the rate of growth of suburbanism increased at increasing rates. By 1960 the rate of suburban growth exceeded that of the central cities and of urbanism as a whole. These trends up through the 1970 census are conveniently summarized in the article by Dennis Wrong, *Portrait of a Decade*.

As a result of this process, the central cities and especially their inner-core have been increasingly occupied by the newest migrants to the cities. These include displaced southern blacks, Puerto Ricans, Chicanos and other South Americans as well as whites displaced from marginal agricultural areas. For example, six major cities have black majorities and eight others are more than 40 percent black. Moreover one-third of all American blacks are found in 15 major cities.

The new migrants occupy to a large extent the same slums as did earlier migrants from Europe some of whom have left the slums for the suburbs and middle income areas in the city while others have been "forced to move" as the slums have grown in size and population due to the volume of the new migration. Since the new populations have not been able to profit from economic opportunities within the city, much of the central cities have deteriorated and become a new source of urban blight. Simultaneously, the migration of middle and upper classes to the suburbs has shrunk the tax and income base of city government at a time when the need for additional taxes to support the poor has increased. As we shall see the problem of the absorption and support of the new migrants is a basic problem for all urban development.

The growth of the suburbs is a product of the new affluence of the middle classes especially after World War II. With this new middle-class affluence, the children and grandchildren of urban immigrants have attempted to escape the congestion of the city. The growth of the suburbs has also been supported and shaped by subsidized, super-highway construction which makes the suburbs available as residential areas to at least 50 percent of the suburban residents who work in the cities. As the suburbs have grown, however, an increasing percentage of suburban employees have begun to work in new suburban industries which have followed the labor force into the suburbs.

These new industries tend to require skilled, professional and managerial workers and not unskilled or semi-skilled workers. In addition, the high cost of suburban housing maintained, in part, by zoning regulations have kept all but a handful of blacks out of the suburbs.

The great expansion of suburban areas was done without plan. In each metropolitan area, a host of different levels of government organizations had separate jurisdiction over essentially one population. Large scale "developments" by single entrepreneurs co-exist with luxury homes and piecemeal development. Transportation facilities, apart from the main arteries, have produced highly urban traffic congestion, while schools, shopping, cultural and civic amenities have lagged behind residential and population growth. As land in suburban areas has become saturated, the cost of the amenities of suburban life has increased and tax problems have begun to harry the suburban dweller. As a result, the suburbanite, through his political representative, has often been unwilling to provide the tax support necessary to sustain the needed financial support to the central city. Thus an economic and political war between the rural areas, the central cities and suburbia has emerged as a major political issue in American politics. Each contending group through its representatives argues its case on the grounds of overwhelming need. Up to this point no one has found a formula for the political or practical solution to these problems.

PORTRAIT OF A DECADE

by DENNIS H. WRONG

The 1970 census will show that the United States has a population some-what in excess of 205 million, an increase of about 25 million since the last census was taken in 1960. This will hardly come as a revelation, for sample surveys taken by the Bureau of the Census since the last complete count pro-vide an accurate annual record of broad changes in the American population. The question has even been raised as to whether the nation might not dispense with a laborious head count every 10 years and substitute the cheaper and ac-tually more reliable sample surveys to keep track of population growth and change. However, only a complete count can provide the detailed knowledge of individual states, counties, cities and smaller areas desired by many users of the census for political, commercial and scientific purposes. Indeed the pri-mary reason for taking a census as prescribed by the Constitution is to dis-cover shifts in the population of Congressional districts before reapportioning seats in the House of Representatives.

When the results of the 1970 census are finally tabulated and submitted to Congress in roughly eight months, they will doubtless contain a few sur-prises—perhaps the kind of unexpected finding produced by special censuses of Los Angeles and Cleveland in 1965. Those studies disclosed that the dis-tricts of Watts and Hough had experienced net losses of population since 1960 and that an insignificant number of new arrivals had come to Watts and Hough from outside the Los Angeles and Cleveland metropolitan areas. Since both sections were the scenes of black rioting in the middle sixties, the conven-tional association of urban racial tensions with heavy black in-migration and resultant overcrowding obviously must be qualified.

Even though the census is likely to disclose little that is not already known about the broad outlines of recent population changes, coming as it does at the end of one decade and the beginning of another, it provides the full demo-graphic context in which to locate the major events of the recent past and suggests the limits framing future social, economic and political trends. Our tendency to "periodize" American history into decades, each with its distinc-tive flavor, has no doubt been accentuated by the fact that censuses have been taken in all years ending in zero since 1790, though perhaps the founding fathers instituted the practice because they were also prone to the periodizing habit.

The nineteen-sixties are generally regarded as a particularly troubled and turbulent decade. And for perhaps the very first time in American history, the turbulence is widely believed to have resulted, at least in part, from the sheer growth of the population. Thus, rather more significance than usual is likely to be attributed to the 1970 census figures on the size, growth and growth rate of the population. In the past the continuing growth of the American population has been viewed with indifference or complacency where "bigger" has not actually been equated with "better." Today, however, fears are widely expressed that population increase is the fundamental cause of our major social problems and that America is at last approaching, if it has not already arrived at, a condition of overpopulation.

Concern over pollution and the ecological crisis is invariably linked to the pressures of continuing population growth. "Zero Population Growth" clubs have been created at some colleges. Several major political figures who have passed the Vietnam test (otherwise they would hardly be on campus) have been booed by student audiences for "copping out" when they have refused to commit themselves to laws restricting all couples to no more than two children. The proponents of a number of popular causes, initially espoused on a variety of moral and ideological grounds, frequently appeal to the specter of overpopulation as an additional argument on their behalf. Equal salaries and wages for women, liberalized abortion laws, tighter marriage laws and easier divorce laws, the distribution of contraceptives to coeds, greater tolerance of homosexuality, communal living arrangements to replace the traditional family, even the fears of genocide expressed by black militants have been justified with references to the "runaway" growth of the American population.

When I recently suggested at a campus symposium that alarm over population growth was excessive and that there were perhaps more immediately effective ways of combating environmental deterioration than prohibiting births, another panelist—a former editor of *Ramparts,* no less—accused me of gross irresponsibility, to the applause of the audience. The gist of my speech was that the population problems of the United States stemmed largely from population redistribution—in effect, from the "urban explosion"—rather than from sheer growth, in contrast to the nations of the Third World, where the need for eliminating rapid growth was a primary one if they were to achieve substantial economic progress.

My critic, who announced that he had difficulty restraining his temper while listening to me, maintained that my distinction between the situation of the

United States and that of the overcrowded countries of the Third World reflected an "obsolete nationalism" if not "imperialism." He went on to cite scarifying figures on the worldwide per capita consumption of resources and the increased strain on them from every addition of a new child to the population. As I pointed out in my rejoinder, his vague and apocalyptic prophecies of worldwide famine and collapse before the end of the century ommitted any reference to the decline of the birth rate in America (and elsewhere) or to the reduction in desired family size reported by contemporary American women in recent surveys. He obviously felt that it was complacent of me at best and immoral at worst even to differentiate descriptively between the demographic condition of the United States and that of the Third World.

Later, an earnest young woman announced that she intended to contribute to a better world by refusing to bear more than one child, by selling her car and taking up hitchhiking and by giving up the use of detergents. She was congratulated by one of the speakers for truly "living her politics."

To what extent will the results of the census provide support for these fears? The answer, unfortunately, is unlikely to be clear-cut. The population increase of 25 million since 1960 is the second largest between censuses in the history of the nation, surpassed only by a jump of nearly 29 million in the nineteen-fifties. But viewed in relation to the population base from the preceding census, the increase in the sixties comes to just under 14 per cent, which—although it is nearly double the 7.2 per cent increase in the Depression-ridden thirties—is the second lowest intercensal increase on record. By 1969 the average increase of the American population was about 1 per cent a year, or less than half the world rate. These figures unmistakably confirm that the "baby boom" of the nineteen-forties and fifties, to which many of the alarmists are belatedly reacting, has come to an end. Yet the lower rates of increase are still well above zero, and the ever-growing size of the base population makes the apparently moderate growth rates somewhat deceptive if we translate the percentages into numbers of people added to the population each year or each decade. (It's like the compound interest formula on savings accounts.)

Censuses, which give us snapshot pictures of the size and composition of the population once every 10 years, cannot by themselves provide information on the continuous changes the population undergoes as a result of births, deaths, immigration and emigration. The key to changes in the growth rate in the United States, as in other relatively advanced industrial countries, is the trend of the birth rate, which is determined by relating the number of births recorded by the National Office of Vital Statistics in a given period to a base population derived from the most recent census.

The slower rate of increase of the American population in the sixties reflects a decline of the birth rate that began in 1957. Yet the present age distribution of the population indicates that proportionately larger numbers of people, and specifically of women, will enter the age groups from which parents are recruited in the seventies rather than in the early sixties. These potential parents are, of course, the products of the "baby boom" after World War II. For example, infants born in 1957, the all-time banner year for American births, reached the age of 13 by 1970 and can be expected to have commenced reproducing themselves by 1980. The sheer numbers now entering the parental ages, a consequence of the high fertility of the fifties, will raise the birth rate in the decade to come even if these young people elect to have fewer children per capita than their parents had.

Thus, the concern over a continued population increase is justified for the immediate future. However, the very depth and extent of this concern, particularly on college campuses, suggests a disposition on the part of those voicing it to avoid the "moderate-sized"—that is, three- or four-child—families of the fifties. The enormous power of the mass media combined with the exposure of larger numbers of young people to the culture of the campus make it altogether possible that decisions on family size and the spacing of children will be directly influenced by fears of overpopulation *before* the more painful consequences of expanding numbers are actually experienced. A zero rate of population growth, therefore, appears within the range of possibility before the end of the century, if not by the end of the nineteen-eighties. Moreover, just as forecasts of "incipient population decline" continued to be advanced by demographers and other observers in the nineteen-forties *after* the rise in fertility was well under way, so the present concern about overpopulation comes *after* a trend toward smaller families has become manifest. The American crude birth rate (the number of births per thousand population) in 1968 was the lowest ever recorded, even lower than in the Depression.

No doubt the very rapid dissemination of "the pill" in the early sixties greatly increased general awareness of the degree to which family size is subject to personal choice. And with the widespread belief in a direct connection between population growth and environmental damage, the choice is readily converted into a moral issue, a matter of social conscience. Americans have used contraception to restrict the number of children they produce for nearly a century, but the invention of new and immensely effective contraceptive methods, together with alarm over the effects of burgeoning population on the environment and the "quality of life," may for the first time have made total population growth a consideration influencing the child-bearing decisions of millions of people. Nor are current anxieties about the medical effects of the pill likely to counteract this new awareness, for alternative contraceptive methods remain available. The American birth rate, in fact, began its decline several years before the mass marketing of the pill and even more years before intrauterine devices (I.U.D.s) became available.

In spite of the concern over the increase in the total number of Americans, the United States remains relatively sparsely populated, ranking behind Britain, Switzerland, Mexico and the Philippines—none of them considered strikingly overcrowded—in population density, or the average number of persons per square mile. The impression of overcrowding in the United States gains plausibility less from the over-all increase in numbers than from the growing concentration of people in certain regions, states and communities. In the nineteen-sixties, as in the past, internal migration made an important, though reduced, contribution to changes in the distribution of the American population. Migration, moreover, has a "multiplier effect": because most migrants are young adults, they raise the birth rate of the areas to which they move and lower it in the areas they vacate.

California gained about 3.7 million people in the sixties, more than twice the roughly 1.5 million gained by Texas and New York, while Nevada, Arizona and Alaska showed the largest percentage increases among the states. Five states—North and South Dakota, Mississippi, West Virginia and Wyoming—experienced sufficiently large net out-migrations to result in small population declines. In general, the West and the Southwest continued to attract migrants from the rest of the country, while the North Central region suffered net out-migration. Between 1960 and 1968 fully one out of every three counties in the United States actually *lost* population.

Most of these counties were in a belt reaching from the agricultural Middle West southward to Texas and Louisiana and eastward across the South to Georgia and South Carolina, and most of them have been losing population ever since the thirties. Nearly *half* of all counties lost population in the fifties. The drop to one-third in the sixties reflects a general slowing up of migration. These facts sharply contradict prevalent visions of the inexorable filling up of the open spaces as a result of a population explosion. Actually, there is *more* open space in the United States today than there was a generation ago, and— even allowing for uninhabitable desert and mountain areas that were once rangeland or sites of mining towns—much of it is actual or potential farmland in the middle of the country.

The most consequential changes of location made by Americans are movements from rural areas and small towns and cities to metropolitan areas. The "urban explosion," rather than a general "population explosion," produces or contributes to the traffic jams, the clogging of transportation facilities, the strain on public services, air and water pollution and the defilement and disappearance of open countryside which create the sense of crisis and claustrophobia felt these days by so many Americans.

The term "urban" is no longer meaningful insofar as it suggests those clearly demarcated built-up areas we call "cities," for the bulk of the growth of the urban population since the twenties, and especially since World War II, has been in the suburban rings outside the central cities. The Bureau of the Census now distinguishes in its tabulations between *metropolitan* and *non-metropolitan* areas, the latter including both farm and non-farm residents of what were formerly called "rural areas" as well as all residents of cities and towns of less than 50,000. The shifts of population from non-metropolitan to metropolitan areas and from central cities to suburbs within metropolitan areas constitute the major changes in American population distribution.

The sixties witnessed a continuation of the trends of the fifties, but at a slower rate. Metropolitan areas grew more rapidly than the national population, but their growth was greatest in the suburbs. The over-all metropolitan rate of growth was roughly 14.5 per cent, as compared with 26.5 per cent in the fifties, a growth rate about 2 per cent higher than that of the population as a whole. Just under two-thirds of our population now lives in metropolitan areas. The metropolitan growth was concentrated in the suburbs, which increased by 26.5 per cent, as compared with a growth rate of 49 per cent for the fifties. By the end of the sixties, central cities had replaced non-metropolitan areas as the slowest-growing areas. Their increase was only 1.3 per cent and such cities as Buffalo, Cleveland, Des Moines, Louisville, New Haven and Rochester were shown to have lost population by special censuses taken since 1960. The 1970 census will undoubtedly disclose similar declines in many more cities.

The suburbs and the real or alleged characteristics of suburbanites received a lot of attention, mostly unfavorable, from sociologists and social critics in the fifties. Although the movement to the suburbs continued throughout the sixties, attention shifted to the problems of the central cities and the economic plight of their residents. The reason, of course, is primarily race: the growing concentration of Negroes in the central cities, replacing white migrants to the suburbs and becoming a larger proportion of the city population when whites move out. Which trend—black immigration or white out-migration—predominated in specific cities will not be ascertainable until the detailed tabulations of the new census become available.

By 1969, however, more than half of the total Negro population, 55.2 per cent, lived in central cities. Washington, D.C., was still the only large city with more Negroes (69 per cent) than whites, but in Newark the population was almost evenly divided, and the proportion of blacks in the populations of

Baltimore, New Orleans, Memphis and Atlanta was estimated at 40 per cent or slightly more in the late sixties. Except for Newark, the only northern city close to 40 per cent was Detroit, which had 39 per cent. Perhaps the racial battleground will shift back to the South in the decade ahead, but this time it is likely to be centered in the urban South.

The gross changes since 1960 in the distribution of the races by residence were not, however, as great as they are often believed to have been. The proportion of the total white population living in central cities declined between 1960 and 1969 by about 4 per cent (from 30 to 25.8), while the suburban proportion went up by 5 per cent (from 33.1 to 38); the proportion of the total black population in central cities increased by nearly 4 per cent (from 51.5 to 55.2) and in the suburbs by just over 1 per cent (from 13.2 to 14.7). Since 1966 the central cities have been losing an average of half a million persons a year, the result of a net white out-migration exceeding the growth of the black population. One-third of the black increase is a result of net in-migration, the remainder of natural increase (the excess of births over deaths). As these figures indicate, the trend toward racial polarization between the cities and the suburbs, which became clearly established nearly 30 years ago, continues relentlessly in spite of widespread alarm and policies aimed at arresting it.

Yet since 1968 there have appeared for the first time signs of a sharply accelerated movement of Negroes to the suburbs, especially the inner suburbs, along with a decline in the rate of growth of black populations in central cities. The numbers involved are still small, but the new trend may be significant. What its continuation might imply for future race relations is uncertain. It could reduce the polarization of white suburbs and black cities, but it could also extend the pattern of polarization outward from the central city to embrace the inner suburban rings as well.

The findings of the new census on the situation of Negroes, especially on social and economic differentials between whites and Negroes, are likely to receive closer and more critical scrutiny than any of the other conclusions. Even the taking of the census and the procedures followed have become a sensitive issue. A few black militant groups urged their followers to refuse to answer the census takers' questions. But a far larger number of black leaders counseled cooperation, promoted the slogan "It pays to be counted" and promised vigilance in overseeing the performance of the Bureau of the Census to ensure a full and honest count.

Sensitive to charges of underenumeration of Negroes, the bureau was determined this year to avoid any repetition of the 1960 census, in which, according to its own estimate, as many as 14 per cent of all Negro males (as against only 2 per cent of white males) were not counted. But since the new census was taken at the end of March, there have been complaints from black community groups that many blacks in the big-city areas were missed again or were unable to complete the mail questionnaire sent to residents of large metropolitan areas. The tabulation of the census has, in fact, been delayed while the bureau investigates these and other complaints.

The issue is crucial because the poorest and most deprived blacks are the most likely to be missed. The statistics would therefore falsely upgrade the socio-economic status of Negroes and understate their relative disadvantages vis-a-vis whites. Such errors would, of course, be magnified in districts with large black populations.

However, even if substantial underenumeration of poor urban Negroes is avoided—or if it is generally believed to have been avoided—the census reports on the condition of Negroes are certain to be subject to varying and conflicting interpretations. During the sixties the Bureau of the Census, in collaboration with the Bureau of Labor Statistics, issued periodic reports on the characteristics of the Negro population. The most recent of these, "The Social and Economic Status of Negroes in the United States, 1969," has attracted some attention from public officials, journalists and social scientists. These findings will be checked against the more exhaustive and detailed breakdowns of the complete census.

This 1969 report showed that Negroes were, as they had been in 1960, about 11 per cent of the population. Their fertility rates were somewhat higher than those of whites, but had followed the same upward and downward movements since 1960. Fifty-five per cent of all Negroes still lived in the South, an 8 per cent decline since 1960. Net migration of Negroes out of the South was still considerable, but continued to decline from the peak volume of the nineteen-forties.

Negro median family income was, by 1968, 60 per cent of the white level, a 6 per cent increase in the ratio since 1960 in the South; however, Negro income was slightly more than half of white income. In the other regions it ranged from 69 per cent in the Northeast to 80 per cent in the West. In 1968 one-third of all nonwhite families had incomes of $8,000 or more, as compared with only 15 per cent in 1960; the proportions for whites were 58 per cent in 1968 and 39 per cent in 1960, indicating a slightly higher relative gain for whites. On the other hand, 29 per cent of Negro families had incomes below the poverty line ($3,553 for a nonfarm family of four in 1968) as opposed to only 8 per cent of white families; in 1959 the proportions were 48 per cent for Negroes and 15 per cent for whites. The decline in poverty was somewhat greater for whites.

The unemployment rate in 1969 for nonwhites was the lowest since the Korean war, but was still double the white rate. Between 1960 and 1969 the percentage of workers in highly skilled occupations increased more rapidly for Negroes and other races than for whites, and nonwhites also experienced a greater decrease in persons employed as laborers, domestic servants and in farm occupations. In spite of large relative gains, nonwhites were still represented in the two most skilled and best paying occupational groups (professionals and managers) by less than half their proportion of the total population. In education, the percentage of Negroes enrolled at every level from nursery school to college increased sharply during the sixties. The percentage of Negro males aged 25 to 29 who had completed four or more years of high school rose from 36 in 1960 to 60 in 1969; the comparable figures for whites were 63 and 78.

I might go on and summarize data on housing, living conditions and health, the family, military status and voting participation. But they tell a similar story of absolute black gains in all areas, some relatively greater than for whites, others relatively lesser, and the persistence of wide differentials favoring whites in most areas. The fact that the circumstances of blacks have improved, however modestly and starting from whatever low levels, needs stressing because I have found that the presentation of the statistical evidence is greeted by students—and not only by students—with amazement and incredulity. Lacking any historical perspective and having so recently "discovered" the unfavorable position of blacks in American society, students find it very hard to believe that any progress can have taken place, especially during the years of the iniquitous Vietnam war. Suspicious of statistical abstraction by contrast with "lived experience" and raised in comfortable suburbs where there was little visible evidence of poverty or the squalor of black ghettos, they often seem to feel that the sheer existence of the latter refutes any quantitative indications of improvement. There is also the tendency, common to liberals as well as those students who define themselves as radicals, to evaluate the present by the ideal standard of full equality, whereas statistical trends inevitably compare the present with the past. As a result, one finds a strong disposition to dismiss the evidence in toto as an apologia for evil, or even as a pack of self-serving lies put out by the "Establishment."

Few of the advances made are remarkable, and the "glass of water" parable clearly applies to them; optimists may declare the glass "half full" while pessimists are at liberty to describe it as "half empty." Both, of course, are right. One may also select from the statistics to stress for polemical purposes either absolute differences between blacks and whites, relative differences or unequal rates of change in a wide variety of areas. All demographic data lend themselves to such manipulation. From the standpoint of proclaimed aspirations, rhetorical commitments and time and energy—if not money—invested at all levels of government as well as by private organizations in efforts to right the historical injustice of the Negro's position in American society, one may readily conclude that a mountain labored throughout the sixties to bring forth a mouse. Moreover, some gains registered by blacks may owe less to policies adopted than to unplanned consequences of other, possibly transitory, circumstances such as a temporarily favorable age distribution among Negroes or the effects on the economy and on employment of the Vietnam war.

Yet there *have* been real gains, and the rate of improvement *has* quickened. The record hardly indicates total neglect, whether "benign" or otherwise. It is unlikely that the fuller data to be provided by the new census will reverse or even greatly modify this general conclusion.

In general, except for the beginning of a trend toward relative improvement in the position of Negroes in several areas, the demographic profile of the nineteen-sixties shows no dramatic reversals of direction either in the overall growth pattern of the American population, in its distribution or in its major social and economic characteristics. Trends that began at the end of the Depression or even earlier in the century continued, though at slower rates. Even the significant decline in fertility commenced, as we have seen, in the late fifties.

Many people have seen the sixties as a crucial transition decade in American life, whether as the beginning of the decline of the republic or as a breakthrough to a new and hopeful social transformation. The demographic indices, however, reveal no startling changes—in contrast, for instance, to the Depression decade, when most major social and economic trends, even rural-to-urban migration, were temporarily reversed. But this is to be expected; population movements have a momentum of their own and change more slowly than our political and cultural responses to the world around us. Often we become aware of and react against the consequences of population trends only when they have already begun, almost imperceptibly, to change. Perhaps the demographic trends of the sixties will be seen in retrospect to have been more of a turning point than is apparent now.

NEGRO MIGRATION TO NORTH FOUND STEADY SINCE FORTIES

by JACK ROSENTHAL

WASHINGTON—The Census Bureau reported today that Southern blacks streamed north during the sixties at a rate nearly the same as the high level of the two previous decades.

The finding, drawn from newly computed 1970 census data, contradicts earlier, widely accepted reports that black migration north had tailed off sharply, falling to about half the earlier level.

Since large numbers of black migrants go from poor farms to urban slums and often require welfare assistance, the finding is likely to figure importantly in the present political debate about revenue sharing and Federal assumption of welfare costs.

More than three-fourths of the 1.4 million black migrants from the South went to five large states where the soaring cost of welfare is a heated public issue.

By far the largest gain was measured in New York, which gained 396,000 black migrants in the decade. California gained 272,000, and New Jersey, Illinois and Michigan each gained about 120,000.

Analysts said there were indications that such migration could well continue and even increase in the next decade.

The Census Bureau also released reports showing significant improvement in three indicators of the condition of housing units across the country.

"The quality of housing went up considerably," Maurice H. Stans, Secretary of Commerce, said at a news conference. He cited improvements in the number of units with basic plumbing facilities, in the age of the housing stock and in the degree of crowding.

The census report on migration showed that as Southern blacks moved north and west, Northern and Western whites moved south in historic numbers.

In total out-migration, New York lost 638,000 white residents. Pennsylvania lost 423,000. Illinois, Ohio, Iowa, Kansas and Washington, D.C., each lost more than 100,000.

The result of this dual movement is a clear continuation of a long-term trend toward dispersion of the black population throughout the country.

The South still contains 53 per cent of the black population, but that compares with 77 per cent in 1940. Since that year, the population of the Northeast and North Central states has gone from about 11 to 20 per cent black.

The total black population increased from 18.9 to 22.7 million in the decade. Blacks now make up 11.2 per cent of the national population, up from 10.6 per cent in 1960.

The black population growth rate continues to be higher than that of whites, but not enough to alter this proportion significantly in the future. Herman P. Miller, director of census population studies, said today he estimated that by the year 2000, blacks might account for no more than 13 per cent of the population.

More significant than the black population's size, analysts said today, is its distribution. Each of the 11 states of the Confederacy lost black population. Mississippi lost 279,000, and Alabama lost 231,000.

These losses continued strong trends evident since at least 1940.

In 1968, however, the Johnson Administration released a widely noted Census Bureau–Labor Department study reporting that these trends had at last begun to change dramatically.

"Average annual out-migration in recent years is about half of what it was in the forties," the report said.

This study, based on survey data, showed a drop in black migration from 159,000 a year in the forties to 80,300 in 1968.

The report released today, based on full census data, shows that the figure for the cities in fact was about 138,000 a year, close to the annual figure of 147,000 in the fifties.

George Hay Brown, director of the Census Bureau, took note of the 1968 findings at the news conference today.

Those findings and the figures released today were estimates, he said. The new data were computed by subtracting births and deaths from each state's population change. The result is defined as net migration.

He said this method was useful to provide interim data until precise migration studies were complete next year. But it also may encompass considerable error, he said.

In any event, Mr. Stans said, "migration of blacks to the North is continuing in the same degree as in the previous two decades."

The Commerce Secretary said, ''I have no doubt that higher welfare bene-fits in the North are a factor.'' But, he added under questioning, ''I would cer-tainly assume that greater job opportunities [in the North] would be the chief motivating factor.''

Other authorities have attributed continued migration as much to the push of poor rural conditions in the South as to the pull of opportunity in the big city.

Details of the 1970 census lent some support today both to these views and to the belief that heavy black migration north may continue.

These data show that the migration rates are highest among young adults in at least seven Southern states. In Mississippi, for example, there were 70,000 black men aged 15 to 24 in 1960. But now there are only 30,324 black men aged 15 to 24, a drop of 57 per cent.

The figures for young black women are somewhat lower.

Since there are few deaths in the 15 to 24 age group, analysts regard it as a significant measure. It suggests, they said today, that as farm mechanization continues to eliminate rural work, young blacks continue to look north.

Meanwhile, whites continued to migrate south and west. The West gained 2,855,000 migrants of all races. California accounted for 2,113,000 of these.

As Mr. Brown, the census director, reported last fall in a speech on the new South, that region as a whole gained about 1.8 million whites, offsetting the 1.4 million black out-migrants. The net gain is the first for the South since the eighteen-seventies. Florida accounted for 1,340,000 white migrants.

The North Central states lost 752,000 in migration while the Northeast gained 324,000, most of them black. Among the state figures are the follow-ing:

State	White	Black
New York	−638,000	+396,000
New Jersey	+336,000	+120,000
Connecticut	+166,000	+ 38,000
Pennsylvania	−423,000	+ 25,000
Massachusetts	+ 23,000	+ 33,000

Today's Census Bureau housing report showed that the proportion of hous-ing units without a toilet and tub or shower dropped in the sixties from 17 to 7 per cent. In 1950, the figure was 35 per cent. The total is now 4.7 million out of 68 million units.

The proportion of units that average more than one person per room dropped from 11.5 to 8.2 per cent of all units over the decade.

In both cases, the highest over-all proportions are in the South. But California, with 522,000, and New York, with 447,000, have by far the most housing units with more than one person per room.

Mr. Stans said that about half the present housing units in the country were built after World War II.

ONE-THIRD OF BLACKS FOUND IN 15 CITIES

by JACK ROSENTHAL

WASHINGTON—Nearly half the nation's black population is now concentrated in 50 cities, and a third of the total is in 15 cities, according to a Census Bureau compilation made public today.

As a result of both migration and natural growth, six cities now have black majorities and the population of eight others is 40 per cent or more black.

The new compilation on minority groups also showed that the two largest such groups, blacks and people of Spanish origin, now include 31.5 million people, 16 per cent of the total population.

Blacks constitute about 11 per cent of the population, a slight increase over 1960. Persons of Spanish origin are about 5 per cent. No comparable figures were tabulated for 1960.

The Spanish-origin population totals about 9.2 million. The black population is about 22.3 million, of which 10.5 million are in 50 cities and 7.6 million in 15 cities.

New York City has by far the largest black population, almost 1.7 million, an increase of 579,000 over 1960. This increase raised the black proportion of the city's population to 21 per cent, from 14.

The highest proportion of blacks of all cities occurred in Washington and Compton, California, with about 71 per cent. East St. Louis, Illinois, Newark, Gary, Indiana, and Atlanta also have more than 50 per cent black populations.

The cities with 40 per cent or more blacks are Baltimore, New Orleans, Savannah, Georgia, Detroit, Birmingham, Richmond, Virginia, St. Louis and Jackson, Mississippi.

People of Spanish origin tend to be younger than those in other groups, the new report showed. Their median age is about 20, against 21.2 for blacks and 28 for the whole population.

Both minority groups, taken as a whole, average considerably less education than the population as a whole, with a little more than a grade school education. The national median is a high school education.

Among younger blacks and people of Spanish origin, however, this gap nearly disappears. The national median for people between 25 and 34 is 12.5 years of education, against a black median of 12.1 and a Spanish-origin median of 11.7.

The new report also showed that, compared with the total population, minority group members are much less likely to be white-collar workers or to earn $10,000 or more.

BROWNSVILLE SINKS IN DECAY AND FEAR

by STEVEN V. ROBERTS

The narrow hallway in 102 Herzl Street is as dark and chill as the wintry street outside. Most of the apartments in the building have been abandoned and stripped bare by vandals. Plaster crumbles at the touch and the stairs groan ominously. On the third floor of this building Mrs. Nancy Dickerson lives with her three children.

The landlord has not been seen there since October. The family has been without heat or hot water through most of the winter, and gets its only warmth by leaving the blackened gas stove on 24 hours a day.

"I'm praying until the gas bill comes," Mrs. Dickerson said. "We'll probably have to go without meat for a few days to pay it. The welfare check won't cover it."

Mrs. Dickerson held her baby, a bright-eyed girl who has been ill with pneumonia. Another child, in school at the time, needs orthopedic care. All are in constant danger from the cold, from fires, from falling plaster.

"Why should I move?" Mrs. Dickerson said to a visitor. "I'd just be moving to another hole. No sense doing that—I'll just stay in this one."

This is life in the Brownsville section of Brooklyn, until about 10 years ago a largely Jewish, working-class community. Today it is largely Negro and Puerto Rican, and largely forgotten.

Row after row of apartment houses—modern brick and masonry structures as well as older tenements—have sunk into decay. More than 500 buildings have been completely deserted. Whole blocks are silent; only the sounds of glass crunching underfoot and the gurgle of water from vandalized pipes echo through the burnt-out hulks.

"If there is a hell," said Vincent Negron, director of the Good Shepherd Mission Center, "many people in Brownsville will take it in stride."

There are signs that Brownsville is no longer completely ignored. Mayor Lindsay, who calls the area Bombsville, recently held a cabinet meeting on the subject and often mentions it in speeches. It has also become a popular stop for visitors, like Governor George Romney, who want a glimpse of slum life. There is plenty to see.

The decline of Brownsville started when the Jews began moving to better neighborhoods in Queens and Long Island after World War II. The exodus was accelerated, according to Major Owens, director of the Brownsville Community Council, when a huge public housing project brought in a large number of Negroes and Puerto Ricans from outside the community.

"When the whites moved out, the landlords just cut off services," said the Reverend James Regan of the Good Shepherd Center. "Brownsville became a place to make as much money as fast as possible."

Rents for deteriorating apartments run from about $60 to $80 a month, but some landlords double these when they find that the city will pay the higher rents for tenants on welfare.

"The stable Jewish population moved out and took all their institutions with them," added Eugene Taylor, a teacher in local schools for 17 years. "There was no organization here, no one to fight for the new residents. The politicians had nothing to worry about."

About three years ago the new community began to organize itself. Financed by antipoverty grants, the residents started rent strikes, pressed city agencies to inspect the worst buildings and record violations, and demanded that landlords make repairs.

"We thought we could get action," Mr. Owens said, "but the landlords just ran. It all happened so fast."

"We pulled a rent strike about a year ago," said Mrs. Ella Thomas, who moved to Brownsville four years ago from Alabama. "But as soon as the landlord saw he couldn't get any more money out of us he disappeared. We all had to move out, and now the building is abandoned."

Many of the buildings are still owned by the original landlords, who pay enough taxes to forestall foreclosure and hope the city will eventually condemn the property for public use. Other buildings are owned by the banks that held mortgages on them. Some of the banks have indicated an interest in making repairs, according to city officials, but the high cost has prevented them from doing so.

Although Brownsville has lost thousands of residents in recent years, 125,000 people still live there.

Located just south of Eastern Parkway, the dividing line with Bedford-Stuyvesant, Brownsville is jammed between largely white East Flatbush on the west and Canarsie to the south, which starts below Linden Boulevard. To the east, across Van Sinderen Avenue, is East New York, a rapidly changing area now showing the same signs of decay and desertion.

Only 4 per cent of the apartments in Brownsville are considered up to standard. The median family income is less than $3,500 a year. The percentage of families classified by the city as poor ranks second only to Bedford-Stuyvesant.

The people of Brownsville rank at or near the top in juvenile delinquency, welfare cases, narcotics addiction, venereal disease and infant mortality. Their life is a constant battle against fear.

Annette Thomas lives with her mother, five brothers and sisters, and her own baby at 70 Herzl Street. The ceiling over her baby's crib leaks and recently she had to flee with the child because of a smoky fire in the backyard and spend the night at a neighbor's.

"There are too many fires here," she said recently. "Last night across the street they threw whisky bottles through every window. One more fire and I'm getting out with my baby. This neighborhood is just bad."

There is a constant battle against rats. Mrs. Daphne Davis of 118 Amboy Street found her daughter playing with a rat last summer that was so big the child was calling, "Here, kitty, here, kitty."

There is a constant battle against vandals. Mrs. Gloria Boyce, director of a community action center for the Community Council, related how a woman would not leave her freezing apartment during the recent cold spell because she was afraid of being robbed. When vandals broke into a neighbor's apartment she pleaded with them to stop, Mrs. Boyce said, and was thrown down a flight of stairs.

"You can wake up in the morning drowning if someone steals the pipes," said Mrs. Shirley White, a cheerful woman who lives at 142 Amboy. "The thieves on our block are nice, though—they turn the water off first before they strip the building."

In conditions like these it is hard to salvage even a shred of dignity. "If you want to have a little something you have to go into debt for it," said Mrs. Davis, her proud, dark face touched with sadness. "You have to struggle very hard to get something halfway decent."

Mrs. Davis is 30 years old. She receives $181 from welfare every two weeks for herself and five children, the oldest of whom is almost 15. Her apartment on an almost deserted street is threadbare but meticulously neat. At night her sister cares for the children while she studies basic reading and mathematics at the Good Shepherd Center.

"They expect you to go without dressing or without eating," she said. "The welfare doesn't give you enough for both.

"I won't go without either," she added fiercely, "even if I have to hustle."

Children grow up without fathers and without security. "My boy dropped out,'' said Mrs. Ella Thomas. "He said he was too embarrassed to go to school in the clothes I could afford to buy him.''

"The kids are crowded in at night with the rats and the roaches, they get up in the freezing cold, and have to fight to get into the bathroom that usually doesn't work,'' Mrs. White said. "Then they get to school and the teachers start fussing at them. And you wonder why they do so badly.''

Mrs. Davis's nine-year-old boy has been expelled from school for unruliness. The boy's father had a stroke and now lives with his mother. "They're at an age where they need advice,'' Mrs. Davis said of her children. "I try to give it to them, but I don't know what to do.''

Life for the few whites who remain is no easier. Mr. S. (he would not give his name) runs a newsstand on Pitkin Avenue from 5 A.M. to 7 P.M. seven days a week to make a meager living. Recently his son got married and he bought him a television set and a sewing machine that the store said cost $570. He has already paid $800 and the store keeps sending him bills. Last summer he was mugged and barely escaped serious injury.

The Lindsay administration is doing more than conducting guided tours of Brownsville.

A $72 million urban renewal project is due to start soon, but the city is still uncertain where it can put all the families who would be displaced by the new construction. Local groups are pressing hard to get those displaced into public housing, but many families are either too large or have too many social problems to be admitted under the strict rules governing public housing prospects. In any case, there would not be enough housing to go around.

Planning is beginning for about 1,500 low-income and middle-income apartments in small, unobtrusive buildings that would not stand out like the stark towers of the existing public housing.

The antipoverty program is providing a range of services from job placement to consumer cooperatives to cultural enrichment to family planning. Next year it is to receive a budget increase from $1.7 million to $3 million. The Community Council, which is the official antipoverty agency for the area, also wants to sponsor its own housing, but the Federal Government has said the council is not old or stable enough to warrant a 40-year mortgage.

Probably the city's most visible effort in the community is its demolition program, which has a goal of tearing down about 500 of the worst structures.

Some city officials think that the large number of abandoned buildings indicates an easing of the city's housing shortage. But most of them are convinced that private landlords in areas like Brownsville are largely unwilling or unable to keep buildings in good repair because it just is not profitable enough.

Because of this the administration is exploring ways to take over some of the better buildings, repair them and turn them into cooperatives for the present tenants. Carrying charges would be used to keep the property up.

Donald H. Ellictt, chairman of the City Planning Commission, said that local workmen could organize corporations to maintain the buildings, thus getting jobs as well as good housing out of the program.

Any such program, Mr. Elliott said, would require vast subsidies, since the tenants could not afford enough rent to maintain the buildings on their own. One possible source of subsidy would be welfare, which now pays high rents for miserable conditions.

If there is some brightness in Brownsville's future, the present remains grim. It is hardest, perhaps, for the mothers whose sons are going off to war.

The night before her son left, Mrs. Gloria Boyce said, "Many of our boys are going to Vietnam. They come back to the same thing they left—no jobs, no education, nothing better. They come back to another war, just like the one they just left."

INNER-CITY DECAY CAUSES BUSINESS LIFE TO WITHER

by JERRY M. FLINT

DETROIT—The weather-beaten plywood board is replacing the gleaming steel and glass skyscraper as a symbol of the American city.

Outside the central city, apartments and air-conditioned shopping plazas and theaters spring up, miles apart but bound together by freeways making anything only a few minutes away from the auto-equipped resident of that outer city, suburbia.

But for those remaining in the central city cores—the black ghettos and the poor and even middle-class white areas around them—it is harder to buy food because the big supermarkets are going and the little stores are boarded up or torn down; it is harder to find a doctor or dentist; harder to fill a prescription or have a suit cleaned because the stores are gone; harder to buy a newspaper; call a taxi; find a pleasant park, a good restaurant or even a good corned beef sandwich.

The traditional commercial services are dying and the old urban cores have not yet been able to adapt to the new commercial pattern.

What is more, years after the racial riots along these same streets and after innumerable pledges to rebuild, the decay has intensified.

Four years ago this week, Detroit's great riot occurred and today the streets, if anything, look emptier, with large stretches of dusty cleared land and even larger stretches of shabby boarded-up storefronts. And reports from other cities—Pittsburgh, Chicago, Washington, for example—are much the same.

In a dozen cities examined as the summer began, the scene on these streets is similar: blocks abandoned, storefronts covered with plywood. Open stores are dingy, the fronts bricked up in the architectural style that dominates the ghetto of the nineteen-seventies: "Riot Renaissance." If anything new is built on the old commercial arteries, it is probably another gas station or a gaudy drive-in.

There are exceptions. Here and there a bright shopping center exists, not matching the glistening ones in the suburbs but reversing the general commercial decay. And some of the old shopping streets, such as 125th Street in Harlem, are still bustling and bright, with a wide range of stores and throngs of noontime shoppers. But they are not typical.

Some blame a lack of Federal money for the continued blight. Others blame the squabbling of citizens groups, or high crime, or burdensome insurance, or freeze-outs by banks and private investors, or inability to gather large blocks of land needed for modern commercial services, or high costs for the obviously unwanted city blocks. Whatever the reason, the imagination and the will to rebuild the city cores seem lacking.

"We don't need the central city, even as a communications center," said Peter Drucker, the social critic. In Europe, he said, "the city was a desirable form of life. In this country it never was. This is a country of anticities.'"

Here are reports on the situation around the nation:

PITTSBURGH—The large core ghetto is called the Hill district. After the murder of Dr. Martin Luther King, Jr., three years ago 100 stores were looted or burned. Most have not been rebuilt, and where the rubble was cleared away there's new debris: beer cans, whisky bottles, trash.

"After the 1968 troubles we cut our hours. We close at 5:30 P.M., not open at night. Our black employees don't want to go out at night," said Leonard Edelson, a white co-owner of the bustling Hill Pharmacy. His store keeps its windows boarded up and is busy because "four major drugstores in the Hill were burned out" and because the welfare business has more than doubled in three years, he said.

He has to send a driver to pick up drugs each day because the suppliers pulled their men from the routes when they were attacked.

"There's nothing here to open up for," said Matthew Moore, a Pennsylvania state coordinator for the National Association for the Advancement of Colored People. "Drugs are flourishing so people are afraid to come out. The Hill is full of winos and junkies. People are afraid to carry money."

"Some services are available," he added wryly. "We control the bars, beauty shops, barbers and churches."

BOSTON—The Boston ghetto stretches from the South End near downtown into Roxbury, its heart, and in it live four-fifths of the city's 105,000 Negroes. More than 50 stores along Blue Hill Avenue, a main thoroughfare, were damaged in the 1967 riot and most have not reopened. Some $56 million in pledges of aid for rebuilding never materialized, but some new black-owned or black-run businesses have opened, replacing white ones.

"So many Jewish shop owners got out of deep Roxbury that it amounted to a mass exodus" after the 1967 riot, said a spokesman for the Anti-Defamation League of B'nai B'rith. In one area 100 stores changed hands. Despite some new businesses and improvements the old core area is still "a business desert," said Robert M. Coard, executive director for the city's major antipoverty agency.

"A very bad situation," said Donald E. Sneed, Jr., president of the Unity Bank, the largest black-run business in New England. "I think we in the community feel we're an island by ourselves in terms of real progress compared to the surrounding area."

BIRMINGHAM—Although the city says it tries to give the same treatment to the streets and sidewalks of Birmingham's ghetto as to other parts of the city, one can see piles of trash lying about. Outside the biggest grocery store, boxes, paper, old produce and other refuse lie around for two or three days.

The only new restaurant in the area in five years, a quick-service hamburger franchise, changed management twice and has closed.

DETROIT—Twelfth Street, once a thriving Jewish commercial strip, then a busy honky-tonk black strip and the heart of the 1967 riot, is practically leveled, and residents must travel miles to find a large grocery or drugstore. Even the pimps complain, "I used to make $100 a day on this street. Now I can't make a dime," one said.

On the east side of the city, on Mack Avenue, 127 vacant stores were counted in a two-mile stretch. A west side resident complained, "I called to have milk delivered and they said they don't have any trucks out here."

Detroit's car makers invested almost $100 million to set up black-owned automobile showrooms in inner-city locations abandoned by whites, but now the companies have decided that even blacks can't do much business there.

CHICAGO—"In the past 10 years I would estimate that the attrition rate of ghetto business is 30 to 40 per cent, as high as 50 per cent in areas affected by the riots," said Pierre DeVise, a social scientist at DePaul University. "Madison Street [on the West Side of Chicago] looks like it was hit by a holocaust. Maybe only one-third of the stores operating there 10 years ago are still functioning. A three-block area lined by storefronts before 1968 lies completely vacant."

"See for yourself. Nothing has been replaced. The only new places are the gas stations moving onto some of this cleared land and one Midas muffler store,'' said Tommy Lee Durham, a black who owns a second-hand refrigerator store on Madison.

Construction of new stores has proved to be a failure in some cases.

Dr. Arthur Falls is a Negro and part of a 16-member syndicate that owns a shopping center in the South Side ghetto. He said $1 million was invested in the center in four years. Now graffiti cover the walls of the stores, four of the seven are vacant, and chicken-wire, plywood or brickwork cover the windows.

There has been fire bombing and thievery and no profits, he said.

TRENTON—In the last five years two large department stores in Trenton have closed and some expect the remaining two to follow. Both downtown hotels are gone. Plans for a downtown shopping mall fell apart, and of the four movie theaters downtown all are expected to be closed by next month.

The seven black neighborhoods in Trenton are serviced by one small and one large supermarket. Bars and liquor stores abound, but a trip downtown is necessary for drugs or hardware, for shoes or to see a doctor.

On the eight blocks of North Clinton Avenue there were 120 businesses in 1950; now there are 60. Every other store window is boarded up; alleys are filled with garbage and broken glass.

In most ghetto areas residents can't buy a newspaper because there are no stands and few stores, and carrier boys are scarce.

''The whites have siphoned off the money and are leaving the city and they try to sell their businesses to blacks like they were doing us a big favor, but it's all because no one else will buy it but a black guy,'' said Albert Robinson, director of Trenton's antipoverty program.

LOS ANGELES—On Central Avenue in Watts nearly all the stores were destroyed in the 1965 riot and about one-third remain boarded up today. There are no major supermarkets in the business strips, Central and Compton Avenues and 103rd Street.

''If I get someone going to Watts in the daytime, and he looks O.K., I demand he pay in advance, and I take him. At night I won't go,'' said a white taxi driver. Services, which were scarce in the area before the riots, have not improved. And jobs and transportation still seem the major concern.

WASHINGTON—Plywood is a big decorating item along Seventh and 14th Streets N.W. and H Street N.E., the old commercial corridors damaged in the 1968 riots. Black-owned stores are increasing but, said Cornelius Pitts, who owns the Pitts Motor Hotel just off 14th and has founded a black business-men's alliance:

"After the riots when whites were selling out to blacks, the new owners were paying substantially higher prices, based on prior volume, than volume justified afterwards. As a result, many have gone out of business, and a lot of the rest are just hanging on."

"I'm dying for lack of business," he admitted.

"I've been discouraged for the last year and a half," said Rufus A. Isley, owner of two clothing stores and winner of a Small Business Administration award a year ago. His side of the 3000 block of 14th Street looks as if the riots had occurred last month rather than three years ago.

NEW YORK—Harlem is exceptional, both within the nation and within New York City. The density of its mobile but constant population of about half a million people is part of a critical set of variables that set it apart even from Brooklyn's larger Bedford-Stuyvesant section.

"Harlem is different and the negatives are more aggravated than in other cities," said Hope Stevens, a prominent black Harlem lawyer who is also president of the predominantly white Uptown Chamber of Commerce.

It does not have to rebuild structures damaged in civil disturbances. Although there was an outbreak of violence following the death of Dr. King, property damage was not as extensive as in other cities.

But spiraling insurance costs, followed by a rise in prices for inferior goods, have been a source of aggravation. This has been accompanied by a high incidence of crime against property. One study by the Small Businessmen's Chamber of Commerce—a predominantly black group—estimated that crime last year cost the community "more than $2 billion."

"The cost of crime," said Mr. Stevens, "is passed back to the consumer. It doesn't drive the businesses out. They simply raise the prices."

Many of the larger white businesses are said to be "up for sale." But as one black businessman put it, "There are no banks or other agencies willing to give the black businessman a loan."

In all the cities studied, of course, many residents of the core areas, black and white, own automobiles and can drive to the suburban shopping centers. Any visitor to Northland, Detroit's major suburban center, can see that a large percentage of the buyers are blacks from the city.

"You don't know what a big thing it is for a black family to get in a car and go out to the suburbs to shop," said a black automobile dealer in Chicago. "That's where half my business goes."

And in some of the central cities, some of the shopping streets are succeeding.

In Philadelphia, not far from Columbia Avenue, a former riot area, there's a striking new shopping center. Progress Plaza opened in 1968 with 17 stores and offices. One of its main backers was the Reverend Leon Sullivan, a leader in the black capitalism effort.

There's an A. & P. supermarket, two banks, shoe stores, a drugstore, appliance store, bookstore and others, all owned or managed by blacks. There have been no failures and the center's stores did $5 million in business their first year, Dr. Sullivan said.

In most places, however, the blight is widespread and deepening. For millions of people, living becomes a little more inconvenient and a little uglier each year.

Mrs. Anita Watson, a 26-year-old mother and part-time college student who lives in public housing on Chicago's West Side, paints a familiar picture.

There are no large chain stores or cleaning shops within walking distance, she says, nor are there milkmen or licensed taxi cabs.

"The grocery store picture is so ridiculous," she said. "During the day milk will sell for $1.12 a gallon, but at night when only one store is open the price is $1.40. And you've got to pay or drink water. If you decide to travel outside the neighborhood and you don't have a car, it will cost you a dollar round trip on the buses."

BLACKS AND PUERTO RICANS UP MILLION IN DECADE

by EDWARD C. BURKS

New York City added one million black and Puerto Rican residents during the nineteen-sixties, and the major impact was a large expansion of the sprawling sections where these minorities live.

The old segregated housing patterns were intensified because non-Puerto Rican whites moved out at a pace matching that at which the new migrants moved in. There was dramatic evidence of this especially in Central Brooklyn, the South Bronx and South Jamaica, Queens.

These are the principal conclusions of a detailed analysis by The New York Times of official 1970 census figures. The study of each of the city's 2,159 census tracts, or counting areas, shows that more than two-thirds of them were either 90 per cent white or 90 per cent black.

The following were the factors in the census picture:

The population of whites (exclusive of Puerto Ricans) dropped by one million between 1960 and 1970. But the actual migration of non-Puerto Rican whites from the city was much greater than a million, an estimated several hundred thousand more. Whites remaining had an excess of births over deaths to trim the net loss of white population to one million.

Of 5.1 million whites (other than Puerto Ricans) in 1970, 4.4 million lived in census tracts that were more than 90 per cent white, and in scores of cases, totally white.

Nonwhites, bolstered by a net in-migration of 436,000, also had a higher rate of births over deaths, and a population generally much younger than the whites.

Where census tracts had a mixed population it was very frequently a case of minority groups having expanded rapidly into old white areas. Many of these were on the fringe of long-established black and Puerto Rican sections.

In that manner, the minority areas grew to two and three times their former size in Brooklyn, the Bronx and Queens.

There were numerous integrated areas—several on Manhattan's West Side, for example, and some in all boroughs. But the main trend, both through migration and natural growth, was expansion of the areas where minorities live.

Dr. Abraham C. Burstein, director of economic research for the city's Human Resources Administration, estimates that 81.6 per cent of the black population in 1970 lived in the 26 officially designated poverty areas here.

During the decade, the black population in those poverty areas grew by more than 380,000—from 980,000 to 1,361,000. However, there was an economic improvement. In 1960, 90 per cent of the black population was in those poverty areas.

While the Census Bureau has not yet released Puerto Rican breakdowns, Dr. Burstein, who keeps close tabs on poverty-area totals, estimates that the over-all Puerto Rican gain in those areas was about 400,000.

On the other hand, he says, there was an outflow of a million non-Puerto Rican whites from the poverty areas.

The Times has prepared racial maps of each borough, using raw figures from the Census Bureau for each of the city's census tracts. In addition, comparisons were prepared to show how such minority areas as Bedford-Stuyvesant, South Jamaica and the South Bronx pushed out into former white residential sections.

A study of the maps indicates that the greatest black and Puerto Rican growth was in officially designated poverty areas.

In Brooklyn, where the racial change was greatest, the black concentration in the Bedford-Stuyvesant area expanded to about three times its former size. By 1970 it stretched all the way across central Brooklyn from downtown to the Queens line. The non-Puerto Rican white population dropped by three-quarter of a million.

During the same period the Puerto Ricans spread into additional areas of East New York, Sunset Park, Williamsburg and other designated poverty areas in Brooklyn.

New Yorkers and New York City agencies accustomed to breaking down races by "white," "Black," "Puerto Rican" and "other" may be confused by Census Bureau nomenclature.

Although in a few months the bureau will have a complete breakdown of Puerto Ricans, the overwhelming majority of them in current figures are lumped with the whites. In fact, census officials and Dr. Burstein agree that about 95 per cent of all Puerto Ricans here class themselves as "white" in filling out census forms.

The final 1970 census figures for the city showed a total population of 7,894,862, a gain of about 110,000 over 1960. The breakdown was as follows:

	1970	1960
Whites	6,048,641	6,640,662
Blacks	1,668,115	1,087,931
Others (mainly Chinese and Orientals)	177,906	53,391

The official count for Puerto Ricans in 1960 was 612,574. Pending the official report by the Census Bureau for 1970, the Division of Employment of the New York State Department of Labor has calculated that the city's Puerto Rican population in 1970 was 1,051,200, a gain of more than 438,000 during the decade. The black increase in that period was 580,184.

If it is considered conservatively that 90 per cent (rather than 95 per cent) of the Puerto Ricans listed themselves as white, then the racial breakdown of the city for the two censuses would be as follows:

	1970	1960
Whites (not including Puerto Ricans)	5,102,761	6,089,346
Puerto Rican whites	946,080	551,317
Blacks	1,668,115	1,087,931
Puerto Rican blacks	105,120	61,257
Others	177,906	53,391
Total	7,894,862	7,781,984

(The categories do not add up exactly to the official total because the Puerto Rican figures are estimates.)

Raymond A. Glazier, chief of the Bureau of Community Statistics Service of the Community Council of Greater New York, another statistical expert, believes that the official Puerto Rican figures for 1970 will be closer to 980,000 than the state's estimate of 1,051,200. Even so, Mr. Glazier now figures the black, Puerto Rican and "other races" population of New York City at 35 per cent of the total and expanding rapidly.

The figures show that whites did not move to integrate. On the contrary, they left growing black areas by the hundreds of thousands. The relatively small amount of integration was in the opposite manner "a spillover of poverty," as Dr. Burstein calls it, with many blacks moving out of slum areas into formerly white-majority areas. In addition, a sizable number of middle-class blacks were scattered about the city in predominantly white sections.

Thus, while 85 per cent of all whites were living in sections predominantly white (that is, where at least three out of four people were white), the corresponding figure for blacks was much lower. Slightly more than a quarter of all blacks were living in census tracts that were at least 90 per cent black. Less than half of all blacks—670,000—were living in census tracts where at least three out of four people were black.

The median age of the growing black population was ten years lower in 1970 than that of the declining white population. For example, the median age of white males here was 33.3, meaning that half were older than 33.3 and half younger. The corresponding figure for black males was 23.1. For females, the median ages were 37.6 for whites and 26.8 for blacks.

The rapid rise in the number of black youngsters is shown by a drop of five years in the median age of black males—from 28 to 23.1—between 1960 and 1970.

In Brooklyn, where the black gains were most spectacular, half of the black male population of 297,000 in 1970 was under 21 years of age. In the Bronx, nearly half of the 163,500 black males were younger than 21.

Median ages for females were generally higher because of their longevity.

In comparison with the over-all 15-county New York–Northern New Jersey "standard consolidated area," the city had a higher percentage of non-whites (23.4 to 16.3); proportionately fewer young people under 18 (28.3 per cent to 31.2 per cent); and more residents over 65 (12 per cent compared to 10.5 per cent).

A look at the different age groups in the city illustrates the migratory trends. Among whites, the biggest drop in population was among adults aged 25 to 64. There was a lesser but still sizable decrease in white children under 14. On the other hand, half of the 700,000 gain in nonwhites was in the age brackets from 5 to 24 years.

A borough-by-borough breakdown of population trends and totals follows:

MANHATTAN—The borough lost nearly 160,000 population. Even the blacks and Puerto Ricans decreased 17,000 and an estimated 40,000 respectively as they migrated to "outer" boroughs. The non-Puerto Rican white loss was much greater, more than 100,000. Only the Chinese gained, as their citywide total reached 68,324, the bulk of it in Manhattan.

Manhattan's over-all total in 1970 was 1,539,233. The approximate breakdown was 923,000 non-Puerto Rican whites; 380,442 blacks; 184,900 Puerto

Ricans; 69,489 "other races" (some of the Puerto Ricans are also listed as blacks).

The residential breakdown was as follows:

Whites (including Puerto Ricans) living in tracts 90 per cent white, 739,000; living in tracts 75 to 90 per cent white, 213,000; living in tracts 50 to 75 per cent white, 104,000.

Blacks living in tracts 90 per cent black, 180,000; in tracts 75 to 90 per cent black, 26,800; in tracts 50 to 75 per cent black, 33,000.

Manhattan median age, 35.4; percentage under 18 years, 21.5; those over 65, 14 per cent.

THE BRONX—The combined black and Puerto Rican population topped 53 per cent, with major growth in the South Bronx, Hunts Point area, Morrisania and Tremont. There was an estimated gain of 24,000, raising their total to 430,500, the highest anywhere in the city. Blacks gained 194,000 and their total reached 357,681. The non-Puerto Rican white population dropped by 420,000 during the decade.

The residential breakdown: whites, including Puerto Ricans, living in tracts 90 per cent white, 532,000; in tracts 75 to 90 per cent white, 195,000; in tracts 50 to 75 per cent white, 293,000.

Blacks living in tracts 90 per cent black, 7,300; in tracts 75 to 90 per cent black, 17,700; in tracts 50 to 75 per cent black, 88,300.

Median age, 29.6; those under 18, 31.6 per cent; those over 65, 11.6 per cent. Total population: 1,471,701.

BROOKLYN—The greatest white decline in the city was recorded in Brooklyn. There was a gain of 285,000 blacks for a new total of 656,000; and an estimated gain of 220,000 Puerto Ricans for a total of 399,600. The non-Puerto Rican white loss during the decade was 740,000 as black and Puerto Rican concentrations built up all through north and central Brooklyn.

While the white population (exclusive of Puerto Ricans) was reduced to 58 per cent of the Brooklyn totals, the bulk of the land area remained more than 90 per cent white. Of 780 census tracts in the borough, 100 reported no black residents at all.

Vast stretches of south Brooklyn areas—Bay Ridge, Borough Park, Bensonhurst, Flatbush, Flatlands, Canarsie and new developments along the south shore—remained more than 90 per cent white.

The residential breakdown: whites, including Puerto Ricans, living in tracts 90 per cent white, 1,419,000; in tracts 75 to 95 per cent white, 202,500; in tracts 50 to 75 per cent white, 109,000.

Blacks living in tracts 90 per cent black, 172,000; in tracts 75 to 90 per cent black, 111,400; in tracts 50 to 75 per cent black, 241,300.

Median age, 20.1; those under 18, 31.4 per cent; over 65, 11.1 per cent. Total population: 2,602,012, of which 1,506,000 were non-Puerto Rican whites.

QUEENS—With Staten Island, Queens recorded a growth of whites, but the black growth rate was higher as major black concentrations in South Jamaica, Springfield Gardens, St. Albans and North Corona expanded substantially.

The blacks increased by 112,000 for a new total of 258,000 out of a new borough total of 1,986,473. Puerto Ricans gained by approximately 14,000 for a new total of 31,400. The non-Puerto Rican white population climbed by about 60,000 to a new total of 1,697,000.

The residential breakdown: whites, including Puerto Ricans, living in tracts 90 per cent white, 1,498,000; in tracts 75 to 90 per cent white, 120,000; in tracts, 50 to 75 per cent white, 43,000. Blacks living in tracts 90 per cent black, 116,000; in tracts 75 to 90 per cent black, 38,400; in tracts 50 to 75 per cent black, 38,000.

Median age, 35.5; those under 18, 26.2 per cent; over 65, 12.4 per cent.

RICHMOND—This was the only borough with a substantial growth in white population and with a white majority in every census tract. In fact, of 98 census tracts, 74 were more than 90 per cent white. There was a gain of nearly 64,000 non-Puerto Rican whites for a new total of 272,800. Puerto Ricans added 2,300 for a new total of 4,800; and the black population, with an addition of 26,000 reached 65,416.

The residential breakdown: whites, including Puerto Ricans, living in tracts 90 per cent white, 224,000; in tracts 75 to 95 per cent white, 51,500; in tracts 50 to 75 per cent white, 21,940.

Median age, 28.2; those under 18, 34.6 per cent; over 65, 8.7 per cent.

U.S. IN SUBURBAN TUR-MOIL

by JACK ROSENTHAL

Rapidly, relentlessly, almost unconsciously, America has created a new form of urban settlement. It is higher, bolder and richer than anything man has yet called city.

Transfixed by the image of bedroom towns in the orbit of true cities, most Americans still speak of suburbs. But a city's suburbs are no longer just bedrooms. They are no longer mere orbital satellites. They are no longer *sub*.

They are broad, ballooning bands, interlinked as cities in their own right. In population, jobs, investment, construction, stores, political power—all the measurements that add up to "urban"—the old inner city is now rivaled, often surpassed, by the new.

This is the Outer City.

And from its massive, centerless development, repeated again and again across the country, spring the most serious implications for the quality of urban life.

In 1940, suburbs contained 27 million people; 2 of every 10 Americans; 19 million fewer than the cities. Now they contain 76 million; almost 4 of every 10; 12 million more than the cities that spawned them.

Once-rustic fringe villages now have their own zip codes, area codes, big league stadiums. They are the sites of luxury hotels and industrial plants, fine stores and corporate offices.

In New York, the population remains about equally divided between urban and suburban. But elsewhere the suburbs are already two, three, four times more populous than the inner cities they surround.

Commonly, 40, 50 and even 60 per cent of those who live in a city's suburbs also work in them. Half, or more, of every retail dollar is spent in the suburbs. More than 8 of every 12 dollars spent on housing construction is spent in the suburbs. About two-thirds of all industrial construction is in the suburbs, in the outer cities of the nation.

Visits and interviews in five geographically representative areas—Baltimore, Cleveland, Los Angeles, Houston and Atlanta—showed that the suburbs are individual, diverse communities with a diversity of problems. In the distant exurban greenery, planners worry about how to channel new growth. In closer suburbs, officials struggle to show that age need not bring decay. In the closest, decay has already begun.

But taken together, the suburbs have, like New York's, become informally federated in many areas. Their residents use the suburbs collectively: as a city, a centerless city.

Mrs. Ada Mae Hardeman is a Californian who says she doesn't really know where she is from:

"I live in Garden Grove, work in Irvine, shop in Santa Ana, go to the dentist in Anaheim, my husband works in Long Beach, and I used to be president of the League of Women Voters in Fullerton."

She doesn't much mind. "I don't miss central city pleasures out here in spread city. Honestly, I have to say I love it."

Now such independence of the city is being massively fortified with concrete. Broad beltways already encircle 10 large cities and will soon rim 70 more—the accidental new main streets of the outer cities.

And the residents of the outer cities have become so independent of the inner cities that it is common to hear people brag that they haven't been downtown in months, even years.

Still, like many inner-city residents who think that the urban world revolves around downtown, they do not concede that the suburban rings constitute an alternate city.

They prize the array of urban facilities of their outer city. But many, as in parts of New York's Westchester County and northern New Jersey, still identify with the image of the pastoral town.

They are alarmed by the consequences of their own growth, like increasing density and pollution. But they still cling to the governmental forms of isolated villages.

They are increasingly willing—even, surprisingly, in the most conservative communities—to endorse *Federal* action to assuage the poverty and blight left behind in the inner cities. But, otherwise, they shrink from these problems, often with indifference, sometimes with anger.

Tormented city officials, like Larry Reich, the Baltimore city planner, may denounce what they regard as unfairness:

"The city of Baltimore makes the suburbs possible because we carry the burdens of the old, poor, black and deviants. Why should we keep carrying the burden?"

But in the suburbs, many people quote with unabashed candor the old troopship cry: "Pull up the ladder, Jack, I'm on board."

And the new outer cities continue—rapidly, centerlessly—to grow:

For all the vitality of downtown Houston, the fashion center is not downtown. Tiffany's in Houston now is a block from the Loop beltway, one small segment of a $300 million retail, commercial and hotel development called City Post Oak. Even in the twilight, the rows of plaza light globes, like luminous pearls, only soften the staggered concrete shapes behind them that stretch outward for eight blocks and upward for 22 stories.

It was once second-rate farmland out amid the slash pine and red clay 15 miles from Atlanta's old warehouse district. Now H. C. Pattillo, who calls himself merely a medium-size local builder, has developed an industrial park, serving local and national concerns alike. It contains long, low, attractive plants, 103 of them, on a 2,000-acre tract.

Roosevelt Field, the lonely, little Long Island airport from which Charles Lindbergh took off for Paris in 1927 is now the Roosevelt Shopping Center, one of the East's largest. In place of the tiny crowd that watched the *Spirit of St. Louis* disappear into the morning fog are the crowds of housewives shuttling from Macy's to Gimbel's.

In Orange County, California, once a sprawling bedroom for Los Angeles, Newport Center, a vast alabaster oasis, gleams against the tan foothills near the Pacific. The floor space in the fashion stores and 18-story office towers already nearly equals that of Manhattan's Pan Am Building, and they are 49 miles from downtown Los Angeles.

"Everybody thinks a city needs to have a center," says Richard Baisden, a political scientist at the new University of California at Irvine. "Well, why does it? Downtown has ceased to have any real relevance. Its functions have dissipated and decentralized out to where the people are."

This decentralization, it is evident from the visits to five metropolitan areas, is nearly complete.

The barges, boxcars and industries that once gave the inner city its preeminence, and jobs, have not disappeared. But now they are rivaled by tractor-trailer rigs, beltways and fork-lift trucks that make desirable such low-rent industrial plants as the Pattillo development in Atlanta.

The central cities, their variety of apartments, flats and homes growing old, are no longer the sole, or even the most desirable, location of housing. For millions, the automobile and Federal insurance for new housing in outlying areas have crystallized the American dream.

"The suburban house," says Edgardo Contini, a noted Los Angeles urbanist, "is the idealization of every immigrant's dream—the vassal's dream of his own castle.

"Europeans who come here are delighted by our suburbs, even by the worst sprawl. Not to live in an apartment! It is a universal aspiration to own your own home."

The movement of people, in turn, has sped the outward spiral of shopping, a movement so rapid that in some cities total suburban retail sales now far exceed those in the inner city.

And now have come the circumferential highways, what Baltimore calls the Beltway, Houston the Loop, Atlanta the Perimeter—and what one developer calls "the ribbon of gold."

Pasadena, Texas, near the Houston Loop beltway, expects to double and redouble its population. This growth will come, says Mayor Clyde Doyal, despite the fact that "we have no bus station, no railroad, no airport; what we've got is a freeway."

In Atlanta, people call the Perimeter the lifeline to development of the outer city. "People are learning to use it, learning to drive faster by driving farther," says Harold Brockey, president of Rich's. "No one says it took me 10 miles to get here; they say it took me 15 minutes."

The beltways are generating yet another level of growth. Suburban development once meant tract homes, schools and flat shopping centers. Now it is typified by monumental complexes like Mario Doccolo's $22 million Hampton Plaza in suburban Towson, Maryland.

Why did he build this gleaming, round, 29-story tower of tan stone—with offices, fine shops and condominium apartments—in the suburbs?

Because, Mr. Doccolo says, *"This* is the city. They're getting out of Baltimore. People go there to do what they have to do and then—zoom!—back out to the suburbs.

"I could see Mohammed wasn't going to the mountain any more, so I said, 'Let's build the mountain out here.' That's what I bet on."

Thus the outer city: people, houses, plants, jobs, stores, space, greenery, independence.

But it is not, at least not yet, the complete city.

Some functions are still left to the inner city. Rapid high-rise office development in many cities testifies to one. White-collar professionals—lawyers, brokers, bankers, government workers—still require frequent face-to-face contact, a central verbal marketplace.

Inner cities also remain culture centers. But many suburban residents are willing to do without downtown museums, theaters and symphonies, satisfying their cultural needs at outlying universities or amateur performances.

Most notably, the inner cities, despite the erosion of their economic strength, are still called on to perform a major social function: caring for the needy and bringing the poor fully into society.

The inner city remains the haven where the rural migrant, the poor black, the struggling widow can find cheap housing, health care, welfare and orientation to the complexities of urban life.

The burden of this function, clear from the straining budgets of every major city, prompts officials everywhere to talk of the swelling new outer cities as parasites.

"The middle class has entirely abandoned the city," says Norman Krumholtz, Cleveland's lean, intense planning director. "Twenty years down the road, it's perfectly conceivable that the city will be just one great big poorhouse."

Where, asks Baltimore's Larry Reich, are the blacks in the suburbs? It is a rhetorical question. He knows the suburbs are less than 7 per cent black, compared with the city's 47 per cent.

Where, he asks, do hippies, many of them children of the suburbs, congregate? Where is the suburban skid row? Where is the fairness?

In Orange County, California, the black population is less than 1 per cent. Yet nearly 7,000 of the county's 10,000 blacks are concentrated in beleaguered Santa Ana.

In Cleveland, a suburban-dominated regional council, overriding city protests, voted a new freeway that would chew up more of the city's eroding tax base.

The speaker is a suburban city manager in California, but his words convey the sentiments of outer-city residents across the country:

"Social problems in the city? People here would say, 'Sympathy, yes. But willingness to help? That's their tough luck. That's their problem.' "

NEW HIGHWAYS SHAPING FUTURE OF CITY'S SUBURBS

by DAVID K. SHIPLER

The sleek new highways begun under the Eisenhower administration are nearing completion at the edges of the New York metropolitan region, and they may have already set the basic course of suburban growth for the rest of this century.

Every graceful multilane ribbon of asphalt that skirts a small town and winds through farmland is like the touch of Midas, transforming old pastures and woods into precious real estate ripe for the developer who wants land for an office building, a shopping mall, a tract of houses.

The metropolitan area is now laced with 575 miles of interstate highways, almost all of them in the suburbs, paid for with 90 per cent Federal funds, 10 per cent state money.

As the region grows—adding a predicted eight million people and enough office space to fill 300 new Empire State Buildings by the year 2000—the highway network virtually guarantees that the growth will lead away from urban areas, into new land, perpetuating the centerless sprawl that has characterized the suburbs built since the end of World War II.

The evidence is visible now in a huge lopsided ring around the metropolitan area, the new line where, in effect, country meets city, where the suburbs thin out, where most land is still vacant.

The ring passes through Middlesex County and northern Morris County in New Jersey, Dutchess, Putnam and northern Westchester Counties in New York, eastern Suffolk County on Long Island and parts of Fairfield County in Connecticut. Here is where the 20th century will leave its final mark.

In five weeks of travel through the suburbs, a team of New York Times reporters found that the power of the highways to determine how land developed, and thus how millions of people will live and where they will work, is surer than all the careful reasoning of government planners or the defensive rhetoric of small-town politicians.

Every day in the outer counties, planners who try to fight sprawl and revive mass transportation by encouraging new development in downtown centers are being defeated by the growth that spreads along the highways, that clusters around the new interchanges.

The highways' influence has been enhanced by the resistance of many suburbanites to growth in their own towns.

Strict zoning that limits development is defended with the greatest passion in residential parts of town. Along highways, especially at the town lines, offices and shopping centers with their badly needed tax payments are often tolerated because they appear to leave the rural nature of the countryside undisturbed.

And yet the highway planners who draw the new routes and thus map the future for the suburbs say they never consider the advantages or the liabilities of rapid growth in one place or another. They never weigh the impact of their highways on the older suburban towns that must compete with the glittering shopping centers.

"We've never been able to be that luxurious," said Nicholas Sinacori, regional chief of the New York State Transportation Department in the Hudson River Valley. He said development patterns were not his responsibility, but rested completely on the shoulders of the towns that controlled zoning.

Highway authorities say they simply try to meet transportation needs, and that in doing so they search for routes where the land is cheapest and the political resistance weakest. This technique brings real estate booms to out-of-the-way places.

"It's gone crazy—it's wild!" exclaimed Robert J. Eckstein, a real estate man in Parsippany-Troy Hills, New Jersey, which is fast becoming one of the region's major crossroads.

Eventually five highways—three of them new interstates—will cross in what was once a small town in Morris County. Even before their completion, the roads have begun to stimulate rapid growth.

In 1950, the population of Parsippany-Troy Hills was 15,290. Now it is 55,112. Since 1961, the total value of commercial and industrial buildings and land in the town has jumped from $14 million to $86 million. The value of all property has risen from $107 million to $483 million in 10 years.

Nine years ago, Mr. Eckstein and a partner bought an old Victorian-style house on an acre of ground for $30,000. Now he estimates the value of the land alone at $85,000.

The reason is simple: Only yards from Mr. Eckstein's property, in swirls of dust, steam-rollers rumble along a swath of brown-red earth, packing it into a roadbed for Interstate 80. On an overpass above, a little local traffic makes use of the short strip of Interstate 287 that has been completed.

"We all knew where Route 80 would go," Mr. Eckstein said. "When 80 is complete, it's just going to be the ultimate hub."

Route 80 will connect the George Washington Bridge with the Delaware Water Gap, and Route 287 will run from the New York Thruway to the New Jersey Turnpike.

Mr. Eckstein realized the potential of this spot, and five years ago he had the Victorian house demolished. And now, near the intersection of these two incomplete highways, he already has a three-story office building under construction.

Elsewhere, development usually occurs several years after the highway is completed, either because local towns along the roads use zoning to restrain the growth for a time or because the highways probe more deeply into the countryside than people need to go to escape the spreading congestion of the inner suburbs.

Acres and acres of brush and scrub oak and pine along the extended Long Island Expressway in Suffolk County, for example, have recently been opened to industrial development by a rezoning decision in the town of Islip. Local real estate men say the rezoning pushed land values from $7,500 to $40,000 an acre.

Development has proceeded further along Smithtown Bypass, which runs for 10 miles from Hauppauge to Port Jefferson, and, with its many intersections, is anything but a modern superhighway.

But, stimulated in part by proposals that a bridge be built someday across Long Island Sound from Port Jefferson to Bridgeport, Connecticut, developers have made the Smithtown Bypass a strip of new car showrooms, Carvel stands, treeless tracts of single-family houses, gasoline stations, movie theaters and even a Holiday Inn. All of this is mixed in with a few remaining potato fields.

In Piscataway, New Jersey, small one-story and two-story offices and factories already have been erected along a newly completed stretch of Interstate 287. And in nearby East Brunswick, so many shopping centers now line Route 18 that planners have come to call the divided highway "the main street of East Brunswick."

Continuing growth of this sort is viewed as ominous for the cities, not only the core area of Manhattan but also such smaller centers as Jamaica, Queens; downtown Brooklyn; Newark, Paterson and New Brunswick in New Jersey; White Plains; Stamford, Connecticut; and Hempstead, Long Island.

The Regional Plan Association has long been campaigning for an end to what it calls "spread city" and a concentration of future development in sub-centers around Manhattan. The planners note that otherwise the region's residents will continue to be slaves to the automobile, since bus and train service need estimated densities of 5 to 10 families an acre to be practical.

But virtually every force seems to be pushing hard away from the downtowns. Relentlessly, developers are driving out, not up, seeking vacant land, pressuring towns to relax zoning, trying to appeal to what they believe is an insatiable American appetite for open space, even if it is merely the open space of a shopping center's parking lot versus the curbside of a downtown street.

Trenton, for example, found itself the victim of this aversion to downtown, according to Eugene J. Schneider, director of the New Jersey County and Municipal Government Study Commission.

Having spent years condemning property and clearing land for a downtown shopping mall, Trenton was able to obtain tentative commitments from four large department stores to build branches on the site, Mr. Schneider said.

Then, eight miles away on Route 1, a developer announced plans for a vast regional shopping center with four department stores. In the face of that prospective competition, the stores bound for downtown Trenton backed out.

Regional planning officials are afraid of the same thing happening to Newburgh, New York, where the State Urban Development Corporation is trying to renew and revive the decaying downtown.

Macy's has made plans for a major shopping center at Fishkill, across the Hudson River from Newburgh, attracted by new Interstate 84, recently opened to traffic, and by state plans to convert intersecting Route 9 into a four-lane highway.

The location of a major shopping center at that intersection, planners reason, threatens to sap downtown Newburgh of what vitality it has retained.

Even government facilities are attracted to the highways. Suffolk County built a complex of county offices, not in a downtown, but on rural land near the Long Island Expressway, Veterans Memorial Highway and the Smithtown Bypass. The state is planning an office building nearby, also shunning a downtown site.

Despite the enormous power of highways to determine the pattern of suburban growth, highway planners interviewed in the metropolitan region said they determined routes and located interchanges, not with regard to their impact on future development, but instead to catch up with growth and meet what they judge as transportation needs.

"Our planning has been one to date of reaction," said Keith Rosser, planning director of the New Jersey State Department of Transportation. "The money is not there to plan intelligently."

Mr. Rosser and others said they picked highway routes where land was cheapest, where the fewest structures had to be demolished and where local opposition was the least vocal. They do not locate highways to influence development in one place or another, they said.

"We construct highways, very frankly, where we're permitted to construct highways," Mr. Rosser said.

The view of the highway network as simply a transportation device that responds to existing development was characteristic of the arguments surrounding the proposal of the interstate highway system by President Eisenhower.

In the 53-page message from the President to Congress on February 22, 1955, recommending such a road network, there is not a single word about the impact of the highways on the cities or on the future development of the suburbs.

Mr. Eisenhower gave four reasons for advocating the 42,500-mile system, of which 31,899 miles now have been completed.

He said that present highways were unsafe, that people were experiencing enormous traffic jams, that poor roads saddled business with high cost for transportation and that modern highways were needed because "in case of an atomic attack on our key cities, the road net must permit quick evacuation of target areas."

In a report, the President's Advisory Committee on a National Highway Program, headed by General Lucius D. Clay, hailed the dispersal that planners are now cursing.

The nation's highways, the committee wrote, "have been able to disperse our factories, our stores, our people, in short, to create a revolution in living habits. Our cities have spread into suburbs, dependent on the automobile for their existence.

"The automobile has restored a way of life in which the individual may live in a friendly neighborhood, it has brought city and country closer together, it has made us one country and a united people."

After the House of Representatives approved the program with a voice vote and the Senate voted for it 89 to 1, Lewis Mumford wrote gloomily in his book *The Highway and the City:*

"When the American people, through their Congress, voted a little while ago for a $26 billion highway program, the most charitable thing to assume about this action is that they hadn't the faintest notion of what they were doing.

"Within the next 15 years they will doubtless find out but by that time it will be too late to correct all the damage to our cities and our countryside, not least to the efficient organization of industry and transportation, that this ill-conceived and preposterously unbalanced program will have wrought."

The 15 years have elapsed. The search in those years for an alternative to the city "has provided residents with the worst of both worlds," wrote William B. Shore, a vice president of the Regional Plan Association, in a recent issue of *City Magazine*.

"In some ways," Mr. Shore declared, "they have little more variety and choice and opportunity than the small-city resident. Yet they are imbedded in a huge urban region—everywhere there are people. Houses march over hill-tops, cut into forests, fragment stream valleys. 'Downtown' is the highway strip."

But "spread city," as Mr. Shore terms it, is cheaper for developers to build, and the expense of new construction has become the major source of fear for builders.

"Everyone is catering to the few who can afford our product," said Robert Weinberg, a partner in Robert Martin Corporation, one of Westchester County's largest builders.

"But that customer can be a supershopper. One misstep is fatal for a builder."

Peter Taylor, a vice president in charge of Levitt and Sons' Long Island region, agrees. "We're a mass builder," he said. "But our market is rapidly decreasing. We've tried to drive the cost down, but we still can't sell to a guy who makes under 17 grand a year."

When the original Levittown was built on Long Island in 1947, Mr. Taylor said the houses were about 750 square feet in area with one bathroom, and the capacity to have bedrooms added to them later.

"Four years after that," he said, "our houses had two bathrooms and could not be added to.

"They were larger," he said. "Now high construction costs have thinned out the market so much, we've almost come full circle. We're selling expand-able houses, and now two bathrooms are a luxury. We're going back to one-bathroom houses."

In the midst of this economic squeeze, land has become the most precious commodity in the suburbs. Wall Street investment houses and large corporations have begun investing large sums in vast tracts in Putnam County in New York and Morris County in New Jersey, according to planners.

Someday, the land will surely be exhausted, gobbled up by campus-style offices, one-story factories, concrete and asphalt. Housing will then have to go up, Mr. Taylor said.

He foresees a megalopolis of high-rise apartments on Long Island. "I tell my kids that they can tell their kids that Grandpa Taylor lived in a single-family house on two acres, and they'll say, 'Yeah?' "

THE OUTER CITY: GROWTH TURNING INTO A MENACE

by LINDA GREENHOUSE

Growth, the snowballing, leapfrogging growth that for so long held out to the suburbs the promise of an endlessly prosperous future has suddenly developed into a shadow across that future.

Everywhere in the new outer cities, politicians, planners and residents of subdivisions that were strawberry patches or orange groves less than a generation ago are taking increasingly worried looks at the growth rates they once welcomed and pointed to with pride.

Here in Orange County, the population doubled in the last 10 years, from 700,000 to more than 1.4 million. But public opinion has turned so decisively against keeping up that pace that the new chairman of the County Board of Supervisors can make a statement nearly unthinkable a few years ago:

"The Chamber of Commerce tells us that growth is wonderful," Robert Battin says. "I see it as a cancer."

In the last decade, the number of people living in the nation's suburbs climbed from 55 million to 76 million. The most recent census figures, still uncompiled, will show that the suburbs contain more apartments, more office parks, more high-rise construction than ever before. A 29-story office tower in Towson, Maryland, a 103-warehouse industrial park outside Decatur, Georgia, a planned city for 430,000 in Orange County tell only a fraction of the story.

Thirty years ago, only 2 out of every 10 Americans lived in the suburbs. Now the suburbs claim 4 of every 10. Only recently have these people come to realize that the city they now live in—the new Outer City—is becoming the city they thought they had left behind, with many of the same problems and responsibilities.

They know they cannot turn Santa Ana back into an orange grove, and for the most part they would not want to. People are seeking, not to reverse the tide, but to hold it—or at least to channel and direct it, to soften the impact.

But for all the numbers and potential power, the outer cities remain largely masses of little islands, unable to work together to harness the forces shaping the future.

So development continues to accelerate beyond the grasp of a Santa Ana, which fears that apartment construction may soon bring in 50,000 new people, more than it can provide services for. Despite Mr. Pattin's fighting words, the Outer City is not yet in control of its future.

The turn against growth was gaining momentum even before the emergence of ecology as an issue in the last year or two. Suburban residents, like those in New Jersey's Bergen County, as well as California's Orange County, had already begun to worry about the traffic jams, the rising taxes to pay for more schools and public services, the spillover of racial problems, the first signs of what one suburban planner calls "the spreading great central crud."

Now the ecology movement has given these worries a new focus and momentum and, even among conservatives, a new respectability.

"Many politically conservative people want the natural assets of the county preserved for their own use, and don't want other people to come in and glop it up," says Forest Dickason, director of the Orange County Department of Planning.

Even in Houston, which its boosters delight in calling a boomtown, one of the city's wealthiest men can muse, "Houston is still not prepared to say no to growth, despite the traffic and pollution. But I personally would like to see the streets rendered passable and the air cleared before I'd invite anyone else to come here."

And in Baltimore County, Dan Colasino, administrative assistant to the county executive, mentioned a proposal to build 25,000 units of low-income housing for blacks and commented, "We don't even have enough for whites. This county is growing very fast—too damn fast."

The rising public wariness toward growth has brought subtle shifts in the balance of power between the private market and the public planners, long the flabby stepchildren of local government.

When 1,700 people crowd into a junior high school auditorium in White Plains, New York, on a Saturday morning to hear the Regional Plan Association's presentation of "The Future of Westchester County," there is no doubt that suburban residents care about what planners have to tell them.

When the public outcry on behalf of the Baltimore County Planning Department, which last fall removed large sections of the county's vacant land from potential commercial development, is so great that the County Council has to withdraw the changes it tried to make on behalf of the developers, there is no doubt that the planners have acquired new muscle.

But visits and interviews around the country produced clear evidence that, despite the planners' new leverage, the private market remains by far the most powerful engine of growth, shaping the future of the new outer city as it once gave form to the old.

The new suburban landscape itself—with its growing concentration of high-rise office buildings, sprawling industrial parks, luxury housing in planned unit developments—offers dramatic evidence.

To support "high-density" development is still bad politics in most suburban areas, arousing such negative feelings that most planners are reluctant to squander their credibility by advocating more apartments.

But the private sector is not only building apartments at an astonishing rate; it is both creating and satisfying a rapidly growing public demand for them.

While many families still live in apartments because they cannot afford to buy houses, an increasing number of suburban middle-class families welcome the imaginative design, convenience and recreational facilities that the new developments offer.

"A child who has grown up in a typical suburb has had his fill of cutting all that grass," said Clark Harrison, chairman of the Board of Commissioners of DeKalb County in suburban Atlanta.

Mr. Harrison offers DeKalb as an illustration of the paradox reflected around the country—that suburban residents denounce apartments and seem to rush into apartments at the same time.

"It's the strangest thing," he said. "People around here complain when they can see a high-rise building through the trees." Yet apartment construction in DeKalb is now outpacing single family homes by 2 to 1, and the ratio is certain to increase.

Just as residents of the outer cities are turning to these new forms of social organization, they are looking to new governmental structures to ease the impact of the growth.

Everywhere people talk as if the forms themselves matter. In Cuyahoga County, for example, civic leaders complain that countywide cooperation on planning issues is impossible with Cleveland and 59 other towns and cities to contend with.

But liberals in Baltimore County, 600 square miles without a single incorporated city, make the opposite complaint. They insist that the lack of community governments makes it harder for individual views to be heard.

Meanwhile, many city leaders say that if only they had metropolitan government—to offset the flight of their tax base and middle class to the suburbs—they would have the resources to solve their problems.

But Houston's experience indicates that structure alone can never be the panacea people seek.

Houston, in effect, does have metropolitan government. A strong Texas law allows it to annex the areas which in other states would become suburban rings.

But instead of using its resources to attack its poverty problems or improve its housing and schools, it chooses to tax itself at the lowest rate of the 25 largest cities.

Its school district, for example, spends $511 a pupil annually, $300 below the national average and less than half of New York's expenditure.

The new public concern about unlimited development has challenged both local governments and the private market. Government's attempts to channel growth have been largely ineffective. For its part, the private market has responded to the challenge with new attention to quality in planning and design. It does not matter whether that change is born of conviction or is merely a concession to the mood of a public no longer willing to pay for unimaginative urban sprawl. The final product is the same, and it is often stunning.

Builders who admit that they might once have been content to put up rows of identical little houses say now that they are willing to spend the extra money that quality design requires.

"Good architecture pays off fast—and it doesn't necessarily cost that much more," said Gerald D. Hines, whose $50 million Galleria has become a new urban center six miles southwest of downtown Houston. "People now will pay that little extra for quality."

Nevertheless, the very scale and quality of the new growth, itself a response to problems of the past, is creating a problem that may eventually make the victories over poor design and unmanaged growth look pyrrhic indeed.

Here in Santa Ana, the seat of Orange County, that challenge is already dramatically apparent. While its population is only a tenth of the county's 1.4 million, Santa Ana already has two-thirds of the black population, a third of the welfare caseload and at least a third of the poor Mexican-American barrios.

Even its better areas, like those in much of the older portions of the county, are vulnerable to change. Eighty-five per cent of the housing in Orange County has been built since 1950. "Like the one-horse shay, it will all wear out at once," says Alfred Bell, principal planner for the County Planning

Department. "Within the decade, our rehabilitation needs will be massive."

And now change stares Santa Ana hard in the face. The city lies adjacent to the 80,000-acre Irvine Ranch, said to be the single most valuable parcel of undeveloped urban land in the world, which already is being developed into a handsome, planned city for 430,000.

The city fears that the Irvine development will be a magnet, drawing people and resources away from Santa Ana.

Unless the Irvine developers can be persuaded to include substantial amounts of low-income housing in their plans, says Carl Thornton, the Santa Ana city manager, "our city will look like downtown Kansas City, downtown Detroit."

And so the cycle begins anew. It appears to be a new natural law that even areas that grew up as satellites to inner cities must, as they themselves grow, create their own poor cores, their own repositories for the infirm, the incapable, the unwanted.

Whether through lack of resources or lack of will, if local government remains powerless to guide the form or pace of growth—to make sure there is room for the poor as well as the rich, for people as well as cars—what is the future for the new outer cities?

Will the private market, motivated by the new public desire for quality, be free to create still newer forms, more daring and imaginative than anything we have yet seen—as different from the present as the glass towers of New York's Lexington Avenue are from the four-story, red-brick tenements that preceded them a generation ago?

Or, operating without consistent guidelines for balancing public and private needs, are the developers of the new cities bound to repeat the mistakes of the old?

Or will local communities themselves, with or without coherent government, somehow be able to compel virtue from the private sector through zoning or new government forms?

Edgardo Contini, a noted Los Angeles urbanist, is convinced that to rely on local governments to save the new cities from the fate of the old is to ensure failure.

"Solutions have to come from a level higher than the problem," he said. "Don't ask for virtue retail. Don't ask local communities to martyr themselves. You are asking them to be noble, and people are not like that. The leadership has to come from the top, from the Federal Government."

The pace of growth this time around is quicker. The scale is bigger, and the stakes, in the Outer City, are vastly higher.

As Professor Richard Baisden, dean of the extension division of the University of California at Irvine, said during dinner at the resort enclave of Corona del Mar:

"I came here in flight from smog and congestion and I've found relief from both, temporarily. But after this, I don't know where people will go.

"I don't know where we can go from here."

PART TWO

METROPOLITAN SUB-COMMUNITIES AND CULTURES

One of the distinguishing features of urbanism, from its very inception, has been the number of cultures existing within the city. This has been regarded as both an advantage and a disadvantage. From the earliest urban beginnings, the variety and freedom offered by the plurality of cultural styles has made the city attractive to all those who would escape from the repressiveness of rural life and provincial society. At the same time, this diversity of beliefs, value systems, religions and cultures has been opposed by conservatives committed to the older culture that once unified the city. In developing a pluralistic society, the city has permitted deviation from past standards which more tradition-minded groups have regarded as sacred. Thus the city has been seen as a source of vice, weakness and degeneracy. While this ideology of anti-urbanism actually developed in the distant past, some of it remains in our present image of the city, and bolsters anti-urban attitudes in both rural and suburban populations. At the same time, for those who would otherwise despise it, the city is attractive as a center of vice, pleasure, entertainment, culture and freedom.

Part of the variety of the city is due to our complex urban class systems. In Part two, we indicate some of the major urban class divisions, recognizing full well that urban classes and their life-styles vary continuously in a multiplicity of ways. It would be very difficult to point to distinct urban classes with sharply defined boundaries. To the extent that we indicate such boundaries, we do so in order to impose some sort of order on the assorted population.

Historically, it has often been assumed that the upper classes are rural in origin, i.e., based on the feudal system of land ownership. While this has been true to some extent, exceptions are significant. Even in ancient societies, as distinct from the village agricultural communes, the city has been a residential, cultural and social center for upper-class landowners, government officials and administrators, and, with further growth, urban landowners and urban plutocrats. With the rise of commerce, and later industry, it became the residential center for an urban upper class that has given much of its own character to the city itself.

Every major city has a distinct local and regional upper class whose wealth has been derived either from the economic development of its region or from the growth of specific industries: automobiles in Detroit, steel in Pittsburgh, finance in New York, and so forth. The characteristics of a particular urban upper class are determined largely by the growth of such industries.

Once an upper class becomes stabilized in any urban area, it begins to develop an elaborate and complex social ritual. Such a ritual usually involves self-segregation within either urban enclaves, or suburbia, or exurbia, and frequently all three simultaneously. It involves balls, cotillions, debuts, private clubs and sports (especially sailing and polo). Some persons in this class are deeply involved in philanthropy, education and patronage of the arts—as board members of major artistic, educational or cultural institutions, as collectors of art and, most recently, amateur artists. The philanthropic impulse even extends as far as running for political office.

One of the interesting aspects of the upper class is that, while the source of much of its wealth lies in local or urban-centered institutions, a large part of its life-style is national and international in scope. Locally based upper classes congregate for recreation, leisure and fun at places like the Riviera, Acapulco and Palm Beach.

In some cases, many members of both the new and the old upper classes have appeared to be "radical" both in culture and in politics. While such a phenomenon is not new (upper-class radicalism existed in ancient Greece, czarist Russia and France before the French Revolution, and continues to develop in American society), it has taken on an anti-middle-class character.

Historically, the city has been the center of artistic, intellectual and bohemian activities. Its atmosphere of freedom has attracted aspiring artists, writers, scholars and aspirants to higher culture. Within the city the culturally oriented discover common interests and often organize themselves informally into coteries, cliques, claques and communities. While their total numbers may be small, their voices are strong, and they provide much of the city's cultural tone. Some are co-opted into the upper and upper-middle classes, and some become leaders of political causes at all class levels. Some live in isolated, bohemian cultural enclaves, and others become self-conscious celebrities, viewing the philistine world, both inside and outside the city, with disdain.

The middle classes exhibit an even wider variety of life-styles than does the upper class. In part, this is due to the fact that some segments preserve older class styles more faithfully than does the upper class. At the same time, being subject to the pulls and strains of new social and economic developments, they incorporate new life-styles in a wider variety of combinations.

Since World War II, American society has seen the growth of a new middle class based on the prosperity and affluence of an expanding American industry. This class has been primarily responsible for the growth of suburbia and for urban middle-class housing developments such as Lefrak City. Other members of that class try to retain an older life-style in the outer reaches of the city. To some extent, the black upper-middle class attempts to maintain stable life-styles both in the changing city and in suburbia. But all groups increasingly are exposed to new sets of problems that correspond to the jet-set psychology in the upper class. Women's liberation as a social movement has made large inroads among middle-class housewives, and bohemians dwell in both the central city and suburbia. Drugs have penetrated deeply into the middle classes, and a radical cultural and political youth movement has arisen that disturbs both parents and the rest of society.

Since the life-styles of much of the new middle class are based on a relatively recent affluence, problems of recession, unemployment and inflation are especially threatening to its members, who have few defenses against economic reverses. In some areas the middle classes, as we shall see, have been aggressively resistant to the penetration of blacks into job markets and living areas. In part, apprehension explains the middle-class unwillingness to respond to the problems that afflict the lower class, both in the central cities and the suburbs. Some lower-class city people defend themselves by emphasizing to a high degree the traditional middle-class virtues. In certain communities, such as Jamaica Estates in Queens, they try to isolate themselves from the rest of the city in urban fortresslike enclaves. Others tend to feel that they have been bypassed by the whole movement of middle- and upper-middle-class life.

The joint effect of the new affluence and the arrival of millions of new migrants into the cities has changed the character of the old working class, many of whose members, by virtue of comparison with the "new lower class," have adopted a middle-class psychology. This new lower class is made up of black, Puerto Rican and Latin American migrants who live in ever-expanding slums under almost unimaginable conditions of poverty, inadequate housing, filth, disease, crime, drugs, violence and ignorance. "Welfare" becomes the major economic basis of existence for a sizable percentage of the urban population. This problem is perhaps the most important one in the entire city.

THE SCENE IN GROSSE POINTE: "WHY GO AWAY? WE'RE ALREADY HERE"

by CHARLOTTE CURTIS

GROSSE POINTE FARMS, Mich.—Anyone who thinks the natives get a little restless around here in the summer doesn't understand Grosse Pointe. It was a summer resort long before it became one of the nation's richest suburbs. And, as any affluent inhabitant is quick to volunteer, in many ways it still is a resort.

The country clubs, instead of being at the end of a long drive out of town, are only minutes away from the adequately behemoth houses. The houses themselves are air-conditioned, at least in part, and a lot have swimming pools.

Private tennis courts are not unheard of, although club courts are a popular gathering place. And there is sailing, boating and water skiing on Lake St. Clair, which, to all intents and purposes, is in everybody's front yard.

"We don't have to go away," said Mrs. Allan Shelden, a native-born grande dame who does. "Why should we? We're already here."

Mrs. Shelden, who pops in and out of such places as the Soviet Union and the Orient, is no longer an athlete. But she takes more than a passing interest in a granddaughter's horsemanship ("I don't like it when she falls off"). And in the autumn, she climbs into a leather pants suit to join the parties that go hunting for pheasant, duck and partridge in northern Michigan.

Mrs. Shelden, one of a handful of grande dames who give Grosse Pointe its glamour, also is a senior member of a Middle Western sodality that believes in hats, gloves and work. She says she doesn't care what people do "as long as they do things." And besides being a devoted patron of the Detroit Institute of

Arts and the Detroit Symphony, she is what she calls "a violent gardener."

She negotiates the 30-minute drive between her house on the lake and her downtown office in a Lincoln Continental ("We're friends of the Fords. I wouldn't dare not have one of their cars") and then walks the three blocks from her parking lot to her office and back again "because it's good exercise."

The office, which she keeps because her civic and charity work is complicated ("and I wanted a place to run my own affairs"), is in the Buhl Building. It was named for her mother's family. Buhl ancestors were granted their land by King George III. In 1855, the family founded Buhl Sons Company, a major wholesale hardware business.

When she was a girl, a time Mrs. Shelden distinctly remembers as being before the advent of the automobile, Detroit's upper echelons lived in town and summered in Grosse Pointe.

Since then, the automobile tycoons, manufacturers and corporate executives have joined the older lumber, shipping and banking families in taking over Grosse Pointe. Together, they have spent their old and new money making it into a deluxe bedroom community, run the population up to 55,000 and given over less important seasons to the business of travel.

They turn up in the capitals of the world, but Chicago, which has never been Detroit's idea of the nation's second most important city, is rarely on their travel agenda. And except for such affable people as Mrs. Shelden, Grosse Pointers have little enthusiasm for either Detroit itself or the suburbs of Bloomfield Hills and Birmingham.

"Everybody lives in Gross Pointe," Mrs. Shelden said, then changed her mind. "Well, not everybody. There's a perfectly marvelous group in Birmingham and Bloomfield Hills—automotive people who do things in the companies."

Frederick M. Alger, Jr., President Dwight D. Eisenhower's Ambassador to Belgium, seemed to agree. His grandfather, Russell A. Alger, was first an Ohio and then a Michigan lumber king ("What's left of our so-called fortune derived from lumber") and President William McKinley's Secretary of War. His father, Frederick M. Alger, was a member of the group that bought the Packard company.

"Detroit feels it's unique," Mr. Alger said in the comfortably furnished library of his big, ivy-covered red brick house. "If it doesn't operate, the whole economy folds up. We're the leading manufacturing town in the country—the backbone of the U.S. economy."

But this doesn't mean that he or his friends have to go into downtown Detroit.

"I don't much any more," said Mr. Alger. "Except on Wednesday when I go in to my club."

Neither he nor his son David Dewey Alger, a Harvard graduate who is going to the University of Michigan's School of Business Administration this fall to specialize in finance, can think of any good reason for visiting any other suburb.

"In my day, there wasn't much traffic between Grosse Pointe and Bloomfield Hills," Mr. Alger said, speaking of his youth. "It's an incredibly terrible drive—an hour and 15 minutes."

In my group of friends nobody ever goes to Bloomfield Hills," said David. "I don't even know anybody there."

Grosse Pointe, which is to Detroit what Bronxville is to New York, Lake Forest is to Chicago and Shaker Heights is to Cleveland, is not as insular as it sometimes seems. It's just that the ultimate goal is life as it is led in one of the five adjoining Grosse Pointes—preferably Grosse Pointe Farms.

The children go East to preparatory school and college when they can meet the academic standards, and a lot of them can. Then they come home and, in David's words, "marry each other, so there's an awful lot of inbreeding."

Most families belong to either the Country Club of Detroit, which has a golf course, or the Grosse Pointe Club, more familiarly known as "the Little Club." It has a marina for power and sailboats. By Palm Beach or Newport standards, no boat qualifies as a yacht.

"There used to be yachts," said the Countess Cyril Tolstoi. "It was much more glamorous in the past."

The Countess, an elegant native who met her late husband in Paris, lives on property first owned by Alexander Lewis, her grandfather. At one time, it was a family farm. When the banks closed during the Depression, she and Count Tolstoi, Leo Tolstoi's cousin, came back to Detroit.

"We thought it would be temporarily," the Countess said, "but then there was the Spanish Civil War and World War II so we stayed. We always intended to go back to Paris."

The Countess, whose house is furnished with French, Italian and Belgian antiques, is a lot less gung-ho about Grosse Pointe than most of her friends.

"Where there was one house there are 50 today," she said as she sipped iced tea. "Nothing interests me here."

This is not quite accurate. The Countess, and such equally old-family women as Mrs. Phelps Newberry—whose husband's forebears made their money in drygoods, shipping, real estate and the law, are ardent fans of the Detroit Tigers.

They go to the home games periodically, or watch them on television. And if a dinner invitation conflicts with a particularly important game, the Countess is likely to refuse. The Frederick Sloane Fords, Jr., are far more interested in sailing.

"One of the nice things about Grosse Pointe is that we have so many different kinds of things to be interested in," said Mrs. Ford. "There are our churches and all our community work. We all do a lot of volunteer work."

Mrs. Ford, wife of a naval architect and yacht designer whose family has long been involved in the manufacture of chemicals and glass (Libby-Owens-Ford Company), has the scrubbed good looks of a typical Grosse Pointe matron.

She is lean and blond, blue-eyed and tan. She plays tennis ("three times a week before the children got out of school") and paddle tennis, and she skis, shoots and sails. Fifteen years ago, she resigned from the Detroit Junior League.

"It seemed so silly to pay a baby-sitter so I could do volunteer work," she said. "What I really wanted to do was work directly with the agencies the Junior League served."

Mrs. Ford, who is known as a "salt Ford" (salt was important in the development of both the chemical and the glass industries) to distinguish her from the "automotive Fords" (Mrs. Edsel Ford) and the "banking Fords" (the Frederick C. Fords), belongs to one of the two Grosse Pointe sororities, Sigma Gamma and Tau Beta.

"We take in young girls when they've finished the ninth grade," she said. "We try to teach them to be good volunteers."

Mrs. Ford is another advocate of the "everyone must do some kind of work" school. But she believes that unless it is constructive, work has no point.

"I want my son to travel this summer," she said, speaking of 18-year-old Frederick B. Ford, "and he's going to Europe. That's more valuable than working in a supermarket."

Her daughter, Susan, a student at Connecticut College for Women, is "working" too. She is enrolled in a creative writing course this summer at Harvard. For Mrs. John Lord, the former Rhoda Newberry, work consists of painting lessons ("Just one abstract. The rest are a lot like Grandma Moses") and tending her spacious backyard.

"We never hire people to make party decorations," said Mrs. Lord, who gets down on her knees to weed her garden. "We do them ourselves. We prefer it that way."

Mrs. Lord's house, which is the equal of villas along the Atlantic Ocean in Palm Beach, has the white walls and cream-colored carpets of a resort mansion. A crystal chandelier hangs over the French living room. The entrance hall is white marble. The bouquets are made of plastic flowers.

In contrast to this and other Grosse Pointe houses is the place W. Hawkins Ferry helped design and build for himself farther out on the lake. It's thoroughly contemporary, a blending of Le Corbusier and Yamasaki, and the glassed-in conversation area is dominated by a nine-foot Giacometti sculpture.

Other contemporary art works, including wall-size paintings, a Picasso and a de Kooning, are counterbalanced by such family heirlooms as a Victorian mahogany table, a pewter and gilded-bronze chandelier and an imposing white marble bust of Mr. Ferry's grandfather, Dexter M. Ferry.

The senior Mr. Ferry, who came to Detroit in 1852, was first an errand boy and then a clerk at a book and stationery store. Later, he was a founder of the D. M. Ferry Company, a seed business. All of Mr. Ferry's flowers are real.

RECURRENT IMMIGRATION WAVES ARE KEEPING LOS ANGELES SOCIETY IN A STATE OF FLUX

by CHARLOTTE CURTIS

LOS ANGELES—Every time it looks as if there is about to be some semblance of social structure in this pastel empire, a new wave of immigration sweeps in, knocking it to bits.

A few institutions and individuals have survived these successive invasions. They have adopted a "the more the merrier" philosophy or withdrawn to such button-down bastions as suburban Pasadena. The rest simply fade into the palm trees.

One's bank account has a lot to do with one's status, and so does personal accomplishment and how long one's family has lived in California. But it is not smart to scrutinize other people's ancestors. Somebody might find out about one's own.

The new leaders are a lot like the first Vanderbilts, Mellons and Astors. They have their own ideas about what an establishment should be like.

They retain membership in exclusive country clubs but use these facilities infrequently. This is because they have all-purpose, do-it-yourself country clubs for homes—backyard swimming pools, tennis courts, spacious lawns, exotic gardens and patios with built-in bars and rotisseries.

They are not much for servants either, but not because help is costly. They simply don't want to be bothered with having to eat at the cook's convenience. And although there are still those who believe there is nothing like an Ivy League education, the vast majority look upon the entire East Coast with some disfavor.

"What's the matter?" a prominent oil man is said to have asked a graduate of Harvard. "Couldn't you get into Stanford?"

The Autumn Cotillion, which is generally accepted here as having society members, had its annual fall dinner and dance last week, and the guest list included only one or two of the Los Angeles names Easterners might consider kindred blue bloods. When asked about this, a member of the new order bristled:

"You don't judge society here by traditional standards. Those old people don't do anything. They don't count. Nobody pays any attention to them."

Before the fraternity rejects Los Angeles (population: 6,500,000) as being beyond the social pale, it had better take another look. The edges may be a little rough, but there are diamonds here, and more in the making. As a group these people could buy and sell Newport and most of Rhode Island. But, as one woman put it, "Who'd want to?"

When they are not flinging epithets at one another's credentials, the various social factions are championing their own leaders. One woman's name crops up again and again. She is Mrs. Norman Chandler, the feared and revered wife of the president of The Times-Mirror Company. By January, she expects to have reached a new plateau.

"I will have all the money I need for my music center," she said. "I have another 800,000 or 900,000 dollars to go."

The center, a three-building complex not unlike Manhattan's Lincoln Center, is a $20,000,000 project. Mrs. Chandler raised about half that amount herself. The largest building is for Los Angeles Philharmonic concerts. The completion of the center, the construction of which may be viewed from Mrs. Chandler's Times-Mirror office, will fulfill a tenaciously held dream.

"I wanted my symphony to have a home," she said.

Dorothy Buffum Chandler, Buff to friends, was born in Lafayette, Illinois, and reared in southern California. She met her husband, who inherited his prosperous newspaper, at Stanford University. She has been active in community affairs since 1935.

In 1959, after almost single-handedly saving the foundering Hollywood Bowl concerts, she became president of the Southern California Symphony Association. It rules the Philharmonic.

She is a tall, handsome woman with a freckled tan. She is rarely seen without her trademark, a gold identification bracelet with "Buff" spelled across the top in diamonds.

"It opens up," she said. "I keep a $100 bill inside. Sometimes I forget to take money."

Mrs. Chandler's favorite dress designers are Balenciaga of Paris and Norman Norell of New York.

"I plan my clothes just as I plan my music center or my house," she said.

She is not sure what she will tackle when the money for the center has been raised. She is a regent of the University of California and a director of half a dozen other civic groups. None provide the stimulation she says she needs.

"What I'm doing is upgrading the country," she said. "I'd like to do something else in that vein. There's no challenge at the University of California. Where could you go? Chairman of the Board of Regents? I don't want that."

The name of another University of California regent, Edward W. Carter, causes virtually no dissension among would-be social arbiters. He is considered society, although he neither seeks nor likes it.

"I have three principal interests," he said solemnly. "Business, education and the arts. I do not play golf."

Mr. Carter is educated (U.C.L.A. and the Harvard Graduate School of Business Administration), cultivated (his office contains a collection of 17th-century Dutch paintings) and successful in business. He is president of Broadway-Hale, the department-store chain.

He, too, is in the final stages of a fund-raising campaign. His goal is $10,000,000, the bill for the Los Angeles County Art Museum—the largest to be built since Washington put up its National Gallery in 1941.

Among the hundreds of others who figure in Los Angeles social disorder are Stuart and John O'Melveny, Mr. and Mrs. Martin Manulis, Mr. and Mrs. Robert Pusey Hastings, members of the copper-rich Mudd family, and the Frank L. Kings. They are not necessarily friends, or even acquaintances.

The O'Melvenys are elderly lawyers whose progenitor was an Illinois judge who rode to California on a horse in 1850. Their firm, which represents such celebrities as Bing Crosby and James Arness, is 82 years old.

"There have been lots of changes since I was a boy," John O'Melveny said. "I can remember when Wilshire Boulevard was a dirt road."

Mr. O'Melveny, a University of California at Berkeley graduate who went on to Harvard Law School wearing a Phi Beta Kappa key, raises cattle, quarter horses and English bulldogs. His 1,500-acre ranch is inside the city limits. At 68, he still ropes and brands his own cattle.

The Manulises, whose elegant hillside house is in Bel Air, are new Californians. She is Katharine Bard of Chicago, daughter of Ralph Bard, Franklin D. Roosevelt's wartime Under Secretary of the Navy. Her husband, born in Brooklyn, is the television and movie producer. He did *Days of Wine and Roses*.

"People out here are lonely on a gala scale," Mr. Manulis said. "They have parties because they don't know what else to do with themselves. The big thing is to put up a tent and invite everybody you know.''

"We like a simpler life," said his wife. "We don't have full-time help."

"We have a little woman named Katharine Manulis who comes in and does dinner every night," her husband added.

Mrs. Hastings, whose civic-minded husband is a Yale and a Harvard Law School graduate, is president of Las Madrinas, a children's hospital affiliate. In December, it will present 36 debutantes at its 29th annual ball.

"If we could have Chavez Ravine," Mrs. Hastings said jokingly, "We'd have more room for more debutantes."

The senior Mr. King is chairman of the United California Bank, Los Angeles. His daughter-in-law, Mrs. Frank L. King, Jr., is Janine Brooks, a third-generation Californian who is descended from New England whaling captains. She and her husband live in Pasadena.

"There's lots of new money," she said, "and people who are willing to spend it. It's not like San Francisco, which has old families. We're full of new families. They keep coming and coming."

When asked about Hollywood, Mrs. King said:

"I don't know why anyone would go there unless it would be to go to a movie or to the Hollywood Bowl."

By November 1, when the San Francisco Opera comes to town, society will be well into what may be one of the busiest seasons in its history. On November 8, the Assembly, a group whose 50 members were born in southern California, will stage its invitational dinner and ball.

And then, on November 14, virtually anybody who wants to be taken seriously will attend the Los Angeles Philharmonic's first performance of the season.

GUESTS AT THEATER FOR IDEAS TAKE UP CEREBRAL GAUNTLET

by ISRAEL SHENKER

© 1968 by The New York Times Company. Reprinted by permission.

The Theater for Ideas is New York's leading exercise in participatory autocracy.

In a third-floor studio loft, 30 worn steps from street level at 112 West 21st Street, the élite of America's intellectuals meet off and on to discuss issues of moment.

Usually they are on—and on and on. The theater is a place for exchanging views, but the intellectuals occasionally leave with the same mental baggage they arrived with, views reinforced, reputations preserved. It is where they go to confirm their worst delights.

Though every discussion has a scheduled moderator and distinguished speakers, the views from the floor are often as pertinent as those from the platform. This is hardly surprising when one reviews the guest list.

Among those who have graced the subrostrum level are such lofty thinkers as Robert Lowell, the poet; Isaiah Berlin, the historian; Daniel Bell, the sociologist; Michelangelo Antonioni, the film director, and Alberto Moravia and Dacia Maraini, the novelists.

Among those who have ventured onto the platform are Arthur M. Schlesinger, Jr., the historicopolitico; the semiprofessional revolutionary Professor Herbert Marcuse; the writer Nat Hentoff, Professor Noam Chomsky, Professor Connor Cruise O'Brien and J. Kenneth Galbraith.

"It's a very lively place," says Alfred Kazin, the critic, "and I often wonder why it's so popular when other places that are more pretentious are ignored. The seats are uncomfortable and it's out of the way. I guess something happens there."

At most, 100 people can share the discomforts and enlightenment. They are usually members of the theater and pay anywhere from $20 (for an individual annual member) to $1,000 (founder-member). Armand G. Erpf is the only founder-member thus far. Mr. Erpf is a prominent investment banker who has a chair named for him at Columbia. He also has a wooden folding chair named for him at the theater.

Recently the subject for discussion was, "What is happening in China?" The moderator was Ezra F. Vogel, assistant director of the East Asian Research Center at Harvard. The speakers were Emile Guikovaty, who was Agence France-Presse correspondent in Peking from 1964 to 1966, and Krishnan Raghunath, who served there with the Embassy of India from 1965 to 1967.

Mr. Guikovaty's opening address was a long *mea culpa,* as he explained the restrictions imposed on journalists and the difficulties in communicating with the Chinese. He told of the time they were digging outside his window, and he was unable to find out whether it was for a subway, an air-raid shelter or water pipes.

"How can you be honest in a country when you don't know what's going on before your eyes?" he asked the audience.

Mr. Raghunath topped that plea of ignorance by declaring that diplomats were worse off. "We never got any trips to Yunan or other internal parts of China," he said.

Mr. Guikovaty promptly returned to his public confession to declare, "There were times when one felt the best way to study the situation was to get out of China."

He was not going to win his fight. From the audience spoke up the Sinologist Professor A. Doak Barnett of Columbia. "It seems to me," said Dr. Barnett, "that academics suffer from even greater frustrations."

That was only the beginning. Having thus established the honesty of their expertise, the speakers and audience proceeded to theories on the how and Mao of China today.

Of the half a dozen questions, for example, that were fired by the political scientist Hannah Arendt, the most probing was, "Who are these masses?"

These masses had been the subject of much speculation, and Dr. Arendt's puzzlement was greeted approvingly. Not that this question or others got very full answers. When only one of Dr. Arendt's six questions was answered, the moderator turned to another member of the audience for more questions. Dr. Arendt is urbane, however, and smiled at her own plight.

Not every evening at the theater goes off as calmly, possibly because not every subject is as remote as China.

Only last May, Professor Marcuse informed his listeners that although democracy had a future, "in my view it certainly does not have a present" because, among other things, the "American society has become progressively insane."

Norman Mailer, who is usually quick on his feet, got tangled in Professor Marcuse's judgments when the novelist complained about the way people drop Dr. Marcuse's name at cocktail parties.

"It's the debasement of the Gothic intricacies of Dr. Marcuse's style," said Mr. Mailer.

There followed this exchange:

Marcuse: "You write much better."

Mailer: "Thank you."

Marcuse: "But I write deeper."

Shirley Broughton is the one who brings the meetings back to the subject. She is a dancer-choreographer-turned-impresario of ideas, and it was she who founded the theater in 1961. Its home is also hers.

"I hate provincial conversation," she explained. "I wanted to break the Broadway system of doing things. I wanted to do things in a more human way—in a place where serious ideas could be considered."

At the beginning the project was called "Sundays at 4." But, as Miss Broughton explained, "you can't always do things on Sundays."

Not every evening at the theater is as heady with the evasion of ideas. Some of the nights are devoted to experimental dance programs. Or small-scale theater presentations. Or music or lectures. Saul Bellow read his first play, *Bummidge,* to an audience at the theater. Mr. Mailer and Eric Bentley have also read from their works.

Miss Broughton says that none of her speakers are paid, but that her non-profit theater nonetheless runs a deficit every year, which she estimates as between $20,000 and $40,000. That is why she is devoting this month to raising funds, offering folding chairs to anyone interested in the theater's play of ideas.

OPULENCE BECOMING A WAY OF LIFE FOR THE MIDDLE CLASS

by JACK ROSENTHAL

© 1970 by the New York Times Company. Reprinted by permission.

Roger McRea is not wealthy, not on a Seattle schoolteacher's salary. So when his old second car broke down last spring, the remedy seemed obvious: a small economy car. But he promptly bought a full-size $3,500 station wagon.

"We needed something," says his pretty wife, Diane, "big enough to tow the boat."

A boat. Two cars. A $34,000 suburban house. A long list of appliances, from a dishwasher to a toaster oven.

The McReas, who get about $14,000 a year from Mr. McRea's salary, outside work and small investments, are neither spendthrifts nor unusually acquisitive.

On the contrary, they typify a vast number of American families for whom in the nineteen-sixties the affluent society appears, current inflation and recession notwithstanding, to have become the opulent society.

In the last decade, the average family's earnings rose in inflation-adjusted dollars from $6,900 to $9,400 and, according to a current Census Bureau report, consumers rushed to buy items ranging from cars to clothes dryers. Many, if they already had one, bought another one.

As a result, more families now have two cars than none and as many families have television sets as have toilets. In little more than five years, the number of families with color television has risen from about 5 per cent to nearly 40 per cent.

Such gains mask the deep poverty that endures among 10 per cent of American families. But even that number has dropped sharply from the 1960 poverty total of 18 per cent.

The new census data, coupled with recent commercial statistics, disclose these major changes during the last decade:

The proportion of the nation's 63 million families with basic appliances—refrigerators, radios, ranges and electric irons—went over 99 per cent. Television sets rose to 95 per cent, clothes washers to 92 per cent, vacuum cleaners to 91 per cent.

There were dramatic increases in the purchase of less basic but familiar appliances. For example, in 1958, when John Kenneth Galbraith, the Harvard professor, first characterized this as the affluent society, about half of the American families had electric coffee makers. Now the figure is 86 per cent.

Consumers have given an equally dramatic welcome to other appliances, for which no 1960 figures are available because the products were not marketed then. About 47 million home hair dryers have been sold since 1961. Some 22 million electric carving knives have been sold since 1964.

There were striking increases in the number of families with multiple cars, television sets and radios. Since 1960, the proportion of families with one car rose from 75 to 80 per cent. But the proportion with more than one nearly doubled, to about 30 per cent. Families in the New York metropolitan area still have the lowest proportion of cars. About 58 per cent have one or more, compared with 85 per cent in Detroit, the leading area.

The proportion of families with one TV set rose from 90 per cent in 1960 to 95 per cent now—which is almost exactly the proportion of families with complete plumbing facilities. The proportion with two or more sets went from 17 to 29 per cent. The average family now has five radios, compared with three in 1960.

The Census Bureau data are contained in a special report on ownership of cars, homes and major appliances based on a sampling of 12,000 households. Data on other appliances have been compiled by *Merchandising Week* magazine. It reports that consumer spending for items like appliances and stereo systems soared from $7.6 billion in 1960 to $13.9 billion last year. Only a quarter of the difference is accounted for by inflation.

Judging by Diane and Roger McRea, such statistics are not surprising. Since they were married four years ago, they have bought—or been given—almost all the standard mechanical or electrical possessions.

To the McReas, both 30 years old, many of these are not evidences of opulence, but necessities.

An automatic washer and dryer? Until their daughter, Lori, was born two years ago, they didn't have them. "I preferred the laundromat," says Mrs. McRea. "I could use as many machines as I needed to get all the laundry done at once. But now with Lori, it's a lot harder to get out of the house."

A freezer? The second-hand unit they bought two years ago is "the biggest bargain we've ever gotten—we can put away a whole cow and have meat for a year."

A blender? It's useful for making baby food at home, Mrs. McRea learned from her sister-in-law. "She keeps telling me how much water you pay for when you but it at the store."

Other things are not necessities at all, Mrs. McRea concedes cheerfully. "The perfect example is our refrigerator." When they bought it, a persistent salesman persuaded them to pay $25 extra for an automatic icemaker.

"We didn't really want it. We didn't need it. But now, it's just so neat to reach in and not mess around with a tray of ice when you only want a couple of cubes."

But even such convenience items are not luxuries to Diane McRea. "Appliances are things you use. For me, the real luxury is furniture."

Still there is a recurring unease. "Roger and I talk about how different our life-style is than when we were kids. For instance, I have trouble remembering what we did at home when there was no TV to watch. I worry about what it is that Lori is missing."

The experience of the McReas typifies millions of families. But it, like the general conclusions of the special census report, masks sharp variations at opposite ends of the income scale.

For example, among families with incomes over $15,000, more than 96 per cent have at least one car (and 63 per cent more than one). But among families with incomes under $3,000, only 41 per cent have cars, leaving three of every five families dependent upon friends or public transportation. Nearly half of all elderly families have no car.

Similar contrasts exist for home ownership, for which the national figure is now 64 per cent, a 2 per cent rise since 1960. Among the over-$15,000 families, 85 per cent own their own homes. Among the under-$3,000 families, 50 per cent do.

The over-all census figures also obscure poverty in other ways. Analysts note that the figures do not reflect the age of appliances and that those used by the poor often are old and in poor condition.

And even then, many poor people are dependent on the appliances provided by landlords. Only half of the under-$3,000 families own washing machines, for example.

DOWN AND OUT
ALONG ROUTE 128

by BERKELEY RICE

Arnold Limberg, Wayne Lees, Phil Blum and David Gernes don't know each other, but they should, for they have much in common. They are all scientists or engineers who live within a few miles of each other in Lexington, Massachusetts, a prosperous, well-groomed suburb of Boston. They are all married, with two children, two cars and comfortable homes. To the extent that salary represents any measure of a technical man's worth, they are all competent, successful men, who until recently were earning more than $15,000 a year. This year, they all acquired a new experience in common—they've been fired.

Of course, no one uses such a crude word as "fired" any more. These days one is "laid off," "displaced," "surplused" or "temporarily furloughed, pending recall." Whatever the corporate euphemism, it applies equally to an alarming number of engineers and scientists in the Greater Boston area. Like the massive layoffs in the West Coast aerospace industry, most of those in this area have been caused by cutbacks in Federal spending for defense and space. But unlike the huge assembly lines on the West Coast, which turn out planes, missiles and other big items of military hardware, most electronics and research firms around Boston specialize in complex systems which require relatively few production workers. As a result, the layoffs here have hit the highly skilled technicians as badly as the man on the production lines.

While no Ph.D. bread lines have formed as yet, the problem of technical unemployment has become a community one. Retail sales are off, the real estate market has softened considerably and mortgage payments are running behind. At a recent farewell dinner given by a departing employe of a Lexington electronics firm which has laid off several hundred men this year, three of the five guests had also been laid off by other firms. At the September board meeting of the Couples' Club of Lexington's Hancock Congregational Church, the discussion concerned jobs, rather than church affairs. One engineer, laid off a few months ago, was doing research in his basement; another had just been laid off for the second time this year by Raytheon; one had been laid off after nearly 20 years with his company; the wife of another engineer who expected to be dropped soon, said, "We just live from day to day."

Similar remarks can be heard these days at dinner parties, church meetings and country clubs in Needham, Wellesley, Newton, Waltham, Weston, Lincoln, Concord, Bedford, Burlington and other suburbs that border Boston's Route 128. In the age of the computer, Route 128 has become Boston's "Golden Horseshoe," and the East Coast center of the electronics industry. Most major electronics corporations have headquarters, or at least plants, here, and hundreds of smaller companies with exotic or cryptic names huddle together in sterile concrete clusters which P.R. men call "industrial parks." In nearby Cambridge, dozens of small research firms have sprung up in the last

ne at M.I.T. and Harvard, and
n 128.

rs and scientists worked in the
est concentrations of technical
f, at least 10,000 of them have
llecting unemployment benefits
estimate that many more have
ill turn up soon. To a statisti-
employment in this region has
aught graduates hired last June
with 20 years of loyal service.
y're expensive, highly special-
n. The young engineers gener-

tting worse. Dozens of empty
ase. Many small firms facing
r companies. Others, like Na-
ptcy. The plague has struck the
ter firm that has dropped from
ll as established national firms
everal hundred men this year,
of its semiconductor divisions,
Greater Boston area. In a state-
rs, Sylvania president Garland
me men in its other divisions,
ul of the impact this action will

ve tried to reduce their budgets

Berkley Rice

Down and out along Rt. 128

Autos allowed of Lexington, Need ham
Wellesley, Newton, Waltham, Weston,
Lincoln, Concord, Bedford and others
Rt 128. Referred to as Boston's "Golden

by cutting salaries 10 per cent. Others have tried to "increase productivity" by getting more work out of the men they've kept. Making them work evenings and weekends represents a painless form of belt-tightening for the companies, since engineers, as "professionals," do not receive overtime pay. In most cases the survivors hardly need to be urged to work harder. "There's a lot of talk about 'pulling together' to save the company," says a still-employed physicist, "but it's actually to save our jobs."

At the larger firms, the only way to be sure who's still around is to check the latest company phone directory. The tense atmosphere among those waiting to see who gets laid off next has led to some fairly black humor. A metallurgist at TYCO Laboratories who was recently given three months' notice soon found many of his colleagues avoiding him as though he had contracted some virulent disease. One of his remaining friends gave him a gift of a leper bell, so that he could warn everyone away when he came down the halls. In the company cafeterias, a standard joke these days runs, "Hey, when are you going downtown for your hack license?" Worst of all are the farewell luncheons for those laid off. "They're really pretty gruesome," says an engineer who has attended several for his colleagues. "There're usually about 20 or 30 guys from the department. They all get up and say what a great guy he was, and he gets up and tells them how much he enjoyed working with them and everything. *Eeyuch!*"

Raytheon, the giant of the local electronics industry, has had the most farewell luncheons lately. Like other large corporations that have had to merge or close down troubled divisions, Raytheon has essentially dismantled its Space and Informations Systems Division in Sudbury.

The Missile Systems Division in Bedford, its biggest plant, has been hurt by cutbacks or "stretch-outs" on its contracts for the A.B.M., SAM-D and Hawk missile programs. (Despite such troubles, Raytheon managed to increase its sales for 1969 to a record $1.28 billion, of which about half came from Government defense and space contracts.)

Such troubles at Raytheon have a tremendous effect on the technical labor market since it is by far the largest employer in this region, and one of the biggest in New England. Before the first cutbacks came in 1969, Raytheon had more than 30,000 men working in plants in Lowell, Andover, Bedford, Burlington, Lexington, Waltham, Wayland, Sudbury and Norwood. Over the past year or so this labor force has dropped by 3,500.

Raytheon may be bigger than the other firms along Route 128, but its dependence on military contracts is typical. While the general recession may be responsible for some of the cutbacks along 128, the basis for the area's previous prosperity has always been defense and space contracts. The names of the largest firms in the industrial parks of the Golden Horseshoe read like a list of the country's biggest defense and space contractors: Raytheon, R.C.A., AVCO, General Electric, Western Electric, Sperry Rand, Sylvania, Control Data, Litton. Much of their Government contract money filters down to the smaller firms in the area. They buy electronic components, subcontract research projects, and hire dozens of M.I.T. and Harvard professors as consultants.

To coordinate all this activity, and to handle the billions of dollars in contracts that go to these firms, the Department of Defense has established its own electronics and research headquarters here. The Air Force, the country's largest buyer of electronic equipment, has stationed its Electronics Systems Division at Hanscom Field in Bedford, a five-minute ride from 128. Out of its 1969 budget of $400 million, E.S.D. alone spent $160 million on contracts to Massachusetts firms. In addition to the Air Force E.S.D., the Defense Department has several other major research installations in this area: the Air Force Cambridge Research Lab, Lincoln Lab and MITRE Corporation, all conveniently close to E.S.D. headquarters at Hanscom Field, plus the Instrumentation Lab (recently renamed Draper Lab) at M.I.T. Together, the budgets of these four research centers totaled more than $200 million in 1969, much of it spent on contracts to local research and engineering firms. Even more important to the local job market, they employ about 6,800 personnel, more than half of whom are civilian scientists and engineers.

In addition to cutting back on contract funds, the Government has also begun "reducing" personnel at its local research centers. Rumors have been circulating for months about impending mass layoffs, and there have even been rumors about a possible transfer of the Air Force E.S.D. headquarters. While the Defense Department continually denies such rumors, public and corporate officials around here are justifiably nervous. Many of them feel the severity of the Federal cutbacks in this area are due more to political spite than simple economics. They claim the Nixon Administration is deliberately punishing Massachusetts Senators Edward Brooke and Edward Kennedy for their lack of support on the A.B.M., the Haynsworth-Carswell nominations and other crucial legislative matters. As proof, they cite the case of last summer's closing of NASA's 800-man Electronics Research Center in Cambridge. In December, 1969, in response to rumors about the center's future, the Administration assured Senator Brooke, who in turn assured his constituents, that there were no plans to close the center down. A few weeks later, just before Christmas, *The Boston Herald* broke the news of the center's closing.

Of the more than 400 scientists and engineers who were put out of work by June, fewer than half have since been retained by the Department of Transportation, which has taken over the facility. A few of the younger, more adaptable men found jobs elsewhere with NASA and other Federal agencies. The rest were simply laid off. Their names automatically go on priority lists for Federal job openings, but with the current contraction in Federal research projects, these lists offer little hope. More than 100 of those laid off are still out of work.

One of them is Dr. Wayne Lees of Lexington, a 56-year-old experimental physicist with a Ph.D. from Harvard. At a salary of nearly $23,000, he had been working on a system for monitoring the cabin atmosphere in space capsules. Unlike most of his colleagues, who began looking for other jobs as soon as NASA formally announced the shutdown, Dr. Lees spent the next few months trying to finish up his research project while he still had the use of his lab. He didn't get around to serious job-hunting until late in the spring of 1970, just before the lab finally closed down. "I was lucky," he says now, viewing his unsuccessful job search with the detachment of a scientist. "Many of my colleagues found nothing after six months of searching. I got the same results with much less effort."

Lees called one technical employment agency and was told bluntly, "There's nothing we can do for you." Actually, even in good times the agencies can't do much for senior scientists like Lees. As he puts it, "If you have a Ph.D. and a few decades of experience, you're selling a commodity the agencies and personnel offices aren't qualified to handle." Such men generally find new jobs through personal and professional contacts, and their job applications involve much more than merely sending around résumés. They must offer a specific proposal on how their talents can be profitably utilized by the particular company. Dr. Lees sent such proposals to 30 or 40 different companies— without receiving a single request for a serious interview. His search for a university teaching or research position yielded equally depressing results.

Asked if he feels his age hurts his chances for a new job, Lees laughs gently, "I'm sure it does. Anyone my age who says it doesn't is just kidding himself."

"How do you know?"

"When you get back a dozen answers saying, 'You are too highly qualified for the position we have open,' it can mean, among other things, that you are too old. Of course, in my case, many companies probably feel I am too highly qualified, or too expensive for them. Actually, I'm quite willing to take a lower-paying job, or one of somewhat lesser professional standing."

If nothing turns up in the next few months, Dr. Lees may try to set up a private consulting service. Until then he seems content to work on a few technical papers, and to repair a battered 1963 Ford he bought from a computer-analyst friend, who has also been laid off. His financial situation is not grave and clearly does not bother him. His wife works part-time as a social worker, and his two daughters are still a long way from the expenses of college. Because of his age, and years of Government service, his severance pay will carry him through the rest of this year. He has also filed for unemployment benefits, which will bring in $74 a week for nearly 10 months.

For Wayne Lees, with 30 years of professional experience behind him, the loss of a job has not been an ego-shattering blow. "I am a physicist," he asserts with pride, "and I still consider myself a physicist, and a member of the profession, even though I am no longer attached to an organization."

A few days after talking with Dr. Lees, I asked Manny Sugarman, who runs one of the best-known technical agencies in the 128 area, about the importance of age in seeking a job today in research or engineering. He replied, "It's not so much a matter of age today as it is an oversupply in a tight market. Age was never much of a problem before in this industry. In a good market I've placed guys in their sixties in technical jobs. Today, in some fields, there simply aren't any jobs. If you're a Ph.D. in solid-state or high-energy physics, I probably couldn't place you even if you were 16."

Louis Rudzinsky, who runs an agency in Lexington, feels the technical job market has changed considerably during the past year, and not only in terms of quantity. A year ago, he says, when the first wave of layoffs came, many of the companies were dropping what he refers to as "marginal" employes, whose loss did not really hurt. "This year they're dropping their really good people. Normally we could move these people right away. Now it often takes months. For many of them, the market for the kind of work they have been involved in has nearly dried up. Because of the Government cutbacks there is very little work around today in radar communications or aerospace instrumentation."

In a market as tight as this, job-hunting can be a frustrating and humiliating experience for men accustomed to the respect due professionals. An engineer with a good deal of management experience recalls wistfully, "In the past, all I had to do was let it be known that I was interested in leaving, and I was soon very busy talking to other companies. This time there was absolutely nothing." A former chief engineer, now making the rounds of agencies (often referred to as "body shops") and company personnel offices, calls the process degrading. "When you walked into people's offices before, you were ushered in, no nonsense about it. When you're job-hunting, you sit and wait, and cool your heels. It really shakes you up."

When jobs do open up, the competition is fierce. A recent ad in *The Boston Globe* for an engineering position produced 400 inquiries in three days. A scientist who had been looking for months finally heard of an opening at a research firm for which he was perfectly qualified. By the time he contacted the firm, there were already 120 other applicants, many with equally perfect qualifications. In the face of such depressing odds, many engineers and scientists have given up the search for a job in their own field. Some are now working as rug salesmen, TV repairmen, bartenders, landscape gardeners. Those who take such nontechnical jobs in the hope of getting back into the industry when the economy improves face the danger most feared among engineers— obsolescence. Even if he tries to keep up in his field by reading the technical journals, an engineer out of work for a year or so can easily lose touch. And even if he does manage to keep up, the companies may wonder about his competence when they learn he has been doing construction work for a year.

Arnold Limberg, a 42-year-old electrical engineer laid off more than a year ago, recalls "times when I'd be working on test procedures, with everyone on my back, and I'd say, 'One of these days I'm going to quit and become a handyman, and have no worries at all.' " He still has a few worries, but he got the rest of his wish. His business cards now read, "Odd Jobs: You Name It, I'll Do It." Instead of the $20,000 a year he earned as an engineer, he now averages about $200 a week—in good weather. He charges $5 an hour for yard work, $6 for painting, and $7 for roofing and carpentry.

At ITEK, a large electronics company with plants in Lexington and Burlington, Limberg had worked on Government defense and space contracts. When the Government began cutting back in 1969, he found himself, along with hundreds of co-workers, "sitting around on overhead, waiting for contracts to come in." Unwilling to wait what is beginning to look like a long time, ITEK has laid off about 1,000 men during the last year and a half. In August, 1969, Limberg received notice on a Wednesday that he would be through that week.

A careful man with money, Limberg had fortunately saved regularly, and had always paid in cash. With few debts, he was able to live off his severance pay, $69 a week in unemployment benefits and part-time work on a neighboring farm in Carlisle. He contacted several employment agencies, made a lot of phone calls, sent résumés to 50 or 60 companies and waited for something to turn up. Nothing did. Finally in November, 1969, ITEK hired him back to work on a new contract, but then dropped him again three months later, in the next wave of layoffs.

"I didn't really worry about it back in August," says Limberg. "This time I knew I had to do something. I sent out résumés and contacted the agencies again, but I wasn't about to just wait around for something to open up. If I had, I'd be bankrupt by now. You don't sit on your pride when you've got bills coming in. You do something or you go broke. I saw enough of that when I grew up in South Dakota in the thirties.''

Fortunately, growing up in South Dakota had taught Limberg how to use his hands and tools, and he decided to try earning a living as an odd-job handyman. He told his wife to tell her friends, and put a classified ad in the local paper. Some of his friends thought he was "nuts," but soon the jobs began coming in: a few days of yard work, raking leaves, chopping wood. Since March, he has built a carport, installed a sump pump, reroofed two houses and painted another. No longer worried about getting enough jobs, he finds the work satisfying and healthy. He's lost 20 pounds of office-work flab, and acquired a ruddy outdoor complexion. With winter coming on, though, he wonders if there will be enough indoor jobs to see him through.

With only half their former income, the Limbergs have had to make some adjustments in their standard of living. They put off some remodeling of their $50,000 home, fixed the old dryer instead of buying a new one, pretty much stopped going out and cut the allowances of their two teen-aged daughters. Arnold's wife, Rita, gave up her morning nursery school job and took a full-time job with an insurance company, where her 17-year-old daughter also works now, after school. Rita hopes Arnold will return soon to his real career, and still feels bitter about the layoff. "How could he spend all those years studying and applying his craft," she wonders, "and then be suddenly told there was no use for him? In such a technical country as ours, surely a man with a master's degree in engineering must be needed somewhere."

Arnold Limberg also hopes something turns up soon, but says he won't return to aerospace electronics because, as he has painfully learned, it's not particularly stable. He now claims he wasn't happy in that field anyway, because of all the desk work, "but it's hard to break out when you're into the good money. Once you break out you find you can do it easily. You find you can do without a lot of things.''

(Shortly after this interview, Arnold Limberg found an engineering position with Reclamation Systems, Inc., a garbage-compacting firm now building its first pilot plant in East Cambridge. Though his new salary is considerably less than his old one, it's more than he made as a handyman, and he looks forward to the new job with excitement. "It's not exotic state-of-the-art work," he says, "but it's important and useful. Besides, it's the kind of work I like to do, working with machines, instead of at a desk."")

While the electronics industry in general has been badly hurt by defense and space cutbacks, the research labs have suffered the most damage. Faced with a shortage of funds, both the Defense Department and the companies have pretty much dropped their long-range research projects. According to one senior research scientist, "You can count on the fingers of one hand the number of companies around here still supporting their own in-house, long-range research programs. They just can't afford to spend money on any work that isn't going to pay for itself right away."

A journey along Route 128 illustrates this hard-nosed policy. AVCO's Everett Research Lab, which had just moved into an expensive new building, laid off about 200 men last spring—a 30 per cent cut. "It all happened very fast," recalls one of the survivors. "One weekend, a few of the top people went through the names of everyone in the lab. Monday morning the list went up, and the number two man in the lab, who had helped pick the guys to be laid off, found his own name at the top of the list. They chopped off a lot of Ph.D.'s and some really skilled engineers. A lot of them are still out of work now, after six months. The place is kind of spooky now. Lots of secretaries' desks with no secretaries, shopping baskets full of telephones, empty offices. The ones who are left are really breaking their backs now—partly because the place is badly undermanned, and partly because they're scared to death of losing their own jobs."

At E.G.&G., a Bedford firm specializing in nuclear-testing devices for the Atomic Energy Commission, a 50 per cent staff cut has virtually wiped out several research departments. When I asked him how the company decided which men to drop, one department head told me, "They don't usually tell you whom to lay off. They just tell you your department doesn't have enough contract money to support its personnel budget. Those who are working on contract projects are relatively safe. The ones who aren't, who are supported by in-house funds, are in trouble. Ordinarily many good people are on in-house funds between contracts, but now they have become a luxury. The ones who are kept on are the ones who can go out and drum up business. Once we've got the contracts, we can always go out and hire a lab full of good scientists and engineers, particularly these days."

Phil Blum of Lexington is a typical example of the good scientist who was laid off because he was not involved in contract research when the crunch came. A 41-year-old physicist earning $16,500, Phil was dismissed last May by Norton Research, a Cambridge firm with the function of coming up with profitable ideas for its parent, Norton Company, a large conglomerate. Norton Research had about 90 employes, including two dozen scientists, of which Phil was one of the best. In 1967, in fact, he was featured as "Norton's Moon Man" in a full-page color ad in *Time* magazine. The ad told how he had created artificial "moon dust" for use by the astronauts training for the Apollo program. His mother and his wife were very proud. Now, three years later, he's been fired. He still has the *Time* ad framed on his wall, but it now reads, "Norton's Moon Man—Bites Dust."

Phil's wife, Peg, can still recall vividly the day it happened: "He didn't call. He came home early and stood there in the kitchen, kind of laughing, but in a strange way. I sort of guessed then. You could almost see it in his eyes. He'd been talking about layoffs for a few months, and it had already happened to several of our friends. Even so, those first few weeks were pretty scary. I don't know what the children thought."

Things were just as touchy around the lab, Phil remembers. "I received two months' notice, so I was still coming in each day. My colleagues sort of stopped talking to me. Maybe they felt bad, or guilty, or something. I don't know. I used to joke about it, but they didn't think it was very funny. They were probably too scared about their own jobs. It was all pretty depressing."

For a short time Phil looked around for another job in research or engineering. He tried the employment agencies, with no results. "I knew it was hopeless," he says, "but I felt I should at least go through the motions. I knew there were no jobs around in my field, and I wasn't going to kill myself looking for no jobs." He had been thinking seriously about teaching even before being laid off, but with only a master's degree he stood little chance of finding a university position. Even the junior colleges have been able to fill their openings with Ph.D.'s in this year's glut market. This left high schools. Phil sent out applications to 24 different school systems within commuting distance of Lexington. The forms were long, complicated and full of such questions as "What does your husband do for a living?" Only one high school had an opening, and he accepted it gladly, just about the time he left Norton in May.

To get through the summer months before his teaching job began, Phil collected his $74 a week in unemployment benefits, and Peg returned to her nursing career, which had ended with the arrival of their two children. Equipped with a master's degree in a field still short of help, she soon found an excellent job at a nearby V.A. hospital for $11,900. Together with Phil's new salary of $9,300, this will mean a larger combined income than before, although Peg is not sure how much longer she will continue working full-time.

Since Phil now gets home first, he prepares the family dinner. To take care of the house, Peg hired a cleaning woman who listed another Lexington couple as a reference. When Peg called them, the husband, an engineer, explained that they were dropping the cleaning woman because he'd been laid off and could no longer afford her.

After many years of research ("much of it was really pretty dull"), Phil looks forward eagerly to his new career. "However, I still feel that in other people's eyes there's less prestige in this job. When I used to tell people I was a nuclear physicist they were impressed. Now, when I tell them I'm a high school teacher, I still can't say it with the same feeling of pride.''

According to Peg, ''Many of our friends think it's wonderful, what Phil's doing.''

Phil is not so sure. ''They may just be saying that. They tell me how much they admire me for going into teaching, but some of them really feel sorry for me.''

Phil has few regrets about being laid off. He spent the summer writing a technical paper, built a sundeck on the back of the house and started a mail-order toy business. He also has a few ideas for patents based upon his research. ''There're all sorts of things I've wanted to do for years. Now I've finally got the time. I'm just coming alive again. I feel like I've been in solitary confinement all those years, and now I've been liberated.''

David Gernes, a 33-year-old electrical engineer who lives over a hill from Phil Blum in Lexington's Peacock Farm section, also feels liberated—so much so, that he is no longer looking for a job. In 1967, after working for several electronics research firms in the area, he and two friends formed their own company, Competition Associates. Working out of a garage in Harvard Square, they turned out high-powered telescopes. Soon they wanted to expand and needed capital. Unable to raise sufficient money themselves, they agreed to sell the company to Ealing Corporation, a large distributor of scientific equipment, which kept them on to manage their operation.

In 1969, Ealing, along with the rest of the industry, began having its own financial problems. Although the telescopes were selling well, and Ealing's executive vice president had just told David he was considered ''a valued member of the Ealing team,'' when his contract came up for renewal in November, he was laid off. He even had to fight for a month's notice. That afternoon he called home from the office and told his wife, Naomi, ''Guess what? I'll be home early. I've been fired.''

The fact that David Gernes had set up and run his own firm did not seem to make much difference to the few prospective employers he located. The fact that he has no engineering degree did. Neither his own contacts nor the agencies turned up anything solid. For three months he sent out résumés and made telephone calls, with no results.

Naomi noticed an obvious reaction to his father's situation in their elder child, 7-year-old Todd. ''He was so used to David working all the time, he became a little worried when David began spending all the time around the house. I think he wondered if daddy was in trouble.'' David recalls those days clearly: ''We'd be talking about some job possibility, and he'd hear us and say, 'Great! Are you going to take that job? When are you going to start?' ''

After a while David gave up the job search and took the family on a three-week driving trip to Florida. During that trip, and the days spent sitting around the house, he began thinking seriously about his career. "What the hell. It was pretty apparent I wasn't going to find any work in my field, so I began to ask myself if I really wanted to continue in this field, and if not, what were the other options."

Fortunately for David, his financial position enabled him to take the time to consider his options. The sale of the Ealing stock he had received when they bought him out left him with more than enough to buy his $50,000 home. He also had rental income from two old houses in Cambridge that he and Naomi had bought and fixed up over the years. This led to one of his options. He had learned a good deal about building with those houses, and had also enjoyed it. In February, a friend asked him to help him find a contractor to construct a small studio, and when the bids came in they were so high that David offered to build it himself. He did, for half the price. It took two and a half months of hard work, but again he found he enjoyed it. The word got around, and he soon had a contract to build a neighborhood swimming pool, which took him through the summer.

"What did your friends think," I asked, "when they saw you, an electrical engineer, hammering nails for a living?"

"Most of them understood, but a few were kind of patronizing. They'd come around expressing admiration for what I was doing, and I'd get vibrations of disdain."

Now, David and one of his old partners, who was also laid off by Ealing, are building a custom laser telescope for the Smithsonian Astrophysical Lab in Cambridge. And after that? "Maybe more consulting work in telescopic control systems, or maybe some more contracting. If I do get back into business again, I don't intend to get back into the kind of rut most successful executives are into. I've enjoyed this time I've spent at home, and I've enjoyed the manual labor. It's very satisfying, and low-pressure.

"As you plummet out of the corporate cloud, you suddenly discover that you've never really had time to develop penetrating relationships with your wife and children. The same with your friends. You see them once a week for cocktails or a dinner party, but you don't really know them. I've learned that what matters is people, rather than things."

Gernes is not the only engineer who has been doing some serious thinking about his career lately. The Institute of Electrical and Electronic Engineers, the largest professional society in the field, has been rumbling with talk of a union for engineers that would protect their jobs and standardize employment practices in the industry. One major obstacle, however, is that many of the

I.E.E.E.'s leaders are themselves executives in this industry. Another obstacle, according to one of the society's officials, is that "the only ones who are yelling about unions are the ones who've been laid off. The others don't want to make any trouble. They're too worried about hanging onto their own jobs. Besides, engineers tend to be more management-oriented than labor-oriented, anyway. In fact, most of them hope to get into management eventually. They get paid well, and they tend not to grumble about working conditions. There's a bit more grumbling now, but with all these layoffs, no one's grumbling out loud in the plants."

When I asked Harold Goldberg, head of the Greater Boston I.E.E.E., why his organization was not set up to look after the welfare of its members, he explained, "Up until now, there was never any reason to. The industry was doing well, and all the engineers were happy. Many people even feel we've had this coming to us for a long time. Since the days of Sputnik, engineers have been the golden boys of industry. People always hear about those wonderful starting salaries for the graduates of M.I.T., but no one hears about what happens to those salaries over the years. They don't increase the way they do in other professional fields. There's sort of a ceiling on engineering salaries."

The average starting salaries for last June's M.I.T. grads were still wonderful: about $17,000 for Ph.D.'s, $12,000 for a master's, $10,500 for a bachelor of science. The problem was finding jobs. According to one of this year's crop, some companies that used to hire Ph.D.'s took people with only master's or bachelor's degrees this year, because they were less specialized and cheaper. They might not be as highly qualified as Ph.D.'s for certain work, but for a saving of $5,000–$7,000 apiece, the companies were apparently willing to take that chance.

Dean Robert Weatherall, director of M.I.T.'s placement office, reports a sharp decrease in the number of available jobs, and admits that some of the listings he does have were "given to us only in a routine sort of way. Unless a particularly brilliant student comes along, many of these companies are not really actively searching." The tight job market has even affected the students' life-style. "We have many more students these days with long hair, who are used to working in blue jeans and sandals. They're not willing to compromise their individuality in order to get a job, but they're finding this is a difficult year to make a stand on clothing or hair. Last year the firms needed their talents so badly they were willing to endure some of these personal traits. Now, there's such competition for the jobs, the firms can choose what they consider the 'normal' applicants."

Even the "normal" graduates had trouble this year. Of the seven new

Ph.D.'s in solid-state physics, only three have some prospects for jobs in industry. One of the others, Bob Hughes, says, "Many of us had several promising interviews, but we all got the same letters back. The standard line was, 'The budget squeeze has forced us to re-examine our manpower requirements.' There are days when you get two or three letters back turning you down, and it's pretty depressing. Then somebody at lunch asks you, 'Well, how's the old job hunt going?' and you feel like telling him to go to hell."

With no prospects for a job in industry, Hughes fell back on a research associate position in his department at M.I.T. His salary of $12,500, though much less than the going rate for Ph.D.'s, is hardly a hardship wage. His colleague, Leonard Tocci, 28, has yet to find anything, but Tocci's wife earns $9,000 teaching second grade. Asked about his plans, Tocci says, "I'll just keep sending my résumés around, I guess, and wait for them to contact me."

He may have quite a wait. Students and deans at engineering schools around the country are beginning to wonder about the wisdom of training more and more highly specialized Ph.D.'s at a time when the country, or at least industry, has less and less need for them. Should the schools restrict the number of students in each field according to the number of jobs available? Should the engineering curriculum be revised in order to turn out more generalists?

Perhaps. But such moves will do little to help the thousands of engineers now out of work. Many of them now recognize that they have no future in their former specialties, and are willing to retrain for another, such as the power industry, which in addition to its shortage of power, also has a shortage of trained engineers. Everyone agrees such retraining programs should be available, but no one has any idea where the funds would come from. The electronics industry, whatever its responsibility, is in no position to do much with the current budget problems. This leaves the Federal Government, which both the engineers and the companies hold largely responsible for the current glut in the technical job market. As one former Raytheon engineer says, "The government has supported these areas for years with fat defense and space contracts. In many fields it was the sole source of funds. Now they come along and say they don't want this expertise any more. They just up and pull out all the funds, and leave us high and dry, with no jobs. What the hell are we supposed to do now?"

Even if the Federal Government did create a retraining program for engineers willing to switch fields, there is still some doubt as to how effective this would be. Manny Sugarman, whose placement agency has been dealing with the technical job market for 15 years, has little confidence that the electronics firms would hire retrained engineers. "Industry today just doesn't accept the idea of transfer of skills," he says. "A senior engineer is just kidding himself if he thinks he can transfer." Talks with personnel men along Route 128 confirm this view. As one of them told me ("but please don't quote me on this"), "Sure we favor a Government retraining program, but let's face it, why should we hire a radar engineer who has retrained as a computer man when we can get hundreds of guys who've been working with computers for years? I know that sounds cold-blooded, but that's business."

It may be good business for the companies, but not for the engineers. A growing number of them are beginning to question the entire system they are caught up in. The Reverend Scott Paradise, director of the Boston Industrial Mission, has talked to many of them and senses "a marked change from the almost universally held view only a few years ago that all these military and space projects are new, exciting and vital to the national defense. What I hear more and more is that most of these projects are counterproductive from the standpoint of society's needs."

Some engineers would like to see part of the energy, money and skill that have gone into these projects diverted to pressing social problems like pollution, housing and mass transportation. In many cases the skills involved are too exotic or specialized for such conversion, but a number of engineers and research companies would be willing to try—if the Federal money were available. They can't switch fields until it is.

While these men ponder the value of technology, others, like Jamie Chapman, a 33-year-old Ph.D. physicist at E.G.&G., consider the current unemployment crisis a threat to the very future of technology. "The first wave of layoffs," says Chapman, "was partly a house-cleaning operation at most companies. But now some firms are getting close to the critical stage. They're beginning to lose people who give them their technical competence. If you let too many of these people go, you are forced to close down a whole department. Some of these research teams took years to assemble. Once you close them down, you just can't build them up again quickly when market conditions change. In some fields we are systematically dismantling entire areas of technology. This is a very real danger to the country's scientific competence."

QUEENS ENCLAVE STRUGGLES TO KEEP SUBURBAN FLAVOR

by FRANKLIN WHITEHOUSE

Jamaica Estates is, in the words of one New York City planning official, "an enclave of well-to-do citizens which is pretty much self-reliant and self-sufficient."

The Queens community also is a grassy and leafy example of how resistance against the tides of urban sprawl may be mounted and how the atmosphere of suburbia in the city may be retained.

The doctors, lawyers, political figures who have resided for 60 years in solidly built houses under the great shade trees of Jamaica Estates have lavished considerable time and talent on keeping the physical aspects of their neighborhood the way they have always been.

This is not to say that there have been no changes since the Jamaica Estates Company, headed by Timothy L. Woodruff, Lieutenant Governor of New York under Theodore Roosevelt, bought the 503 acres of land from the city in the early nineteen-hundreds.

Many of the original houses built by Mr. Woodruff and his partners have disappeared. The Grand Central Parkway has come through the neighborhood. And the ethnic make-up of the community has changed from time to time.

But the Jamaica Estates Association, which is celebrating its fortieth anniversary this year, has been successful over the years in retaining the Estates as a section of Jamaica consisting almost entirely of single-family homes, with apartment houses only on the perimeter.

In fact, it was the approaching expiration of deed restrictions on December 31, 1929, that led to the formation of the residents' association.

The deed restrictions, written in by the Jamaica Estates Company, specified that only detached, one-family houses, two stories high and with an attic, could be built. No flat roofs were allowed. And no house was to cost less than

$6,000, exclusive of land. In some areas of the tract the minimum cost figure was $10,000.

Stables and garages were allowed, but they had to be set back at least 80 feet from the sidewalk line and at least 10 feet from side and rear building lines.

The story of the community is recounted in a book entitled *History of Jamaica Estates* written by Thomas J. Lovely, an area resident for 37 years and a teacher in Jamaica High School for 45 years. Mr. Lovely, commenting on the aspirations of the original company directors, wrote, referring to an exclusive enclave on the Hudson River, "Hopefully, [Jamaica Estates] would become a second Tuxedo Park."

Certain modifications in design have arrived in the Estates since then, such as the single-story, flat-topped ranch houses built since World War II. And, with rising real estate values, houses now range in price from about $40,000 to as high as $200,000.

And, too, a 16-story apartment house, the Camelot, is nearing completion in the southwest corner of the Estates along Hillside Avenue. The height of the light tan, brick structure is more than a half dozen stories greater than the older apartment houses in its vicinity. But Judge Peter M. Horn, an association founder, is not disturbed by it.

Judge Horn, who retired last January from Family Court after 30 years on the bench, said there was little community objection to the Camelot. The community, he said, had won a fight to remove an alternative to the apartments—a new intermediate school the residents contended would cause congestion and would cut the tax rolls at the same time.

Rents in the 342-unit structure will range from $185 a month for a studio apartment to $615 for a top-floor, three-bedroom unit, according to Hank Sopher, president of J. I. Sopher & Co., the renting agent.

Jamaica Estates is bounded on the south by Hillside Avenue, on the north by Union Turnpike, on the east by 188th Street and on the west by Home Lawn Street and Utopia Parkway.

The 1,700 houses within its borders have been built in several stages since about 1910. They range from columned Colonial houses in red brick with white shutters to the imposing stone-and-timbered Tudor houses along the grassy mall of Midland Parkway, the entrance to the Estates.

Few development homes are included in the total because wide-open tracts of land were not available in the Estates. Gaps between existing houses were eventually filled in with houses of custom design.

Judge Horn built his present three-bedroom stucco house on Avon Road in 1926. With its cathedral ceiling and stone fireplace in the living room, the house cost about $20,000 to build at that time, Judge Horn said. He added that he would insist on "at least $60,000 for it now."

Efforts by the Association succeeded in 1930 in obtaining a zoning classification that effectively barred apartment buildings in most of the Estates. An extension of that zoning to a larger area was secured in 1935, according to Mr. Lovely. In 1938, a new zoning regulation that limited property use to single-family houses was passed. It was challenged and upheld in a fight that was carried to the New York State Court of Appeals.

The opposition to the zoning, according to Mr. Lovely's account, consisted mainly of speculators and owners of vacant land who argued unsuccessfully that it would be economically unsound to have such zoning in the city.

"The building boom that followed proved to the contrary," Mr. Lovely wrote in his book.

The 275 homes that were occupied in the early years of the association have grown to 1,715 on the Estates's 88 square blocks. The 35-member association in 1929 has grown to about 1,000 members, each of whom pay $5 annual dues, plus a special $5 assessment for the book published this year.

In the early years, such prominent people as Chauncey Depew, a two-term United States Senator, and Anna Held, the actress, built houses in Jamaica Estates. So did Michael Degnon, an engineer who built the first subway in New York in 1904.

Now, the Estates are home to about 200 doctors as well as such figures in government as State Supreme Court Justice Frank D. O'Connor, the former president of the City Council, and Bernard E. Donovan, Superintendent of Schools.

Judge Horn said the Estates are "pretty much all white" with four or five Negro families living in the eastern sector. The Jewish population, he said, is not as heavy as it once was. Second- and third-generation Italians have been moving in in increasing numbers in the last 10 years, he added.

David H. Brown, a lawyer and real estate broker with offices on Union Turnpike, said there was currently a dearth of houses available in the Estates and he doesn't see any leveling off of demand.

As evidence of the rising market, Mr. Brown cited two houses built about 15 years ago on Hovedon Road for $35,000 each. The houses—both one-story brick dwellings with three bedrooms, although one has more extensive improvements—were sold recently for $60,000 and $70,000 respectively.

Mr. Brown noted that even though Long Island communities such as Roslyn might have more land and newer houses, the annual taxes that he pays on his own $75,000, 18-year-old house in the Estates ($1,200) is less than half what the bill would be on a comparable house in Roslyn.

A typical lot in Jamaica Estates, Mr. Brown said, measures 100 feet by 50 feet.

The lower taxes and the shorter commuting time to Manhattan jobs were cited by Mr. Brown as reasons why young people ''who are making it financially'' are moving in increasing numbers into the Estates, which Mr. Brown nevertheless characterizes as ''not a young neighborhood, it's middle-aged.''

CO-OP CITY'S GROUNDS: AFTER THREE YEARS, A SUCCESS

by ADA LOUISE HUXTABLE

The motorist speeding by Co-op City on the Hutchinson River Parkway in the Bronx sees only its looming apartment towers. The visitor finds a world of its own, set among 22,400 trees. The vast middle-income housing cooperative built by the United Housing Foundation, a non-profit trade union federation, opened three years ago to critical notices about its lack of design distinction. Today, it has one of the most successful landscaping jobs that ever turned a lemon into lemonade.

No other housing project in New York can make this statement. There is nothing comparable in scale or standard of design. The city's public housing site plans and grounds have been stamped out of the same bleak, unimaginative mold for years, and middle-income housing has faced such rapidly rising costs that landscaping is a luxury.

The green world at Co-op City is no mean achievement because its base is flat, hydraulic fill—300 acres of salt sand. It started as a desolate limbo. There is only one original tree still on the site.

Now, $5.4-million later there are 177 landscaped acres (the rest is building) by the New York firm of Zion and Breen Associates. These are the landscape architects who gave you Mr. Paley's small, exquisitely sophisticated park on 52d Street.

At the base of Co-op City's towers they have created a gently rolling terrain. Wet sand was pumped in for low hills that hide the traffic beyond the development's carfree superblocks.

The fill is covered with topsoil and sod, and the grass is embellished with masses of willows, Lombardy poplars, London plane trees and Japanese black pines that had to be gotten from California when local supplies ran out.

There are sand gardens with pine islands surrounded by borders of wooden blocks that are cheaper and prettier than concrete. "We had all that sand and it saved money," says Robert Zion.

Groups of poplars screen garages, and willows fill awkward spots between buildings. A 31-acre open park adjoins the educational park and schools being built by the United Housing Foundation, which will be turned back to the city on completion.

A two-story shopping center surrounds a paved court with three ivy and willow islands. A fourth island is a hillock covered with artificial grass of the kind used in stadiums, meant here for children to play on while parents shop. It is worn bald with constant, passionate use.

The same imitation grass appears in other hard-use play areas. It sounds dreadful, but looks fine because there is so much of the real thing around it.

There are no formal playgrounds. Well-selected equipment including tee-pees, climbing devices and simple wooden forms, are scattered through the sand gardens and across the lawns, often as an effective kind of sculpture. Handsome natural rock outcroppings are also utilized.

Paving is of London block, a prefabricated stone that can be easily replaced in sections, and flat cobbles. It borders the apartment houses, where trees will grow to form canopies overhead.

Groups of townhouses are given a more unified, urban setting with "wall to wall" London block inset with ivy beds and willows. A contractor had to be set up with special machinery to make the block, which is commonly used in England and Scandinavia.

Nothing like it is commonly, or uncommonly, used here. Attractive, patterned paving shown in architects' housing drawings is always the first casualty of costs. Asphalt walks and parking lots shatter planners' dreams and designs.

The only blacktop at Co-op City was put in at the very start, and was rejected immediately by the landscape architects and the client. As the job went on and rapport increased with the designers, U.H.F. became increasingly open-handed.

At one point, small trees were removed and larger ones substituted at the client's request. The $5½-million has been spent on land-fill, planting, drainage, pavement, lights and street furniture. All are of exemplary standard.

There is some argument about whether U.H.F. hired Zion and Breen as landscape architects and site planners under their own steam or under pressure by the city's planners. But the result is a successful demonstration of how to humanize housing that many people thought was beyond help.

The huge buildings were raised to permit passage and views through at the ground. Everything has been done to soften the project's gigantism at eye level, where it counts.

Curiously, Co-op City residents have had to unlearn their inhibitions about using the land. Many were graduates of other U.H.F. projects, conditioned by standardized chain-link fence and keep-of-the-grass formulas.

Early "grievances" included the fact that there were benches on the grass. The designers' emphasis on variety to relieve the scale and sameness of the structures led to squabbles about "equality" of treatment.

Today, Co-op City is neither the purgatory nor the heaven that its critics and champions predicted. It is a functioning community. Only New York—a city of 8 million snobs, skeptics and desperate survivors—could have swallowed a new town of this size within its limits without a ripple. Anywhere else in the world, there would be a steady stream of visitors to see how a community of 45,000-going-on-60,000 takes shape.

Co-op City has none of the chic new-town esthetics or life-style cachet of a Reston, Va. It will never be in the fashionable planning spotlight like the new town on Welfare Island being built by the New York State Urban Development Corporation. Zion and Breen are also the landscape architects for Welfare Island, where they are already running into the asphalt-paving syndrome.

But it has 15,372 well-planned apartments that are no mean achievement in New York's stumbling housing numbers game.

And there is now a younger, more sophisticated management at U.H.F. that is going far beyond the foundation's sterile patterns of the past. In the next project, it may be possible to raise your eyes from the ground.

FRICTIONS INVADE A UTOPIA

by STEVEN R. WEISMAN

A few years ago, prospective tenants were exhorted and cajoled into joining Lefrak City's "Magic World of Total Living" in Queens.

"All in All . . . A World of Difference," the brochures said. "Soundproof! Fireproof! Spacious! The boldest and most advanced creation in housing . . . The City of Tomorrow!"

Besides the ballyhoo, rents for new tenants were slashed. Prizes were passed out with new leases. For some, the owner guaranteed no rent increases for six years, which angered nearby landlords who couldn't promise the same.

Today the huge Lefrak complex in Elmhurst no longer stands out as much as it did. Its 20 brick towers share the skyline with other high-rise apartments along Queens Boulevard, which Lefrak City used to dominate. The citywide housing shortage, plus rents that still compare favorably with equivalent apartments elsewhere, has meant a fairly contented, and stable, population.

Nevertheless, Lefrak residents have found that, by joining the "City of Tomorrow," they haven't exactly bypassed the frictions of today.

Scaffolding along the walls appears now and then as workmen replace crumbling bricks. The elegant upholstered furniture that adorned the lobbies has been replaced with wrought-iron chairs and tables bolted to the floor. There are a couple of burglaries each week, perhaps by Lefrak's own tenants. And there is the problem summed up by an 18-year-old named Steve, who said:

"It gets awfully boring here, you know what I mean? There's no place to go. You get hassled. You just sit here and stare at those big brick walls, man. The only thing to do is get high. Then the walls look real cool. If you don't get high, it's a drag."

Lefrak City began rising in Queens 10 years ago, the $150 million undertaking of Samuel J. Lefrak, the ebullient president of the Lefrak Organization, which has housed hundreds of thousands of New Yorkers. Its 18-story towers sit on a 40-acre tract bounded by the Long Island Expressway, 57th Avenue, Junction Boulevard and 99th Street in a neighborhood variously given as Forest Hills, Elmhurst or Rego Park.

At the building's base lie amenities that can meet residents' needs without their ever having to set foot outside the complex. There are caterers, beauty salons, cleaners, gift shops, a health club, restaurants and food stores. An office building for the Social Security Administration in one corner employs 3,000 people, some of whom live just next door.

In addition, Lefrak's superblock contains loads of parking space, tennis and basketball courts, playgrounds and three swimming pools, which, though they charge admission, are jammed with people on a sunny afternoon.

"It's a concept which I admire," said Teddy Gershon, a 41-year-old interior designer whose family is in its ninth year at Lefrak. "It's a complete city, a city within a city, you might say. It's not utopia, but you can't fault management for that. Lefrak gives you service. I'm happy here. If I was unhappy, I'd move out."

If Mr. Gershon has any complaints, they center on his fellow tenants, who can be abusive to the property and indifferent to the activities of their children. "Kids have to do something they can do," he said. "That's why we formed a Little League team. Now we're trying to organize football. It's kids who have nothing to do who can get into trouble."

The "trouble" he was referring to was drugs and vandalism, but the extent of the problem varies, depending on whom one talks to.

"It's a jungle here," said an orange-haired woman as she looked up from her poolside card game. "To tell you the truth, I'm afraid to go out at night, and I certainly wouldn't let my daughter go out."

"Even if she did, I wouldn't," the daughter agreed gravely.

"Let me tell you," added the woman, who said she was afraid to give her name, "you see bands of kids—junkies, believe me—they wander around, they snatch your purse. They break windows and mark up the walls. They don't care. Oh, I hate this place."

For many other tenants, too, security is one of Lefrak City's biggest unsolved problems. Some feel that Lefrak's own tenants are partly responsible, and security people agree.

"You've got more than 20,000 people here," said John Timmes, a rangy former police sergeant who directs the Lefrak Organization's security forces. "What do you think is going to happen? But 99 per cent of our tenants are decent, good people. It's like any place else. In fact, Lefrak City is better than most of New York."

In the last few years, Mr. Timmes has directed the eviction of about 30 families for "undesirability," often those with unruly or drug-prone children. "We just kicked a family out this week," he said.

Mr. Timmes commands the 70-man security force for Lefrak City along with his wife, Kay, from a small set of rooms on the first floor of one of the buildings. The Lefrak patrolmen, in chocolate-colored uniforms with the ubiquitous "L" insignia emblazoned on their caps, are organized in four platoons and carry walkie-talkies.

As Mr. Timmes asked one of his men to demonstrate the walkie-talkie, a voice squawked in, "Tenants are complaining that kids are all over the cars in Section 2. Check it out."

"This is unrehearsed, this is unrehearsed," said Mr. Timmes. "Now you see our men are going to rush right over to solve the problem."

Later, he explained that all patrolmen were given full security checks and ordered to keep their hair short and shave all beards. He also said that he had guards who spoke Spanish, Hungarian, German, French, Italian, Greek, Czech, Yiddish and even Chinese to deal with Lefrak's polyglot populace.

A major problem, according to some residents, is an area called Section 5, which they say is a haven for youths using drugs.

"On a Saturday morning, you see people strung out all over that area," said Sheldon Russakoff, the president of the Lefrak City Tenants' Association, and a part-time adviser to a narcotics rehabilitation center in Queens.

"I know half the junkies in Queens. I know that junkies come in to make their deals. It's the biggest narcotics traffic center in Queens. And nothing is done about it."

Two groups of people, at least, disagree with Mr. Russakoff's assessment—Mr. Timmes and the Lefrak people, and several of the youngsters themselves.

"There's some heroin," said Jimmy, a 17-year-old whose father is a "What-do-you-call-it . . . an executive, but mostly it's pot, a little hash, some ups and downs, not too much acid.

"Listen, the junk [heroin] you get here is too expensive and it's no good. You can't get high on it—I tried once. Those people all strung out," Jimmy laughed. "It's wine, man. Cheap wine. Last week I got stoned on beer."

Another youth said that adults get so angry at the young people congregating below their windows that they often pelt them from above with eggs, water-filled bags, aluminum cans, ice, bottles and—once—a 30-pound power generator for the elevator taken from the roof.

Many people at Lefrak City agree that some security problems are better now than they have been. A couple of years ago, the youths tended to gather in gangs that would fight among themselves, or with other gangs that came in from neighboring Corona or Flushing. But that seems to have passed.

On the other hand, there is no problem for an outsider's getting into the building lobbies, and up on any floor, where there might be un unlocked apartment. Access to the basements is open. The buzzers from apartments to the main doors are often inoperable, but that doesn't seem to matter, since the lobby doors are open, and there are no doormen.

The lobby doors are supposed to be locked, and the Lefrak people try to explain why they are not. "I've got crews going constantly to fix locks," said Dennis H. Chaleff, managing director of Lefrak City. "So you fix it, and the next thing you know, a tenant loses his key. What does he do? He busts the door open."

The same problem exists for other maintenance—the removal of graffiti, the repair of cracked plaster, the replacement of stairwell handrails, the fixing of lights in dangerously darkened corridors, the extermination of mice. But for all that, the city reports only a few minor code violations in Lefrak City.

One recurring problem, however, involves the elevators. There are 60 of them, with at least a few almost always out of service, tenants say. Again, the Lefrak people maintain they cope well under the circumstances, but this explanation fails to impress some tenants.

"I walked down 12 floors just this morning, with an elderly woman right next to me," said Daniel J. Spooner, who is legal counsel to the tenants' association. "And look," he added, drawing a sheaf of old yellowed newspaper advertisements from his briefcase. "They advertised doormen. After we moved in, the doormen disappeared!"

The doormen did disappear. But the Lefrak security people say their removal has enabled them to add more patrolmen, providing greater flexibility for protecting the apartments.

Most of the problems arising in Lefrak City seem to be those that would emerge in any community of 20,000 individuals. Tenants complain about each other's fights, loud noises (easy to hear in neighboring apartments) and dogs (which, though illegal, are permitted by authorities unless other tenants complain).

"I have a feeling that things may be worse here because people are packed in so close together," said the Reverend Jack T. Merritt, a boyish-looking Baptist minister from Texas. Together with his wife, Mr. Merritt runs one of Lefrak City's two religious-oriented centers—the other is Jewish—on the premises.

"But I'm not sure," Mr. Merritt added. "Actually, I like it here. If there's a real problem, it's that too many kids are left unsupervised. They need room to play, and the young ones can't walk to the parks alone. A lot need love and attention. It's sad."

"The same thing with senior citizens. A lot of them live alone, with no place to go. We're opening up our center to them, so they can play cards and get together. That kind of thing is really lacking in Lefrak City."

Officials of the tenants' association, which was incorporated only nine months ago, agree. In addition to taking on management over repairs and security problems, they are in the midst of setting up narcotics education programs and recreation for older people at the Jewish Center.

"There's one thing for sure," said Mr. Russakoff, the president of the association. "The Lefrak people don't care about how people live here. You'd think they'd help out, help people get together here. We have to fend for ourselves. You'd think they'd lend a hand, maybe have a social, a *kaffee-klatsch,* or something. But no. They don't care."

"Their only utopia is in heaven," said Mr. Chaleff in response to Mr. Russakoff's complaints. Many tenants agree with him that Lefrak personnel are prompt in making repairs when they're needed and solving problems when they arise. If there's something missing after all that, it's hard, they say, to see what the Lefrak Organization can do about it.

"After all," said Mr. Chaleff, "Mr. Lefrak is a landlord. He's not a social director."

"THIS PLACE MAKES BEDFORD-STUYVESANT LOOK BEAUTIFUL"

by RICHARD ROGIN

Thaddeus L. Hall, Jr., and Arthur Molinelli don't pretend to be sociologists, architects or realtors, and they aren't exactly in the line of conducting house tours. In fact, Hall and Molinelli are patrolmen who work a unique plainclothes assignment out of the 75th Precinct, a small red-brick castle at Liberty and Miller Avenues in the East New York section of Brooklyn. They are known as the vacant-house team. And if you are looking for one of the best (and certainly the safest) field studies of the desolate ghetto heart of East New York, especially its sad inventory of perhaps 1,000 empty, derelict buildings, most abandoned by their owners, not to mention sidelights on other local crises such as the very high incidence of crime and fire, they are your guides.

The team mostly covers a 270-block beaten zone inhabited by more than 100,000 people, predominantly poor blacks and Puerto Ricans. It is an area which has suffered a precipitous physical decline in swift transition from an overwhelmingly white middle-class community.

The zone is bounded on the west by the Brownsville border at Van Sinderen Avenue, on the east by Fountain Avenue near the Queens line, on the south by New Lots Avenue just up from the integrated Spring Creek housing projects, new one- and two-family homes and the wild shore of Jamaica Bay, and on the north by Atlantic Avenue. Atlantic is known locally as "the Mason-Dixon line" since above it the population remains white and middle class toward Highland Park and the cemeteries.

This region of misery is made up largely of old frame and brick one- and two-family dwellings, either attached or with tiny flanking yards, and three- and four-story red-brick and dirty yellow-brick buildings. Many of the old houses, built fifty or sixty years ago, barely qualify as homes. There are also several hundred empty, mostly two-family, houses foreclosed by the Federal

Housing Administration in the past few years whose tinned-up doors and windows and rickety porches are a depressing legacy of lost hopes. This ironic impetus to the abandonment problem came about, according to local critics, because the F.H.A.'s effort to help low-income families purchase homes was flawed by incomplete investigation of run-down properties and consequent inflated appraisals and mortgages.

The low landscape is marked by lots, even whole blocks, filled with ragged piles of old bricks and timbers, and half-demolished structures which are being knocked flat in the Central Brooklyn Model Cities area. (Through a wide range of community programs and construction, the federally funded Model Cities program hopes to revitalize slum areas.) The abandoned buildings—some once home for 20 families and often still structurally sound—give the neighborhood a ruined, bombed-out appearance.

Abandonment also plagues Brownsville, the South Bronx and Harlem, threatens to turn 20 other New York City areas into "veritable ghost towns," as a housing official put it, and is a critical problem in other cities across the country. It is only the most visibly dramatic aspect of the familiar and calamitous housing crisis in New York: massive deterioration, limited new production and a desperate apartment shortage, especially for low-income families.

The vacant houses in East New York, many in the Model Cities tract, are now burned out, vandalized, shattered, filled with old shoes, smashed furniture, forgotten dogs and a sour effluvium of neglect and despair. Professional "strippers" often brazenly drive up in trucks in broad daylight and remove the copper, brass and lead plumbing, the sinks and radiators for sale to scrap-metal dealers. Windows and doors are sealed with tin or cinder blocks or left open and broken. Scores of buildings have had the tin coverings or the metal gates which uselessly guard empty stores ripped away and the interiors ransacked, gutted and heaped with rank debris.

The sidewalks and streets are littered with garbage, wind-whipped newspapers and rotting mattresses. A smashed telephone booth lies on its side in the middle of the sidewalk, the phone coin box ripped out. Broken glass is always being crunched underfoot. A group of boys play basketball in the street, driving for lay-ups toward an orange metal hoop and wooden backboard attached to a wooden power pole. An automobile hulk smolders at the corner. A little girl swings from the end of a thick rusty wire which dangles from the second-story fire escape of an empty brick building.

Behind many of the shabby doors in the decayed inhabited houses, ovens burn day and night with their doors open in a desperate attempt, whatever the gas bill, to warm icy overcrowded apartments. Families endure without heat or hot water, occasionally without water at all. The oases of well-kept housing seem overwhelmed by the bleakness.

"There's no vest-pocket badness," says Mrs. Lillie Martin, a large black woman who is director of East New York Housing Services, an agency of the antipoverty East New York Community Corporation. "It's just all bad. East New York is not a sound community. There's too much turnover. It's a constant struggle for survival, that's what it's become."

East New York isn't off the edge of the map, though sometimes it must seem that way to its residents. The score or so of four- and six-story buildings—either public housing or publicly assisted under the sponsorship of community and other nonprofit groups—now being finished as part of the Model Cities project, the scattering of rehabilitated houses, the rubbish-free lots surrounded with new silvery cyclone fencing, courtesy of Model Cities, are all the comforting light-at-the-end-of-the-tunnel which bureaucrats have a rare talent for spying more often than the rest of us.

To be a tourist in this region is a depressing and helpless experience. To be an impoverished resident in that blasted urban heath—almost like an anonymous survivor in a Beckett play—must surely drive one deeper into the perpetual crafty rage, the anomie and stupor of the city, the common madness of the urban poor.

One day last winter, I joined Hall and Molinelli on their empty building patrol. Hall, who grew up in Brownsville, is a burly, bearded 33-year-old black man who dresses like a street guy in casual clothes and a black leather car coat. Molinelli, a white East New York native who is 25, tries for the role of a dope-addict-hippie with almost shoulder-length hair, muttonchop whiskers, old army fatigue jacket, fringed blue jeans and sneakers. He somewhat resembles the movie actor Michael Pollard.

They make an odd pair, walking quickly and alertly around the battered area. The neighborhood hustlers, of course, know a block away that they are "the Man"—and know that under their coats, on their left hips, both carry small .38-caliber police specials.

The team was started by the 75th Precinct's Captain George J. Cerrone (now Deputy Inspector) in May, 1968. He is very proud of its record of 350 arrests since then and what he says is a reduction of fires in vacant buildings. Consider what has happened to a neighborhood, though, when you have two policemen assigned to full-time reconnaissance of abandoned buildings, routinely checking out complaints from school principals, block associations, merchants and individual residents and on their own. Hall and Molinelli often stake out a house at night for narcotics addicts, burglars who break through into adjoining buildings, furtive intruders who want nothing more than a few pieces of pipe and arsonists. (In 1969 the Fire Department said that although .5 per cent of all buildings were abandoned, they were responsible for 17 per cent of structural fires, 27 per cent of major fires, and a "terrible percentage" of injuries to firemen.)

As we headed south on Van Siclen Avenue, the two policemen warned away some kids who were jumping off the decrepit wooden roof of an abandoned garage. A large frame house across the street had been reduced to its present ramshackle state in two weeks, Molinelli said, when an old woman who had lived there for years moved out after trying unsuccessfully to sell the place.

At 412 Schenck Avenue, a solidly constructed four-story yellow-brick building at the corner of Sutter Avenue, the two men climbed upstairs, checking the devastated rooms. There was a smell of leaking gas. Molinelli called police communications on his handie-talkie to notify the Brooklyn Union Gas Company to come and turn it off.

Later, Molinelli gently lifted a little girl out from a garbage-piled empty storefront on Blake Avenue where she was playing. Then the men went into the N. & J. Meat Company at 937 Blake Avenue at the corner of Ashford Street to talk with the owner, Nathan Levine, who said his market had been burglarized nine times in the previous two months. To make things worse, there had been a fire several weeks before in the apartment on the floor above the market and the tenant had moved, leaving the building vacant at night. Even though Levine had cinder-blocked the street door to the apartment and the upstairs windows, thieves had ripped away the metal gate on a bakery next door, which had been empty for a year, and had entered the market by smashing through the adjoining wall and ceiling. They stole cash registers and adding machines.

"I have no insurance," said Levine, a worried-looking man in his early fifties, who has had a thriving business here for 10 years, staying on while many of his fellow merchants fled. "I don't even call the police any more. I don't know what to do. I'm at my wits' end. I inquired about a dog. My wife says close it up and go. I have a good business. I have eight men working. We do well. There's just no end."

"The Blake Avenue market area," Molinelli told me later, "once it's dark down there, it's sort of a little jungle."

In a vacant two-story frame house with red asbestos shingles and yellow trim at 336 Vermont Street, Molinelli stooped amid the rubbish in a stripped upstairs bathroom and discovered three glassine envelopes. One of them was blood-smeared. He said they had contained heroin. "Drug addicts will make no noise at all,'' he added. The house was across the street from the rear of Intermediate School 292 at 300 Wyona Street. Molinelli said that this building and at least 300 others should be demolished immediately but that the demolition program, except in rare emergencies, moved very slowly.

Next door, in 338 Vermont Street, an abandoned four-story brick building, Hall cautiously pushed open apartment doors at arm's length. ''In all the years I've been going in these vacant buildings,'' he said, ''I've never found a body yet. I hope and pray my luck holds out until they get all these buildings demolished.''

Passing another abandoned house later on, Molinelli said, ''You can't exist next to a building like this. They hit your main pipe one night and your house is flooded. One building becomes vacant, before you know it the block is gone.''

We turned the corner from Belmont Avenue down Elton Street, past a collard garden, with Hall quietly leading the way into 470 Elton Street, a three-story red-brick building with shattered windows that appeared empty even though a light glowed dimly in the first-floor hallway. Inside, the policemen's suspicions were confirmed when they heard the telltale noises of strippers. They swiftly arrested three men with a bag full of wrenches and screwdrivers who had just started to work on the pipes in an upstairs bathroom and the brass tubing from the boiler.

A stocky woman wearing a coat came out of the rear first-floor apartment shouting incoherent obscenities at everybody. Her apartment was inexplicably filled with old tires. There was no heat, no hot water. In fact, she said that since some of the pipes had already been removed, there was no water at all. Yet the woman and her husband, who had apparently once been rent-paying welfare tenants there, continued on as squatters in the cold, foul house.

Eventually, criminal trespass charges against the three strippers were dismissed in court because the police were unable to locate the landlord, who has to make the complaint. The address given for him in the official city records turned out to be another nearby abandoned building—there was no phone number—and he was not listed at a forwarding address which Molinelli got from the post office.

The house at 470 Elton Street was added to the precinct's list of vacant buildings and Molinelli notified the local welfare center about the couple who were living there. Relocation, of course, is another difficulty since not only is housing inadequate in East New York and other poor sections of the city, there just isn't enough of it to go around.

Molinelli later drove me past his old home, a two-family two-story brick house at 383 Milford Street at the corner of New Lots Avenue. He had lived there for the first 22 years of his life. He said it had been sold in 1967 for $15,000 to a real estate agency and then resold to a Puerto Rican family. His family had moved to Howard Beach, Queens, and the house had been abandoned a year later. Now it was decaying and cinder-blocked, the yard cluttered with garbage and old timbers.

"This is the house my grandmother lived in for 55 years," Molinelli said, "since she came to this country from Genoa. It was beautiful. We had 40 rose bushes in the back. It was what you call picturesque. Now it's like the neighborhood dump there. My grandmother sees this, she'd have a heart attack.

"This place," he added, referring to East New York, "makes Bedford-Stuyvesant look beautiful. In 10 years, it was completely destroyed."

Until the nineteen-fifties East New York was a predominantly white, middle-class neighborhood made up largely of Jews and Italians with enclaves of Russians, Poles, Lithuanians, Irish and Germans. Then suddenly it began to undergo the ethnic and economic transformation that has taken place in many New York neighborhoods.

Public housing projects went up in neighboring Brownsville, uprooting residents there, and they, together with other displaced people from Central Brooklyn and Harlem, moved to East New York. Many were welfare families for whom the city found apartments in the area. This has led to criticism by many East New York residents, blacks and whites, especially homeowners, that the city "dumped" welfare clients in the community, dragging it down.

In a neighborhood described by residents as "very desirable" even as late as 1960, whites now panicked at the influx of poor minority persons and homeowners feared their property values would collapse. Blockbusting, with its tragic catalogue of onerous second mortgages and rapid foreclosures, was rampant in the early nineteen-sixties, accelerating the ethnic change. Black and Puerto Rican home buyers, anxious to escape the ghetto, only became victims once again on what a consultant to the City Commission on Human Rights called a "debtor's treadmill." The population in the core section swung to more than 80 per cent black and Puerto Rican; the remnant was made up mostly of elderly whites, either unwilling or unable to move.

The vicious, dreary cycle of expectation and fact commenced as welfare tenants arrived in greater numbers and landlords, in general, fearfully certain that their properties would be wrecked, collected all the rents they could and let the building run down. There were victims and villains on both sides. The tenant's attitude became: The landlord doesn't give a damn; I don't give a damn. Mutual self-destruction prevailed. Convinced the neighborhood was sliding into the lower depths, the banks gave up on block after block, and mortgage money became scarcer and scarcer. Decay and abandonment proliferated.

In a futile attempt to reverse the rising tide of deterioration, early in 1966 the city designated a 40-block zone a "disaster area." It underwent the intensive scrutiny of a housing inspection crackdown. But the inspection enforcement backfired, according to Sheldon C. Katz, vice president of the Community Housing Improvement Program, a group which claims a membership of 2,600 landlords with upwards of one million tenants concentrated in Brooklyn and Queens. Coupled with the declining neighborhood, he says, it scared away many owners because of the several thousand dollars needed for repairs to correct the violations in a single building. The tenants, of course, saw it the other way: profit-greedy landlords finally being called to account.

"What the city never calculated was that owners would walk away," says Katz. "Owners started to desert, to stop paying their taxes. You just can't expect people to run property without making money. If you think they'll do it out of social responsibility, you're kidding yourself. Now you've got an area that's really sick. The landlord is a bastard—that's the basic city attitude."

Vito P. Battista, the conservative Assemblyman who represents most of the ghetto area, attributes the dilapidated housing in the district mainly to tenant vandalism. "We've had more damage in East New York, Brownsville and the South Bronx than [resulted from riots in] Newark, Watts and Detroit put together," he says. "But nobody wants to print it."

In the summer of 1966, after a history of gang wars, the neighborhood did erupt in destructive racial disorders among blacks, whites and Puerto Ricans. An 11-year-old boy was killed by a sniper and damage and looting were extensive. Fearful residents were reported fleeing the district, carrying furniture on their backs. The riots were the new Mayor Lindsay's baptism to the city's brand of street warfare and led to the Urban Action Task Forces.

Later in 1966, a year when everything seemed to happen in the community, the city and East New York residents banded together, determined to stop the spiral of housing decay. Planning began for Model Cities construction in the area—programs which are now regarded with considerable local bitterness as having fallen far short of the promised goals. Residences and businesses, if they survived at all, often endured between abandoned buildings or alongside vacant lots. Sutter Avenue, for example, a once-thriving commercial street, became virtually an eerie stretch of boarded-up, empty and burned-out stores interrupted only by garbage-strewn lots.

As the dolorous nineteen-sixties wound down in East New York, landlords found themselves caught between what many housing experts agree was insufficient rent-controlled income and soaring costs for maintenance, heating oil, taxes, insurance and mortgage payments—if they could get mortgage renewals at all. Fearful of property damage and city-ordered rent reductions for housing violations, burdened with poisonous landlord-tenant disputes, unable to sell, they gradually let go. The final and perhaps most significant factor in the complex process of abandonment was a failure of confidence by the landlord not only in the building, but in the block, the neighborhood, even the city, which went beyond all economic reason.

Albert A. Walsh, city Housing and Development Administrator, says that neighborhood blight is the critical factor in the abandonment crisis in East New York, not rent control or tenant vandalism as the landlords charge. (Abandonment has struck in cities where there is no rent control.) Another cause, he says, is that many poor nonwelfare families in the area are not able to pay even the controlled rents. Another factor, often cited by residents as responsible for pulling down the community's housing stock in such dismal fashion, is the role played by the banks. "Fifteen years ago the banks suddenly, arbitrarily, decided that East New York was no longer the type of mortgage risk that they cared to take," says John J. Mullally, a 41-year-old lawyer who is chairman of Community Planning Board 5 and a lifelong East New Yorker. "Perhaps the neighborhood would have deteriorated, perhaps a racial change would have been brought about by the open operation of the market," he goes on. "But pulling out of the market precipitated the change and left scars on the face of East New York. The scars are the abandoned buildings and the whole blocks that are burned out."

"We are very discretionary how we put our mortgage money," counters William Gatehouse, mortgage officer for the East New York Savings Bank. "We haven't pulled out completely. It's not good business to invest in a good building on a block where there is deterioration, abandonment."

"You will find banks, lending institutions in this city," says Administrator Walsh, "who have drawn lines on a map on their wall and they simply will not make a mortgage within certain areas." Landlords, too, he adds, come to the same conclusion, no matter what the rents are.

It is within these boundaries that a scenario is played out, called "End Game" with Beckettian irony by Professor George Sternlieb, a Rutgers University urbanologist who last year finished a massive study of rent-controlled housing for New York City. In End Game, according to Professor Sternlieb, the landlord skimps on repairs, taxes aren't paid, the building is milked for maximum rental income (though rents are often not paid for a multitude of reasons), essential services such as heat and hot water end. Finally, the landlord walks away. In a given situation, perhaps he has gotten all he wants out of the building; perhaps he doesn't wish to invest any more on the chance of future gain. The tenants move or survive amid junkies, drifters, fires, muggings, thefts, vandalism. Ultimately, the building is vacant and the city usually takes over a gutted shell for tax delinquency, foreclosing in an *in rem* proceeding.

Illustrative of the city's housing dilemma is a 20-apartment building in East New York that through the winter seemed to teeter on the edge of Patrolmen Hall's and Molinelli's list and the abandonment statistics. It is a decaying but still structurally sound four-story red-brick walk-up at 552 Shepherd Avenue, between Blake and Sutter Avenues, a block made up almost entirely of inhabited one- and two-family houses. Last December, the building was said to be fully occupied, housing about 70 people. In happier days, probably when it was built in 1927, the name Shepherd Arms was cut into the stone over the entranceway.

As winter came on, the house was snarled in one of those landlord-tenant tugs-of-war, so familiar in the ghetto, marked by charges of tenant destruction and countercharges of landlord neglect. Most of the tenants, almost all of whom are on welfare, were on a tacit rent strike because they said there had been no heat or hot water for months. The landlord was in the midst of legal proceedings to evict several of them. The tenants had organized themselves and had contacted East New York Housing Services, the East New York Urban Action Task Force and East New York Legal Services, the antipoverty law offices, for aid. Welfare rent checks had been cut off, the tenants said, and before that, they claimed, some of the money had gone for such expenses as electric heaters and increased gas bills.

The building was actually being run by a court-appointed receiver, another clue to housing trouble. The last landlord had failed to make his mortgage payments and in April, 1969, the mortgage holder at that time, the Brevoort Savings Bank (since merged into the Metropolitan Savings Bank) had a receiver appointed by the Kings County Supreme Court. According to the bank, this move was designed to prevent the landlord, known in the trade as a "milker," from collecting rents without servicing the building—and thus to protect the bank's investment during foreclosure proceedings. But receivers, too, have been accused of being milkers.

Aside from forgone interest payments, the bank's stake was the principal on the mortgage, which amounted to about $25,000. The court appointed I. Edmund Frohman, a Brooklyn real estate management specialist who says his Monarch Management Corporation runs about 30 houses, to operate 552 Shepherd. Depending on where one stands, Frohman then became either the villain of the scenario or another hapless victim that the building had claimed, or some of both.

When I first came across the Shepherd Arms late last fall there were overflowing garbage cans out on the sidewalk in front, broken windows, mailbox doors ripped off in the lobby, no front doors, the usual sour run-down-building smell, peeling paint, chunks of fallen plaster on the floor, a leaky roof over the stairwell and scraps of old food on the stairs. The apartments were full of cracked and peeling paint, gaping holes where the plaster and boards had fallen away, leaking pipes, complaints of roaches and rats, faulty toilets and, most important, repeated angry claims by many tenants—seemingly supported by city inspectors—that there had been no heat or hot water for at least seven months.

The building had been repeatedly checked by city housing inspectors—a mid-November inspection had recorded a cumulative total of 153 outstanding housing violations—but no real improvement seemed to have happened. City records at that time disclosed that only a single $5 housing fine had been assessed since the receiver had taken over, though the city reduced the rents approximately 30 per cent last December because of the lack of heat and hot water.

The city's Emergency Repair Program had spent about $1,250 on the building in two years, fixing the boiler and the oil burner, delivering heating oil, plastering and repairing a broken pipe—with no repayment from the landlord. Joseph Mazziotta, the city's chief housing inspector, with whom I once visited the building, seemed proud that the city had kept the building going and habitable for two years so cheaply. He said it would cost the city $15,000 to order the building vacated, with the resultant relocation fees. Then, of course, it would fall prey to the perils of vacant buildings and cost the city additional thousands of dollars in lost taxes and demolition expenses.

One November afternoon, the tenants said, a city-ordered fuel truck had delivered 900 gallons of oil, enough for about two weeks of heat, just ahead of a fuel delivery which the tenants' council had pooled its money to purchase, thus saving its money. And on another cold morning the red minivan from the Emergency Repair Program was parked outside and workmen were rehanging the old front doors, which Frohman said he had removed because kids used them as swings, and installing a new interior lobby door to keep the heat in. A private plumber, contracted for by the city, was repairing a leaking hot-water pipe in the basement. The boiler, working on city fuel, was humming away and the building was finally warm for a while.

At the Housing and Development Administration headquarters in downtown Manhattan, a clerk studied the thick manila folder which contained 552 Shepherd's Emergency Repair Program file and said, "An average bad building." The stocky, white-haired Mazziotta, who wears American and Italian flag pins in his lapel, added with the cheerful cynicism of someone who has spent a quarter-century amid the ruins, "Some are bad, some are worse, and we have some good ones. Every day you say, 'This is the worst.' The next day you hit something worse."

The Shepherd Arms carries the other usual burdens of buildings in distress. Through the quarterly payment due last January 1, there was a total of more than $15,000 in delinquent real estate taxes, water and sewer fees and interest charges on the building. On April 1, if the oldest tax bill is not paid, the building will be four years in tax arrears. It will then be technically subject to city acquisition for nonpayment of taxes, a procedure which usually takes up to a year to complete.

Set against the tax delinquency, according to Frohman, there was nearly $14,000 in back rents due through the end of last December on an annual rent roll of $17,600, excluding the superintendent's apartment. The rents officially ranged from $55.18 to $99.45 for three- and four-room apartments.

"If the rents would come in," said Frohman, reflecting the optimistic side of his ambivalence about 552's future, "it could be the finest building in that particular area or in all of Brooklyn. I've taken buildings that were worse than this and brought them back to life. I hope to be able to pull it out."

But usually Frohman, a portly, bearded young man with a mod flair, was saying, "This is going to be another abandoned. It isn't going in the right direction. This thing isn't going to last to spring."

For the tenants, it wasn't lasting at all. "Been living this way for so long," said Mrs. Valencia Herndon, the tenants' council president, with quiet anger late last fall, "I know you can't live no place without paying rent, but you would like some services." Before the city brought it back, Mrs. Herndon said, there had been not only no heat, but no hot water or baths for the children for seven months, the same period she said she hadn't been paying rent. According to Frohman, Mrs. Herndon owed 13 months' rent.

"Believe me, this used to be a beautiful building," added Mrs. Herndon, who had lived in 552 Shepherd for six years. "Now I have to chase junkies away shooting up with dope on the top floor." She said her rent was $86 a month for four run-down rooms which were occupied by herself, her three children, her sister and her two children. Mrs. Herndon's oven was on, the door open, warming a bit of the apartment.

"This whole area is going to be taken over by the city, sooner or later," she said. "The landlord figures he'll get as much money as possible before the city takes over."

In a first-floor apartment where a kitchen wall seemed about to collapse because of a leak and the bathtub appeared to be sinking into the basement,

Mrs. Bloscine Brodie said, "I'm trying to get into a project, any project. I won't have holes hanging down over my head."

Mrs. Esther Banks, a 32-year-old welfare mother who lives in the Shepherd Arms with three of her children, told a Legal Services staff member one afternoon, "Believe me, honey, I'm searching like hell to get out of here, to run. I want to get away." She had lived in 552 Shepherd for two years. Mrs. Banks and 10 other black women tenants and two small children were meeting with Legal Services attorneys to detail counterclaims against the landlord and discuss the possibility of petitioning the court to appoint an administrator, superseding Frohman, to collect rents and make repairs.

Frohman, who had periodically served dispossess orders on almost all of the tenants, claimed eviction wasn't his goal, because it was a costly, prolonged process, he lost rent and vacant apartments were subject to vandalism. Despite all this, he had sued four tenants for back rent and last December the court decided in his favor, subjecting the tenants to eviction.

Eviction, Frohman said, was really what the tenants wanted, or to have the city order the building vacated because it was unsafe—which was why, he charged, they intentionally vandalized it. Despite reports on the squalid conditions in welfare hotels, Frohman said last fall, before the city announced it would try to phase out their use, "if the city issues a vacate order, it means emergency housing, which means everything from the Americana on down."

The tenants, of course, knew all about welfare hotels and preferred even the Shepherd Arms to that fate. They also knew that emergency housing wouldn't give them much of a chance at high places on the 135,000-family waiting list for public housing (a new city policy supposedly sets a higher priority now). As to Frohman's charge that the tenants were purposely damaging the building, Mrs. Dorothy Payne, a welfare mother with three children who had been living there for almost four years, said, "You can't destroy something that's already destroyed."

What is the future of 552 Shepherd? Until a couple of weeks ago, the heavy odds were that the city would acquire it for tax delinquency and become the official landlord of either an abandoned, gutted shell, prime for demolition, or another rancorous, occupied slum building. But in early March, the Metropolitan Savings Bank sold its mortgage for a mere $5,000 to a real estate businessman who wanted, as a bank official said, to "resurrect" the Shepherd Arms with his own capital and without evicting the tenants.

The bank and the new mortgage holder (who will become the actual landlord after foreclosure) maintained that with perhaps $15,000 to $20,000 worth of repairs, 552 Shepherd could be fixed up a bit and turned into a profitable rental operation within two years. To help make this come true, the prospective landlord said, he had a tax-abatement proposal pending before the Housing and Development Administration.

To a city skeptic, the acquisition suggested more a tax shelter, or a speculative holding action by simply paying off the oldest tax bill to keep the building out of the city's hands. For beyond the prospect of whether any minimal repair work is done or is financially successful, the landlord surely has his eye cocked on an attractive investment incentive which would more than make up for his liens and city emergency repair bills: city condemnation of a property currently assessed at $60,500, probably the minimum he would receive.

This might occur because the building, which lies within the unofficial site of a $70 million educational park now in the planning stage, would be demolished to make way for that new construction, which is tentatively scheduled for completion by 1976. But what if that doesn't come off or not as soon as planned—leaving whole blocks to decay for years in administrative limbo— and what of all the other 552 Shepherds throughout the city?

While strategies ranging from low-income co-ops to a $700 million New York City Housing Development Corporation are proposed and pondered, everyone in the city waits and waits for housing money from Albany and Washington. The Shepherd Arms begins to resemble a foul museum exhibit showing what dismal shelters mankind inhabited in the big American cities circa 1970.

"You're developing a cancer which is practically self-feeding," says Professor Sternlieb. "Good housing on a block crumbles in the face of the frequency of abandoned structures. There are significant hunks of New York City where the private housing market has gone out of business.

"In East New York, there has been abandonment not only by the owners and tenants but by the city. All the medicine we've brought to bear has been too little, too late. It [abandonment] is happening now, it will continue to happen and it will spread. One of the things it isn't is the bad guys versus the good guys. It's rougher than that."

Just how rough it continues to be in East New York was revealed again on a return visit to the neighborhood on a bright brisk morning this month. Only one, somewhat negative, improvement was evident: the demolition program had accelerated, flattening sizable tracts, and, according to Patrolman Molinelli, was now keeping pace with abandonment.

The house at 470 Elton Street was empty and tinned-up, but the heroin addicts' refuge at 336 Vermont Street, across from the school, was open and fire-scarred.

The scene at the Shepherd Arms was, if anything, more dismal, though warm. The building seemed shabbier than ever and there had been, taking the most favorable reports, steady heat for only the past month, after an intermittent supply during most of the winter. The city had put in another $1,000 through January, fixing the boiler and providing heating oil. At one point, the pipes had frozen and burst when fuel had run out.

East New York Housing Services had provided some residents with extra blankets and electric heaters during the icy intervals. Six apartments were reported to have been without water for a while. Nobody had been evicted, but five tenants, including Mrs. Herndon, had found homes elsewhere, leaving vacant apartments. For almost a year, the Department of Social Services has not been referring welfare cases to the Shepherd Arms because of what it calls "hazardous" violations. The tenants' council had collapsed, no rents at all were being paid and only the rumors and promises of new ownership and the coming of warmer weather seemed to break the residents' deep despair.

In the heart of winter, Mrs. Esther Banks had stood barefoot in her apartment in a damp litter of fallen paint and plaster, her voice harsh with rage: "We have no place to go. We're just buried in this dump. We're lost souls. Five-fifty-two Shepherd is a lost continent. There's no hope, no future, no nothing. We're just in an inferno of hell right here."

Now, in early March, I told her about the prospective landlord's intentions and asked if she still felt that the Shepherd Arms was a doomed place for "lost souls." Her worn, brown face relaxed for a moment with a trace of hope. Then the everlasting anguish returned. "I'm going to be that way until something is done," she said.

THE GHETTO EXPLODES IN ANOTHER CITY

It was Newark's turn last week.

The pattern of racial violence that has scarred city after city across the nation, leaving in its wake the debris-littered streets, the burned and looted shops, the dead and the injured—and always new legacies of hatred and bitterness—came to the city of 405,000, a 20-minute ride across the Hudson River from New York.

By late last night, as national guardsmen, state troopers and helmeted policemen patrolled the torn streets of Newark's Central Ward—the Negro ghetto—the toll rose to more than 20 dead, with over 1,100 injured and over 1,600 arrested, and property damage in the millions.

But the even larger toll was starkly defined by New Jersey Governor Richard J. Hughes, who said Newark was a city in the grip of "criminal insurrection"—a state of "open rebellion." Perhaps even more succinct was the comment of one national guardsman, who said, "This is just like two countries fighting."

It is the "two countries" that have always been at the heart of the violence that exploded in Harlem and Bedford-Stuyvesant in New York in 1964, in the Watts district of Los Angeles in 1965, in Chicago's West Side and Cleveland's Hough in 1966 and in Cincinnati, Buffalo, Boston, Hartford, Waterloo, Iowa and a score of other communities this spring and "long hot summer," whose end is not yet in sight.

There is the country of the whites—relatively prosperous, unencumbered for the most part by insurmountable social and economic barriers, free to shape its own destiny. And then there is the country of the Negroes—a country whose capital is the ghetto, whose constitution states that "all men are created equal, but Whitey comes first," and whose statistics still spell out a largely unchanging picture, despite new laws on the books, of higher unemployment than the whites, poorer education, poorer housing, poorer—you name it.

"I do not believe there will be any mass violence in Newark this summer," said Mayor Hugh J. Addonizio last May. The Mayor, a Democrat and former Congressman with a liberal voting record on civil rights and other issues, was not being a blind Pollyanna. Newark, half of whose population is Negro—the largest proportion of any city in the North—had been comparatively free of serious racial trouble. Mayor Addonizio, with some justification, credited efforts by his administration at improved community relations as a factor.

But the Mayor—like other mayors across the country—had only limited power to deal with the basic combustible elements that keep every Negro ghetto in the country today at the flash point.

For the past 15 years, Newark has been struggling to cope with a growing low-income population. In 1950, the city had the highest proportion of dilapidated housing in the nation. A slum-clearance program has helped somewhat, but it has barely touched the worst ghetto—the Central Ward.

In recent months, Newark's Negro community has been agitated by efforts by city officials to clear some 50 acres in a shabby Negro neighborhood for the site of the State College of Medicine and Dentistry. They have also been protesting about the rising unemployment of ghetto residents, and about an attempt to appoint a white city councilman to a post on the Board of Education, rather than a Negro now serving as the city's budget director.

The explosion, when it came, was touched off—as has so often been the case in racial riots—by a relatively minor incident.

Last Wednesday, Negroes gathered at the Fourth Precinct station house to protest the alleged beating of a Negro taxi driver by police. Tempers rose, and the demonstrators let fly a hail of stones and bottles that broke almost every window in the police station.

Then the violence spread as Negro youths roamed the streets, smashed windows and looted stores, and hurled rocks at police.

On Thursday, the rampaging grew worse. Negroes, some now armed, firebombed stores, battled with firemen trying to control the blazes and took up positions on rooftops to exchange shots with police. In the early hours of Friday morning, Mayor Addonizio, declaring the situation "ominous," telephoned Governor Hughes for national guard reinforcements.

About 2,600 national guardsmen rolled into the city in convoys of jeeps and trucks. But the sniper fire, the violence and the fury mounted, and hospital emergency rooms were soon overloaded with scores of injured persons, many in critical condition.

At times, amidst the scenes of riot and destruction that made the city look like a battlefield, there was an almost carnival atmosphere. Negro housewives calmly invaded shops and supermarkets that did not bear signs saying "Soul Brother"—a kind of password among Negroes during the riots—and walked off with everything they could carry. Said one woman as she lifted bread off a supermarket shelf, "The brother's got to take everything he gets. Whitey ain't about to get up off of anything unless you make him."

Nearby, several teen-agers danced and laughed in the street as two of them held aloft sticks with yellow wigs on them. "We've scalped the white man!" they shouted. Governor Hughes, touring the shattered city, said bitterly, "It's like laughing at a funeral."

It was a wild and violent funeral of sorts as the Governor, the Mayor and other officials sought yesterday to restore law and order. "The line between the jungle and the law might as well be drawn here as any place in America," Governor Hughes said.

But that was only one line. Beyond it lay other lines against which the Negro is pressing with ever-increasing force and impatience, precipitating in return a sharp white backlash. The struggle has riven the civil rights movement itself, with the militant "black power" elements increasingly challenging the moderates to act now and act strong, because the waiting has been too long.

PART THREE

ETHNIC COMMUNITIES, BOUNDED AND UNBOUNDED

From the oldest civilizations onward, the city has been the site of diverse ethnic populations and communities. Ancient cities were located at seaports and travel junctions, which enabled alien populations and cultures to penetrate indigenous agricultural societies. The foreigner was always denounced because he brought with him alien ideas which might undermine and threaten the values of the host society. In addition, the upper classes in almost all societies are drawn from different ethnic and racial stock than the indigenous population. Historically, a major avenue for achieving class dominance was military conquest. As the conquering migrant class settled into local society, its ideas of ethnic and racial superiority became a major constituent of the indigenous class culture.

In the United States, ethnic interpenetration has been more extreme than in most areas of the world, because the entire development of the country has been based upon successive waves of immigrants. As members of each ethnic wave achieved mobility and dominance, more immigrants poured into the cities to become the new lower classes. This process of European and Asian immigration into the United States continued until the mid-1920's. When mass immigration from Europe and Asia was cut off in 1924, the mass migration of blacks was already under way, and was in full force after World War II. Then came the Latin Americans, mainly Puerto Ricans. The relaxation of immigration laws in 1968 once more allowed the entry of new but smaller waves of immigrants from Europe, Asia and the Middle East.

The port and industrial city has always been the first point of entry, and sizable numbers of immigrants, especially in the 20th century, have settled in cities. As a result, ethnic communities of all varieties and ages have emerged in urban areas. Initially they tend to concentrate in ghetto communities, occupying successively the same ghettos from which older immigrants have been displaced or have moved out as they achieved economic success and residential mobility. Some ethnic groups have clung to their areas of original settlement and have become successful there. In other cases, where the number of immigrants is relatively small and they do not come in waves, the problem of establishing an ethnic community is difficult and does not necessarily result in a pattern of concentrated settlement. Immigrants from a relatively progressive industrial society may bypass the older ethnic ghettos and create more advanced ghettos. Some groups are unable to bring with them the skills, the wealth and the status which they held in their place of origin. Status and skills are not necessarily transferable from one society to another, because of differences in technology, culture and status systems. Their possessors may be declassed with respect to American society but retain their prestige and status within their own ethnic community. Those who can maintain their skills, wealth and prestige may easily be accepted at comparable class levels.

Other groups have struggled to maintain their culture in their patterns of settlement, often creating a minority culture which may be more unified and concentrated than it was in their homeland. Among some ethnic groups, conflicts emerge between earlier and later immigrants in the same group, as illustrated in the two articles on Chinatown. Most ghetto areas, however, are occupied by a plurality of ethnic groups whose struggle for common space can be a source of inter-ethnic problems.

In urban areas where there are well-defined centers of ethnic concentration, the different ethnic groups within a center may vary widely in density. In fact, there is an uneven flow of people from one area to another, and rarely is one area exclusively occupied by a single ethnic or class group. Since the mix of given neighborhoods is continuously changing, ethnic ''boundaries'' are never permanent, and legal and administrative attempts to fix such boundaries on the basis of residence are negated by the continuous process of ethnic movement within the city. As a result, successive attempts to redefine administrative districts—whether school, health, election, police, sanitation or fire department—seldom reflect current reality and will sooner or later atomize a given residential area.

Any particular neighborhood or public space, then, may be jointly occupied by several ethnic and class groups. Members of such communities within the neighborhood may sometimes be virtually unaware of the co-occupancy. When they are aware of it, the result may be either ethnic cooperation against external threats or neighborhood conflict. Also, such ethnic and class mixtures may include social isolates who belong to no community or who belong to another community outside the neighborhood.

The effect of these class and ethnic mixtures and of the fluidity of boundaries can give the city a great deal of its variety, charm, freedom and looseness. On the other hand, it can become the source of tension and friction.

EL BARRIO'S WORST BLOCK IS NOT ALL BAD

by DAVID and SOPHY BURNHAM

For a godless age there are a surprising number of religious institutions on the block. There are 16 "churches." They range from the Puritan fury of the Pentecostal Church, which forbids smoking, drinking, drugs, television and make-up, to the vague apprehensions of *espiritismo*.

Lenz is a spiritist, and attends sessions in his aunt's house.

"Well . . . you see that when a person dies it all depends on if God picked him up in time, rest in peace, or otherwise he could be around. We believe that every person has their own god to guard them that way, and also that they have other persons that are put on them in the side; and you have bad spirits and good spirits, you know. Some of them give you—well, it's hard to say."

He believes that the troubles in his family are caused by bad spirits, and the envious thoughts of the living. And certainly his family has had its troubles since coming from Puerto Rico 18 years ago. Fourteen children have been born to the family. Lenz's father, a diabetic and subject to blank spells, is retired from his dishwashing job and lives on welfare, though he sees no irony in his dutiful continuance of his union dues. Four of the surviving sons are drug addicts, three of them with arrest records. One son was killed by the police, another by a junkie when he sold him ersatz dope (a common enough activity on the block, but it was this family's son who was killed for it). A few weeks ago, a third son shot two men with a shotgun after a gambling argument. He is hiding from the law. One girl committed suicide; two daughters have illegitimate babies of their own. It is easy to understand Lenz's paranoia.

"You see, a lot of people on the street, they envy us," he explained. "I don't know why. And they always wish that we would all get in trouble, things like that. . . . When you think of a person mentally," he added, "it hurts more than if you put a voodoo on the person, believe it or not."

Espiritismo, Espiritistas. Many people on this block believe in the spirits, that the dead come back and talk to the living. They attend spiritist meetings;

they buy powders and potions to put in their bath water, to wash away their sins. Sometimes they cleanse the house with special leaves and herbs to get the spirits out.

But these are individual beliefs, and if Lenz and his father and aunt believe in the spirits, his brother Fernando does not. He looks up, gentle eyes sparkling: "Well, it's that there's no proof and no history on it. It comes to a dark end. In other words, it begins nowhere and ends nowhere. So there's no proving it. That's why people don't even argue over the religion of it." As for the Catholic Church, it "does not approve of it. But also they don't argue the point."

This is in keeping with the morality of the block: Live and let live. Keep quiet about what's not your business.

A block in El Barrio—Spanish Harlem—despite all the speeches and studies and community-action programs of the last years, remains remarkably foreign to most Americans, who have never lived in the crowded, dirty world of aging, six-story tenements, or talked to the people who live there—the parents, the children, the wage-earners, the welfare-takers, the healthy and the sick. Another reason why the area is hard to understand is that most studies of this world have focused on only one of the dark aspects of its life—the lack of family stability, or the decaying housing, or the drug addicts, or unemployment, or the obviously unsuccessful schools—and failed to portray the stable families, the industrious working fathers, and the teen-agers who have rejected drugs, the large numbers who grow strong and survive.

The block in which Lenz and his family live has been more completely portrayed. The work was begun four years ago by Dr. Bernard Lander, a New York sociologist, his brother Nathan and Dr. H. P. O'Brien of Notre Dame, and was supported by a series of grants from the Lavanburg Corner House, the Office of Juvenile Delinquency and the Vocational Rehabilitation Administration. A rare picture has emerged by now of one period in the life of the block and some changes in the life-styles of its residents.

The 25 tenements facing the 630-foot street are of red brick, most of them blackened with grime. They seem to press in on the street. Two buildings have been abandoned, their windows broken, their insides gutted by fire and emptied by thieves. Between some of them are sudden open spaces where a building has been torn down and the empty lot has become filled with rubble and beer cans. In contrast are five freshly painted tenements on one side of the street which are being renovated by a local housing organization, Metro North.

When the study began, 2,500 people in 640 families lived on the block. Today, after the removal of a few tenements, there are 400 families of 1,750 individuals. Three out of every five residents are Puerto Rican, almost all the rest Negro. The population is far younger than that of the city as a whole; every other person is under 21.

A complete census of the block found that two of every three families are headed by men; the rest by women. Of these family heads, more than half had not finished school, more than half were unemployed, a quarter were on welfare, a third made less than $60 a week. Rent, compared with the rest of Manhattan, seems low; two-thirds of the families pay between $25 and $45 a month for a three- or four-room apartment.

The block was built in 1906 to accommodate a wave of Jewish immigrants from the Lower East Side (upper Manhattan was opened to construction two years earlier with the completion of the first subway). The houses were "new-law" tenements. Among other reforms, every room had to have at least 70 square feet of space. Every room had to have a window.

The Jews were supplanted by the Italians and the Italians by the Puerto Ricans and Negroes, but the housing did not begin to get really bad until 1953, when the city designated the block for public housing, and then did nothing. The landlords, awaiting renewal, stopped making repairs; and during the next 15 years the block gained its reputation as a "bad" block.

Sixty per cent of the people on the block have lived there for 10 years or more, despite the fact they say they want to move, and most look back to a golden past: "It's not the street. It's the people who moved into the street. See, 'cause . . . it was a very good neighborhood. I mean it was quiet. It was. I couldn't say it was clean, but it was quiet, and they didn't have a lot of burglars and murders that they have now. It's just the dope and the marijuana that's being brought into the street that's messing up the street."

Since one of the advantages of poor accommodations is low rent, the poorest people tend to remain on the block; and the poorest are also those with the least education, the least resistance to and the fewest outlets for frustration, the highest incidence of ill health, mental disturbance and unemployment. The interior of the housing on the block has often been described: brown hallways with their rotten stairs and the acrid smell of garbage; cold apartments with overflowing toilets and moist, peeling paint. Housing probably is the worst problem because it is always with you. Your son can be a junkie, or your daughter in trouble with the police, and this is a worry, gnawing at the back of your mind. But if your roof leaks, it leaks on you and all around you. You cannot get away from it.

None know this better than the people who live there. About eight years ago the neighborhood formed Metro-North to do something about housing in a seven-block area. This organization is completely self-supporting, financing its two offices, supplies and phone bills with bus outings, dances and private donations. In the last three years it has fought the city bureaucracies, organized the tenants in run-down buildings, obtained vacate orders from the buildings department, relocated numerous families from dangerous buildings, and finally acquired about $12 million in private grants to buy and renovate 17 tenements—an example of concerned citizens' action that would make any middle-class family proud.

Though most of the work of Metro-North is in housing, in 1965 it persuaded the city to build a vest-pocket park on the block. It is a bare asphalt slab, more like a parking lot than the usual leafy image of a park, but to the residents of the block it is an achievement. It was Metro-North which forced the city to limit the height of the new public housing in the area. Metro-North is now associated with some of the antipoverty projects—the Youth Corps, educational counseling, tutoring and summer camps for children.

But this, of course, is only a beginning; the block's major problems remain. The fighting gangs are gone now, and apparently there are fewer crimes of violence, but the street—almost without shops, seemingly deserted on a cold winter day—is a marketplace for drugs. A bookie hangs out here. A numbers racketeer. Two pushers. Youths watch for fags to service for $5, money that immediately will be converted into a bag of heroin. Girls walk the streets. You can find almost anything here, and the activities permeate the lives of everyone, whether they participate and approve or not.

The fact is that the majority of the people on the block do not participate even peripherally in the life of crime, beyond a regular bet on the numbers. Crime is often a matter of definition. In some cases, it is simply an accommodation to a situation. And on this block, if there is considerable crime, particularly of a sort that is not found in well-off areas (numbers, pushers, fences), there is also a surprisingly conservative, even middle-class morality.

Of the 50 teen-age members of the old fighting gang that was centered on the block, for instance, three are now in the rackets, eight or ten are addicts; but three are members of the police force, one is a lieutenant in the Marines, and the remaining 30 or 35 have also "gone straight." It seems to be a matter of growing up.

Look at Angelina, the 19-year-old mother of an illegitimate child, who admitted she smoked pot when she was 14, shoplifted, roamed the streets. She doesn't do that any more.

"It's not lady—it's not for a woman. That's men's stuff. Boy's stuff."

The block is composed of 1,750 individuals as different as characters in a good novel. There is the short, heavy woman, a social worker, with direct brown eyes and a finely arched nose, strong, proud, self-sufficient. She has lived on the block with her husband and four children for 40 years. She sent one son through college. And there is the woman whose two daughters are lesbians—and it is a sad commentary on the neighborhood that the third will probably be one, too. (There seems to be a lot of lesbianism on the block. Many girls are drawn to it, either from fear of the hit-and-run tactics of the boys, or else because they grew up in state institutions where homosexuality is common. Lesbianism does not prevent accidents, though; and what does a mother feel when she discovers that her 14-year-old daughter is a lesbian—and later watches the 14-year-old belly swell with pregnancy anyway? "I thought you liked girls! And a boy, who you don't even know where he lives.")

A large number of people on the block believe that ability is more important than pull or "who you know." Many of the 25 per cent on welfare are ashamed of receiving it, though others accommodate themselves to it quite cynically. There is Johnny, a Negro, whose wife is on welfare despite her paying job. Sometimes he lives with her, sometimes with his girl friend on another block, and sometimes he even gives his wife some of the $80 a week he makes as a full-time social worker. There is the addict whose wife and four children live on welfare on another block. They have an apartment for $75 a month, and he told her to stay on welfare because even though he has a job he can't afford both the rent and his habit. "If I was an investigator and see that dump I would notify the city," he complains.

If some people abuse the welfare agency, the agency sometimes returns the favor. One caseworker, for example, tried to dissuade an ambitious youngster from learning a trade. "He say to me, 'Why don't you just go to work and forget the problem of going to school?' I told him if I go to work . . . I'm going to get a job washing dishes, somewhere, going for 15 dollar. That's what he requested I do." This youth is now working on a B.A. degree at City College.

Perhaps drugs have the most to do with the evil reputation of the block. One-twentieth of all the deaths from overdoses in Manhattan in 1967 (20 out of 400) occurred on this block, and despite continued and frequent arrests, the block has maintained its reputation as a place to get heroin. Cars with Jersey plates cruise down the street, looking for a connection. Yet only a small proportion of the block's population, less than 2 per cent, uses heroin.

The Lander study shows inexplicable changes in drug usage, periods of high consumption followed by periods of decline. Just now the block is going through a high. Four years ago, Lander interviewed 60 nonaddicted teen-agers living on the block; today a third of them are addicts. About 100 addicts hang around the block, two-thirds of them, as might be expected, Puerto Rican. While about one-third of the Negro addicts are female, only three out of the 24

Puerto Rican addicts are girls, and these three have become addicted in the last year or two.

If a third of the teen-agers have become addicts, however, two-thirds have not. Why one boy will succumb to drugs and another will resist defies explanation. One tentative finding of the Lander study shows that those tempted to drugs appear to come from the more stable and economically secure families. "Perhaps they turn to drugs because they are in a better position to see just how tough it will be to break out of the block," Lander speculates.

"I remember when I was 18 I started using drugs," said Thales, a Negro, 23 years old and one of eight children. "I used to sit alone, and just being alone used to bother me so much, because then I was by myself, and I started thinking. I was so disturbed I didn't know what to do. Everything was bothering me. . . . I don't get along with my father. I'm not clean the way I want to be. I haven't got the clothes I want. I never have the money. . . . I'm not asking to have a pocket full of money all the time, I don't never have no money. I got to go to school, and I'm failing in this subject and I'm failing that. . . . I felt quite sure I wasn't going to graduate. And I said that if I didn't graduate, man, that's going to hurt my mother."

Eventually he turned to drugs. "This thing was A-O.K. It's different. My emotional problems aren't solved, but I don't feel them. They don't bother me. I'm high, man, I don't have to worry 'bout nothin'."

There is a lot of talk on the block about drugs—OD's (overdoses), copping (procuring drugs) and skin-popping and mainlining (intramuscular and intravenous injection). Every now and then the addicts go to a hospital for a cure or to reduce the amount of heroin they need. An addict named Ralph has tried to kick the habit 11 times, and each time, the first day out, as soon as he can, he mainlines.

Yet heroin gets different holds on different people. Some addicts lead quite normal lives. There is the man on the block who has been using heroin every day for 10 years, skin-popping only, never putting it in his veins. There is another who mainlines only on weekends, and holds a regular job during the week.

These and other facts about heroin and its use are not given recognition by the politicians, perhaps because the politicians have found, in addiction, a handy devil on which to blame the city's ills. It is far easier and cheaper to view heroin as the cause—rather than the product—of trouble, to talk about cracking down on the addict rather than to make meaningful improvements in housing and schools.

On the block the feelings of the nonaddicted toward the addicted is ambivalent.

"What's the worst thing you can do?"

"I don't know. Be a junkie, I guess. I don't know."

Many denounce the addicts as the cause of all the block's problems; others express understanding, even acceptance. "They're human beings, but they just have problems, too," said one 16-year-old girl.

For the most part the block lets the addicts alone, partly perhaps because there is little to be done anyway, partly out of total lack of arrogance.

"Yeah, some of my friends are addicts. I treat them just the same. 'Cause once, I told something to a friend of mine, and I think he told me, you know, not to treat him that way. And I figured he was right. 'Cause it wasn't any of my business what he was doing, and I realized I was wrong. . . . I see them in the street, I talk to them."

On the block there is a distinction between an addict and a junkie. An addict has pride. A junkie will stoop to anything to support his habit. "He'll hustle his own sister. That's disgusting. I can't see it. I feel that if you have a habit, support it. . . . Be a man about it. . . . If you got to steal, go steal. It's a job like any other job. You make faster money, and you deprive people of other things, but it's a job. . . . They require certain skills, and stealing is one of them."

One young man, speaking of his addict brothers, recalls with pride, "They did a lot of stealing, but not from our house. . . . They respect my mother and respect my father. If they did anything, they did it outside. The door was open to them 24 hours a day."

The 33-year-old mother of six children, a heroin addict, prostitute and thief: "They say that drug addicts lose their shame. I don't think so. I come from a religious family. I have a lot of scruples. I'm very easy to be hurt. I want to raise my kids right."

The block is not afraid of the addicts. Addicts usually are not violent. "They just support their habit by stealing. They're only like a rat. If you corner them, they have to jump you. Because they are—the point is, if they would go to your house and you will be there, they won't enter. They're just as scared as anybody."

Not all addicts on the block steal to support their habits. At least a third of them, according to Lander's study, have regular jobs or are supported by their parents or a working husband or wife.

So the addicts survive. They scrounge and get by, and for the most part live unmolested on the fringes of the block. Moreover, it seems eventually some of them stop.

While Lander found that during the four-year period of his study one-third of the kids began taking heroin, he also discovered that about one-third of those with a drug history—22 out of 60 addicts and former addicts—had quit. It seems they reached their late twenties and early thirties and simply stopped. On the average they had been off drugs for three years or more. All but three stopped without the assistance of the various government programs.

Unlike the addiction-prevention agencies, which appear to have reached almost none of the people on the block, welfare and schools touch many. Of the quarter of the families on welfare, some get off the rolls quickly, others remain on welfare for years.

"Yes, welfare helps, because it's a salary, just like being a husband to some women," said Juan, a young man who lives on the block. "But to others, it's a hold-back, the chain that's holding him back."

The schools are not wholly admired either. "Yeah," said one young man, looking back on his education, "we used to go to the classroom and the airplanes flying all over the room, and then in a hour you have finish another class and there's a different program. You weren't in one place long enough to learn anything."

One girl said she felt most of the teachers "just come for their money, they don't teach you, they let you do what you want and everything." But there were exceptions. "I had two good teachers in junior high school. Both of them were science teachers. They're interested in the kids. They make Saturday trips; they try to teach you what you don't understand. A lot of things."

If the welfare system and the schools often fail at the task of developing citizens capable of standing on their own feet, it seems clear that the system of criminal justice—the police, courts and prisons—is often equally irrelevant to the problem of crime. Many on the block, especially the young people, admit that they commit illegal acts on a fairly regular basis. For the teen-agers, for example, the weekly shoplifting trip down to Macy's or up to Incredible Alexander's in the Bronx is a regular Saturday entertainment like going to a movie.

"Why do you steal?"

"To get what we wanted. Pocketbooks and clothes."

They go in groups of twos or threes, the girls in their cliques, the boys in theirs. One girl will stand guard watching for the store detectives, while her friends stand at a rack of chain belts, trying them on, choosing the one they want. At the all-clear, they rip off the price tag and move out of the store. Sometimes they are spotted by the detectives and they hit the door running, and race across the street, dodging among the cars, to collapse laughing a few blocks away.

They rarely are caught, partly because they are very adept, partly because the stores find it cheaper to accept a certain amount of shoplifting than to hire enough clerks to wait on each customer. One store detective estimated that his staff catches one of five of the shoplifters, about half of whom are middle-class. When the slum kids are caught, he said, "the Puerto Ricans break down and cry; the Negroes are cool, tough."

Often the youngsters don't bother with the long trip downtown. They pocket an item from stores in the neighborhood as they have undoubtedly seen adults do. Sometimes, more rarely, the kids will steal on order, the casual comment by some adult that he could really use a radio becoming the signal for a profit-making transaction.

The kids on the block experiment with drugs (one addict said he first tasted heroin when he was 11), "scheme" (pet) the girls, sneak into the subways, break into cars, hang around and get bored, rubbing up against the police as they roam the streets. No backyard or open field gives them the buffer against the law which is available to the suburban young. Despite this constant confrontation, however, a check of police and F.B.I. records shows that surprisingly few persons on the block have ever been arrested—or given, if under 16, a Youth Division card. Only one out of 11 on the block has any kind of police record. (Checks on similar blocks in Washington, D.C., and Chicago showed much more police activity than in New York.)

As of 1964, about one in four of those between 11 and 20 (128 out of 488) had been picked up by the police. Most of the charges were trivial. About a third of them were for truancy, running under subway turnstiles, disorderly conduct and fighting. About one in 10 was for either assault or burglary.

The charges brought against adults were more serious. There were seven for robbery, three for shoplifting, two for purse-snatching and 16 for petty larceny. The single largest category of crime charges against the adults on the block involved drugs—crimes which seldom involve unwilling victims.

If surprisingly small numbers are arrested on the block, an even smaller proportion ever get to court or prison. According to police records, only 11 per cent of the boys between 11 and 20, and only 30 per cent of the adults who were arrested ever went on to court. These figures raise the questions whether the larger police force many call for would actually reduce crime and whether efforts would not be better directed to the schools, which at least have direct contact with almost everyone living in the area. Particularly so since what contact the block has with the law hardly seems to contribute to a higher sense of morality. There is an almost unanimous lack of respect for the police there, a widespread belief that they are corrupt and brutal.

"One of my friends got killed by a cop," a pretty young Puerto Rican girl remembered. "The cop was drinking and they say he came out of a bar on 103d Street, and the kid was running and some lady was yelling, and he got shook up and he shot him in the back and got him killed, and he died."

"Had your friend done anything?"

"I don't know. You really don't know what happened 'cause the cop told his story and that's all the story. It was still wrong 'cause he coulda shot him in the leg or something, but he shot to kill."

She added, " 'Cause you're a Puerto Rican or Negro, they just take you in the car and beat you up and then take you to the precinct and everything."

Tonio was beaten up that way and returned home with his face swollen as evidence of the treatment. Also Peter, who tried to escape from Elmira prison. "They beat him on the body. They did not beat him on the head, 'cause they probably would have killed him. But they beat him with rubber nightsticks."

A young man was asked whether the police accept bribes.

"Oh sure, they do that all the time."

"Have you ever seen it yourself?"

"Giving them money? Oh sure."

"Who would it be?"

"Bookies. All over. Everything."

A runner for the numbers racket was even more definite. "They, you know, they come around the first of every month. There is the cop which you call the captain's man and he comes around and he picks up for the captain and then the cop on duty he gets paid, too."

"Aren't there any honest cops?"

"Yeah. You get an honest cop on Fifth Avenue someplace. You can't have honest guys around a block like this."

It is estimated that the residents of this one short block bet $270,000 a year on the numbers game (50 cents per person, six days a week). If this figure is multiplied by the 130,000 people in the local police precinct, it appears that each year about $20 million is being gambled on numbers in that small corner of Harlem. The size of this operation makes believable the rumors that some of the $10,000-a-year plainclothesmen charged with stopping gambling receive $1,000-a-month payoffs.

This one block in El Barrio has been studied and analyzed for 10 years. It is a living laboratory, the subject of TV documentaries, books and articles. Reporters and sociologists have been drawn to this block, tantalized by its reputation as a haven for prostitutes, crime and drugs, enjoying it vicariously, indulging their *voyeurism*—until the block is sick to death of it.

It is easy to see crime and evil when you look at a block. It is harder to see the good, since the good people are often "good" merely in a negative sense—that is, refrain from performing certain acts. Yet the good people on this block are often good positively and overtly—even though what they do is still overlooked. They have found $12 million to rehabilitate their housing, started programs for the addicts, stopped the old fighting gangs (there are two shopping bags full of guns and other weapons at the bottom of the East River, collected 10 years ago from willing gang members). They have organized social clubs to keep the children occupied, manned the antipoverty agencies, and in a hundred quiet ways are trying to change their block.

CHINATOWN IS TROUBLED BY NEW INFLUX

by MURRAY SCHUMACH

At Bayard and Mulberry Streets, among congested tenements, is Public School 23, one of the few schools left with the outdoor fire escapes of the last century. Inside it is immaculate. The school's monthly attendance frequently exceeds 99 per cent, about 10 per cent above the city average. Nearly all the students are of Chinese origin.

"They enjoy school," says Mrs. Grace Mok, a teacher there who grew up in Chinatown and was graduated from this school, and whose children, who are now married, did the same. "That's the trouble sometimes. They enjoy school so much they'll come to school with fever, with whooping cough, with measles."

Yet at Seward Park High School, where 600 of the 4,000 students are Chinese, the dropout rate for them often reaches a surprising 15 per cent.

This contrast is one result of the immigration wave that has been drastically altering Chinatown since the repeal of the immigration quota system in 1965. About 25 per cent of the 45,000 residents of the community arrived in the last two years. The boundaries, once generally regarded as Canal Street on the north, Park Row on the south, Mulberry Street on the west and the Bowery on the east, extend uptown to Grand Street—with some clusters near 14th Street—and to Essex Street on the east.

Gangs of loitering dropouts have become as commonplace in Chinatown's narrow streets as the smiling children, the aromatic restaurants, the stores of exotic merchandise and the camera-clicking tourists.

"The Chinese are a people New Yorkers tend to neglect," says the Reverend Denis Hanly, pastor of the Roman Catholic Church of the Transfiguration, which took root at Mott and Park Streets in 1848, a couple of decades before the section began changing from Irish to Chinese.

The problems of this community, which have been obscured by those of black and Puerto Rican areas, are serious. They include the following:

Housing shortages have resulted in payments of "key money" ranging from $500 to $2,000 for tenement flats.

Language problems have made it difficult for Chinese immigrants to get jobs and obtain education.

Debts incurred in getting to the United States have obliged wives as well as husbands to work. Sometimes children, after school, stand beside a sewing machine at which their mothers are working.

Crime, mainly robbery, but with some purse-snatching and mugging, has grown in this area, once known for its low crime rate.

"There's a great need for help in Chinatown," says Percy E. Sutton, Manhattan Borough President, "and no special attention is being paid. But I'm determined that within a year we're going to get a language laboratory there. I think it's terribly important."

The lack of what has come to be known in the area as "sur-English" has been the main cause of the difficulties of students in high school, according to many community workers in Chinatown. The language problem is much more serious among adolescents than among children in the grade school. These bilingual workers point out that very few of the community's school dropouts were born in this country.

Part of the trouble has been the reluctance of the Chinese-American community here to press for government assistance. A recent study of Chinatown by Chinese-speaking college students, under the auspices of Columbia University and the Ford Foundation, found that, "The Chinese have always relied upon their family or relatives in times of need, and children are expected to take care of their parents in their old age. Thus few are willing to accept welfare."

In addition, the Chinese Consolidated Benevolent Association, with some 60 member groups, the Establishment of Chinatown, has been challenged by the Chinatown Planning Council and the Chinese Youth Council, both largely publicly financed, which direct their appeal to the young, arranging English classes and seeking jobs.

There are indications, however, that, except for a tiny Maoist-directed group, efforts are being made to reduce frictions. Representatives of the different groups join in meetings with public officials and a number of men in the dissident groups, in private conversation, seem in basic agreement.

Though residents of Chinatown are learning how to use the government—they have even staged a few demonstrations—the dominant qualities of the community are still self-reliance, industry and ingenuity.

Residents are buying many of the area's tenements and factories. Volunteers teach English and the Benevolent Association operates the New York Chinese School, after regular school hours, which teaches Chinese and Chinese culture to more than 2,600 children. At the Chatham Square branch library, the children burrow tirelessly among English and Chinese books.

An example of the Chinese businessmen's resourcefulness is the line of men at the curb every weekday, at Elizabeth and Bayard Streets, at 10 A.M. and 3 P.M. They are restaurant workers who are picked up by car and driven to and from restaurant jobs in Queens, Long Island, New Jersey and Westchester County at the expense of the restaurant owners.

One of the major assets of Chinese-Americans is their mobility. Unlike some minorities, if they have the money they can live almost anywhere in the city or suburbs.

But there is some concern—most people agree it is very little—about the possibility that if hostilities break out between the United States and Communist China, they might be put in concentration camps as security risks.

David Ho, executive director of the Chinese Youth Council, says, "The great majority of the Chinese here have faith in the American Government. They don't feel insecure here. There are only a few who are worried about this."

That Chinese-Americans do not take this possibility very seriously is a tribute to them. For many years they were persecuted in this country. Early immigrants were brought to the United States as cheap labor in the goldfields of the West and as railroad laborers.

They began settling in New York City, driven from the West by the humiliation of being limited to the most menial work. Sometimes they were even lynched.

Despite this unhappy history and present problems, the adaptability of Chinese immigrants here is reflected by the cheerfulness of the children. Says Mary Gee, a young woman who has never moved from the Chinatown tenement in which she was born:

"The little kids are happy."

CHINATOWN STRETCH-ING BORDERS INTO LITTLE ITALY

by ALFRED E. CLARK

In Public School 23, at Bayard and Mulberry Streets, there is a faded, 40-year-old photograph that shows two Chinese pupils in a graduating class that was nearly all Italian. Now all the pupils at the school are Chinese.

In the block south on Mulberry, once the center of lower Manhattan's Little Italy, there were seven Italian restaurants not long ago. Now all but one are gone, and in their place are shops and restaurants owned by Chinese.

There was a day when Chinese residents of the area were clustered together in a few blocks, not daring to venture north of Canal Street, even for a stroll.

"Maybe it was the traffic, but many also were afraid they would be beaten up," an elderly Italian resident recalled. "Now, they're not only across Canal, but they're buying houses and flats as far north as 14th Street."

Pressed by sharp increases in immigration from Hong Kong and Taiwan, they are moving well beyond the two or three blocks that once made up Chinatown.

"The Chinese are not only buying buildings in old Chinatown below Canal Street, they are becoming owners of buildings all along Mulberry Street," said Louis DeSalvio, a Democratic district leader. "They are also buying buildings on such streets as Henry, Catherine, Division and Elizabeth.

"Eventually, at this rate, most of the landlords here will be Chinese, and there may not be any more Little Italy."

Although precise figures are not available, old-timers say that in the nineteen-thirties the area had 100,000 residents of Italian descent. Now, partly because of moves to Queens or the suburbs, there are thought to be no more than 30,000 in Little Italy, and that figure has been passed by the increasing Chinese population in the area.

Fifteen years ago, New York City recorded the birth of 651 children of

Chinese descent; in 1967 the figure was 1,025, and most of them live in the expanding Chinatown.

"It's not like the average reaction of so many who, when they can make enough money, want to move out to the suburbs," said Norman Lau Kee, a lawyer.

"The Chinese feel safe and at home here, they want to be with their own people," explained Mr. Kee, whose office on Mott Street is at the center of the traditional Chinatown.

The most rapid phase of the influx that has widened the boundaries of Chinatown began in 1962, when 15,000 people from Hong Kong and Taiwan were permitted to join family members in the United States. Even more came in the succeeding years, as the quota system of the old immigration law was abolished.

There followed what James Typond, an insurance and real estate broker on Mott Street, described as "a veritable population explosion.

"For decades those who migrated from the China mainland were men seeking to work and earn the money to bring their families here," he said. "Then, Chinatown was a small section centered about Mott and Pell Streets and Chatham Square.

"Now the Chinese people are seeking to rent living quarters almost anywhere, but it is right here that most want to live and work."

The railroad flats, street-level stores and even cellars are in brisk demand. Chinese syndicates are paying what one resident called "the top dollar" for properties, and Chinese tenants are paying rents so high that they surprise real estate experts.

"Don't let the outside of some of these tenements fool you," said one long-time resident. "Many of the apartments have been beautifully decorated and are as nice as any of those in fancy neighborhoods."

Five years ago, Mr. Typond and others in a syndicate built a six-story cooperative building at Bayard and Elizabeth Streets, with a doorman and elevator. Of the 168 families living there now, all but five are Chinese.

A block away he is planning to build a 12-story condominium on the site of a grimy second-hand clothing-store arcade. The site will also house a 900-seat motion picture theater for Chinese films.

Two blocks west on Mulberry Street, another Chinese syndicate bought two dilapidated buildings not long ago and tore the interiors out. They added an elevator, two penthouses, air-conditioning and a white brick façade.

Before the renovation, five-room apartments in the tenement were renting for $45 a month. Now three-room apartments go for $175, and all the occupants of the building are Chinese except for an Italian superintendent.

Michael J. Greco, a condemnation-law expert familiar with Chinatown, said he was "amazed" at the prices recently paid for some tenements, prices that he said seemed "far in excess of market value."

"Yet the demand for property in the area is strong," he added, "and when the tenements are renovated, their original sales prices look like bargains in retrospect."

There is plenty of available money in Chinatown. Some attribute the wealth to traditional Chinese thrift; others say that large amounts are coming in from Hong Kong.

"Surprising as it may seem, the Chinese in Hong Kong are very much afraid that Communist China will decide one of these days, possibly within the next two years, to take over Hong Kong," said Albert V. Saducca, president of Noma World-Wide Enterprises, Inc., which has a Christmas tree-light factory on Taiwan.

On a recent trip to the Far East, Mr. Saducca concluded that some Chinese there, apprehensive about the Communists, were sending money to relatives here for safekeeping.

The unusual boom in Chinatown has brought its own kind of inflation. Mrs. Assunta M. Sirota is now being charged $2,000 a month for the old-fashioned drugstore she operates at 70 Bayard Street. She considers the rent, produced by a succession of quick increases, to be excessive, and she has taken her Chinese landlord to court over it.

But, reflecting the relative peace of the coexistence between the two ethnic groups in the area, Mrs. Sirota has also learned enough Chinese to deal with her customers in their own language.

Despite some tension between the two groups, the Chinese have also learned from the Italians, as Joseph Nonna, a brisk, silver-haired Italian butcher pointed out the other day.

They have come to understand Italian ways and to like Italian foods. In fact, Mr. Nonna recalled happily, "I even saw a couple of Chinese youngsters eating spaghetti on their pizzas."

ASTORIA'S RELAXED MELTING POT

by MURRAY SCHUMACH

A visiting detachment of evzones, the famed skirted warriors of Greece, will be on hand in the Astoria section of Queens today for ceremonies accompanying the demolition of an old mansion.

On the site will rise the six-story Athena Pericles John Lantzounis High School, the first Greek secondary school in the United States. It was named after a Manhattan real estate man and his wife.

The school, across the street from St. Demitrios Greek Orthodox Church, 31st Street and 30th Drive, is the latest proof that this middle-class community, some 20 minutes from Times Square by subway, is entitled to its claim as a "league of nations."

At a single school serving the area—Public School 166—records show students born in 28 nations other than the United States. The children have an international dance festival, for which they make their own costumes and an international food party, to which they bring home-made delicacies of the country of their birth.

"The foreign-born parents are very demanding of their children," says Robert S. Abraham, principal. "They come to us and ask why the children are not getting more homework."

In this international enclave, bounded by Broadway, 49th Street, the East River and Riker's Island Channel, are: a candy store, which includes among its numerous imported publications foreign fashion magazines that sell for as much as $6.50; a Scottish bakery; a Greek sidewalk espresso-cum-bakery; bocce courts; expert soccer teams; devotees of Irish hurling; and groceries and restaurants to serve such cosmopolitan palates.

Some tensions have developed beneath the apparent serenity of Astoria. One of the most interesting is among the Greek community of some 30,000 persons, about a fourth of the neighborhood. The older immigrants worked hard, saved diligently, bought the little home, lawn and backyard. But among the newer immigrants are a number of Cypriotes who arrived with means, who speak English well, who have been successful in business, have sent their children to private schools.

In acquiring homes, they have forced up the price of some unpretentious houses to $70,000. There are reports of some houses going for $90,000.

They seem to be able to buy and sell land,'' says Mrs. Irene Dafnas, who settled here as a girl, and whose daughter and son grew up in Astoria. The Reverend Dr. John Poulos, pastor of St. Demitrios, sighs and says, "If only Greeks would stop fighting among themselves."

Slightly larger than the Greek colony, and more strongly entrenched, is the Italian settlement, many of whose members are second- and third-generation Astorians.

State Senator Nicholas Ferraro, who has lived all his 40 years within an eight-block sector of Astoria, points out that most candy stores post placques, issued by churches, vowing not to sell pornographic magazines.

"The people here are dedicated to the education of the children and to own their own home. The whole community is like this."

On almost any pleasant day, homeowners can be seen painting doors, fixing stoops, working in gardens, putting glass in windows. Men and women in this community are accustomed to doing much of their own home repairs.

The desire for education is hampered, according to Mrs. Annaliese Krieger, Czech-born president of the Parent Association of P.S. 166, by a shortage of persons to teach English to children.

Among the men and women born in Astoria, however, Senator Ferraro says, assimilation has been working well. The Irish, for instance—almost as numerous as the Greeks—are often at Italian social affairs.

The area, he says, is very active politically, with about 50 per cent voting in primaries. Nominally Democratic, it is conservative. Astoria supported Mr. Nixon in 1968, and went for Mario A. Procaccino, the Democratic candidate for mayor, last year. It also tends to favor its own. Thus, Senator Ferraro ran well ahead of the Presidential ticket in 1968, and was very close to Mr. Nixon.

"It's enjoyable to campaign here," he says. "You know everybody."

The community and family flavor of Astoria figures in its business enterprises too. Even Steinway and Sons is looked upon here not just as a maker of famous pianos, but as a family enterprise of Astoria.

There is a supermarket that failed twice as part of a major chain operation, but is now very successful as a family business. Employees and customers know one another on a first-name basis.

This community feeling is one reason that Steinway Street, in the vicinity of Broadway, has continued as the important shopping section for so many residents of Astoria. It is a reason for the apparent success of so many stores along Ditmars Avenue, the main stem of the Greek community.

Originally known as Hallett's Cove, after the first settler, William Hallett, who in 1754 received from Governor Peter Stuyvesant a patent of 1,500 acres, Astoria became a village in 1839.

Some authorities believe that in one of the taverns, where farmers, en route from Long Island to Manhattan, waited merrily for the tide to change, the manhattan cocktail was invented. The general atmosphere of controlled conviviality and neighborliness continues.

THE WEST SIDE: A POLYGLOT OF RACES, CREEDS AND CULTURES

by RICHARD F. SHEPARD

Manhattan's West Side sprawls unspectacularly northward from 59th to 125th Streets, an immense checkerboard of wealth and poverty, of black, white, yellow and brown, a three-mile-long tract that is simultaneously running up and running down.

There is nothing typical about the West Side or about the more than 300,000 people who live in its new high rises, its squalid single-room occupancies, its aging apartment hotels or its distinctive brownstones. It is nobody's turf, everyone's home. It is not overwhelmingly black, white or Spanish-speaking; it is, impressively and inextricably, all three.

Yet the West Side is beset with change as people flow in eddies of income and race around certain blocks while others move in and out. The poor, usually Negroes and Puerto Ricans, complain that they are being squeezed out by high-rent construction that brings in the middle classes. The wealthier are fearful of criminal elements among the poor. For all the complaints, few want to leave the West Side and they do so only reluctantly.

Estimates, inexact and projected from the 1960 census, put 100,000 Puerto Ricans (and other Spanish-speaking people) on the West Side. There are perhaps 60,000 Negroes and 200,000 whites. White is an un-New Yorkish term and few New Yorkers say they are white and let it go at that.

West Side whites are largely Jewish and middle class. There are also the Irish, remnants of what was one of the largest communities on the West Side, and the white Anglo-Saxon Protestants, particularly academic out-of-towners in the region around Columbia University.

The West Side is also blessed with Oriental spicing—Chinese, Japanese and a few Koreans. There are Japanese shops selling foods, fans and Fujiyama posters to Orientals and Occidentals. Along Broadway, there are few blocks without a Chinese restaurant or a laundry, a few yards in and down the stairs.

What is the attraction of the West Side for those who live there, mingling on the street and in the stores and in the schools, away from the ghettos, whether gilded or gloomy, where like types tend to congregate? For some, the lure is its very cosmopolitanism. For others, it is the West Side's convenience to the business and cultural centers of New York. Yet others have drifted in because it is the only place where they can find a relatively inexpensive apartment with thick walls and high ceilings and baroque flavor.

Mrs. Alfred Prettyman lives in a seven-story, 50-year-old apartment house on West 97th Street with her husband, who is an editor at Harper and Row, and their three children. She travels to Brooklyn College, where she is going for a graduate degree in political science. The Prettymans are a black family that is determined to remain on the West Side.

"I love the West Side, it's the least sterile part of the city," said Mrs. Prettyman. "It has its own special atmosphere, different in a way from the East Side. There are a lot of Spanish people and customers as well as a strong Jewish and black clientele.

"On the West Side, you see interracial couples, the young, the old. You've got cultural pluralism here. There's nothing to force you to leave because of what you are."

The block between Columbus Avenue and Central Park West on 84th Street is quiet, a mixture of brownstones and apartment houses. Near Columbus is the Spanish American Grocery, a neat little hole-in-the-wall run by Victor Rodriguez, a Puerto Rican who came downtown several years ago from El Barrio in uptown Manhattan.

"Not many Puerto Ricans around here," Mr. Rodriguez said, reflecting the block-by-block cantonization that is New York. "They are all over there," he said, waving vaguely westward toward Amsterdam. "Here are Haitians, Dominicans, Cubans. Now some Mexicans have moved onto the block. They like beer, oh, they like beer. The Dominicans like beer, too, but better *platanos*—bananas."

At Amsterdam and 84th Street is La Gran Esquina Barbershop, subtitled "Your Barber and Friend from Santo Domingo." The shop, which is a bit more modest than the great corner it takes its name from, serves a Spanish-speaking clientele, many of them, like the management and staff, Dominicans.

"If they came for me, they couldn't take me away from the West Side," said Miguel Almonte, the white-haired proprietor. "Some Dominicans moved away from here, but they all came back. We have our friends here, our own people. The life here is *mas decente*—more decent."

The West Side's newest language, in quantity, is French, sometimes Creole, the French dialect spoken by Haitians who have set up housekeeping in the neighborhood. Their community center, the Haitian Neighborhood Service, opened not long ago at Amsterdam and 84th in what was once an Irish bar.

"There are more Haitians in Brooklyn," said Lyderic Bonaventure, the center's director, as he nodded in reply to a "Bonjour" from one of the many visitors who come through looking for advice on education, housing, jobs and adjustment. "There are, I believe, 20,000 of us between 72d and 110th.

"We don't find that our social interests are particularly with the Negroes or the Puerto Ricans. We feel closest, I would say, to the Dominicans. They come from the other part of our island. The Brooklyn Haitians have their own community, more or less, but Haitians here like the facilities on the West Side."

The Asociación Cultural Hispano-Americana, 200 West 84th Street, is one of dozens of storefront locations working for and with West Side Puerto Ricans. There is a large room for meetings and a tiny office, in which Efrain Rosa, its president, was sorting index cards.

"The West Side is very complex," said Mr. Rosa, in an excess of understatement. "A large number of Puerto Rican professionals or semiprofessionals live here, proportionately more than live elsewhere. We are in a new generation of Puerto Ricans, who have higher standards. But many poor Puerto Ricans here are being displaced by the urban renewal."

Puerto Rico shows itself on the West Side on Amsterdam and Columbus Avenues, the *bodegas,* the "botanical gardens" that sell dream books and herbs, the tiny clubs where the members spill over onto the sidewalk and where soap boxes or old straight-back chairs make instant poverty-style outdoor cafes. Puerto Rico is also evoked in the clattering Spanish of curbside congregations and in the blaring wails of the loudspeakers outside of the "disco" stores where one can buy phonograph records of the latest Latin pop tune or of the ballads sung by the *jibaro,* the Puerto Rican who lives far from the town.

McGlade's Restaurant and Tavern, 89th and Columbus, is an old-fashioned Irish pub, with a polished wooden bar and tables where a customer can get Irish stew with his beer.

"Most of the Irish picked up and ran, there are not many left," said one customer, Bill Flynn, a fair, brawny man born on the West Side. "Those of us who are left live mostly in the new low-cost housing."

In a bar and restaurant on Broadway north of 110th, Joe Fats, a neighborhood regular, reminisced on his Irish youth in the West 140's some 30 years ago.

"You couldn't walk down a different block from your own without getting a fight," he said. "Down here? Down here is like Miami. It's quiet. There's still some Irish but most of them have all moved up to Inwood."

The middle-class West Side Jewish community is still active, vital and extensive, although Marjorie Morningstar, the heroine of Herman Wouk's bestselling novel of life on the West Side, would be more likely to show up as an East Side girl were she created today. Until the last 10 years or so, the West Side was the goal of Jewish families whose breadwinning was successful enough to take them to Central Park West or West End Avenue from the Bronx or Brooklyn.

Today older families are moving to the new luxury buildings to the east of Central Park and the young-marrieds are off to the suburbs. But there are many Jews among the white middle class who have lately moved into the West Side, into its Lincoln Towers, its Park West Village, its renovated brownstones.

Certainly, the plethora of Chinese restaurants, delicatessens (kosher and not), its several Israeli nightspots and *felafel* (an Israeli counterpart of the hot dog) cafes, as well as its many large community-conscious Jewish centers give visible evidence of Jewish life on the West Side.

Refugees from Hitler's Germany and Austria made the West Side their home, one smaller only than their settlement in Washington Heights. Today the refugees are an aging and fading element of West Side life, although they are still to be found enjoying their *torte* and *kaffee mit schlag* in places such as the Eclair on 72d Street.

The American Congregation of Jews from Austria, small in comparison to the massive centers and synagogues built by earlier generations of West Side Jewry, is on the second floor of a building at 92d and Broadway.

"We have no youth, it is bad," said Albert Gaertner, the courteous and dignified executive secretary of the congregation. "We used to have *jause*—in Vienna, that was a late-afternoon tea party. We still have a *Kaddish* memorial services for the dead on November 10, to remember the day of Nazi pogroms in 1938. But when our old people go, this will probably dissolve."

John Kawaguchi was born in Seattle, a Nisei of Japanese parents. After he was mustered out of a combat unit in World War II, he settled on the West Side and now works in Forlini's, a tavern-restaurant at Broadway and 111th Streets.

Mr. Kawaguchi is one of several hundred Japanese who make the West Side their home. Some of these Japanese were once part of a small but cohesive Japanese settlement in the tenements where the Lincoln Center for the Performing Arts now reposes. Others are part of the large overseas Japanese business community in New York. The Japanese stores on the West Side not only serve local trade, but weekend visitors from the entire metropolitan area. Japanese Protestants and Japanese Buddhists also come to the West Side to worship.

The New York Buddhist Church occupies a sort of townhouse on a service road that rises above Riverside Drive at 103d Street. It is a fittingly tranquil retreat, set far enough back to muffle the noise of traffic and at the same time to give anyone who cares to contemplate a contemplative view of the Hudson far below. In a wall niche, near the entrance, is a massive statue of Shinran Shonin, the sect's founder. He is dressed coolie-style and he is muscular, far different from the holy men who are pictured in Occidental religions.

"We have 800 people who come here to worship," said the Reverend Harold Odo, one of the church's ministers, as he exhibited the beautifully ornate 15-foot-high altar. "Of them, 25 per cent are American Occidentals. The rest are mostly Japanese."

"The West Side is the only area in New York where rich and poor are both moving in," said the Reverend Henry J. Browne, an earthy Roman Catholic priest who heads the Strycker's Bay Neighborhood Council with headquarters at 89th and Columbus. "There's an interaction. The people with money here know more about the poor than they do anywhere else. Rich and poor used to be geographical terms. It's social here."

BLEECKER STREET: A FRENZIED CITY IN MINIATURE

by MICHAEL T. KAUFMAN

For all its length of 22 blocks Bleecker Street cuts through differences of age, race, nationality, sexuality and outlook, mixing urban sophisticates and heartland rustics, derelicts and the chauffeur-driven in a frenzied distillate of city life.

The street begins at Eighth Avenue, in the western part of Greenwich Village, with a three-block sector of fey antique shops and fifth-floor one-room walk-ups that rent for $119.66 a month. As it moves east it traverses an old Italian neighborhood where hares hang by their back feet in butcher-shop windows and old women shrouded in black buy sea urchins and squid at outdoor stalls.

Two blocks on, it changes again, this time into a district of bars and theaters where teeny-boppers, bohemians and insurance salesmen come to play and preen.

The concentrated diversity has spawned a sense of joy, an incentive to walk and look and flirt. It has also created a concentrated tension. For many it is a street of hustles and hassles.

Now, many of the local businessmen say, a new and unwanted group of derelict men has moved in.

The Village has always had derelicts, they say, but in the past they were occasional drunks and bohemian beggars. Now there are junkies and more dangerous people. Cars are broken into regularly, they charge, and people are accosted, insulted and menaced with a new seriousness and greater frequency.

It is 8:30 Friday night and outside Art D'Lugoff's vast Village Gate restaurant-nightclub complex a staggering drunk is bumping into couples. Two of the many Tactical Patrol Force policemen who saturate the area on weekends approach him. "Take it easy, move along," they say.

"Go to hell," he screams, and goes on to shout a rash of obscenities.

He tries to wave off the policemen, who put his face to the wall and handcuff his hands behind his back.

"I'll be out in the morning, you ———," he yells, and then, turning his body to show his wrists to the passers-by, he blurts out, "Look, they put handcuffs on a 63-year-old man."

"That's Fred. We know him. All us guys that drink wine know him," says a thin little man with a pint of muscatel sticking out of his back pocket. "He's no good as no good can be."

The informant is Danny O'Brien, who is not one of the newcomers. He has been in the area for 20 years. Before that he was in the Army and drove race cars and was known as "Suicide." On his right forearm there is a tattoo that says, "Joey Chittenwood's Auto Daredevils." Suicide is 62.

He lives around the corner from Bleecker on Sullivan Street where he has a basement room rent-free in exchange for carrying out cans of trash. He also makes about $4 a day pulling a cart and picking up scrap paper and cardboard.

For the rest, he panhandles in units of 53 cents—the price of a pint—and if his touches give him a chance he'll tell them how he won the California midget-car racing championship and he'll show them his scars.

He was doing that the other night when a friend shuffled over. "Danny, I need eight cents," he said, showing a quarter and two dimes in his palm. And Danny, flush from recent success, reached out saying, "Here, take a dime."

It is Saturday night at the same place. Bleecker and Thompson. An air-conditioned chartered bus pulls up outside the Greenwich Hotel, where for $1.99 a night male winos and welfare cases and a few hippies, too, can get a four-by six-foot room with a bed. ("No visiting in rooms allowed," says a sign in the lobby.)

From the bus come 24 couples of the Rochedale Village Mystery Club. They have just been to a Times Square studio where the husbands and wives spent an hour painting designs on the bodies of four naked girl models.

They debarked and filed into the Show Boat Cafe for two drinks, each member wearing a small button with his or her name. Alan Sims, a 32-year-old electrician, who like all the club members lives in Rochedale Village, a middle-income cooperative development in Queens, was enjoying the night. "It's different, you know," he explained.

"Every two months we kick in $20 a couple and one of us arranges the evening. The rest of us never know what it's going to be until we get there. We've been hypnotized and once we had a stripper stripping on the bus. We come down to the Village a lot."

Now, as he spoke above the strains of an organ-guitar jazz duet, he was playfully barraged with volleys of peanut shells from his fellow club members.

"We got teachers and policemen and you name it in the club," Mr. Sims went on, fending off a hail of shells.

"Hey, did you see these?" said another man in the group as he passed Mr. Sims four Polaroid snapshots taken of the naked models, their bodies bedizened with the dabbings of the club.

Within two blocks of the Show Boat there is the Circle in the Square, where Eugene O'Neill's *A Moon for the Misbegotten* is playing; the Bleecker Street Cinema, where *Vietnam in War* is showing and the Andy Warhol Theater with its current attraction, a movie called *Flesh*.

In the same radius, Tim Hardin, the singer, opened this weekend at the Cafe au Go Go, the site of the late comedian Lenny Bruce's arrest for obscenity and now a favorite of the young college and dating crowd. There is also the Village Gate, where Herbie Mann, the jazz flutist, was performing and the Bitter End, a showcase for young talent, where The Critters were singing.

And in the same two-block circle there is a place where tourists can squirt paints at revolving pieces of cardboard to make their own "original abstract designs," and a shop in which portraits in charcoal are done by artists lined up like barbers and a store where handwriting is "scientifically" analyzed by computers. There are also street peddlers selling $2.50 yo-yos that light up when they are unleashed.

All of which adds up to noise, movement, money and fun.

The Italians are being squeezed from both sides, high-rent apartments from the west and the spread of the entertainment area from the east. The younger generation is moving out, the older one is dying.

For 25 years Cornelius Fellin has operated a restaurant, Fellin's, at 216 Thompson Street, just off Bleecker.

In the back next to the tables he had perhaps the only indoor bocce alley in New York. Older neighborhood people played the game, which resembles bowls, late into the night.

Last week, he closed the alley.

"There's no one left to play, the old people are gone and the young do other things," he said sadly over a plate of linguini. "But it's dying in Italy, too, it's being killed by Lambrettas and television."

Fletcher (he prefers to keep his last name to himself) is a 23-year-old black New York University student who lived in the Greenwich Hotel some years back. Now he lives on 10th Street, but he spends much of his free time on Bleecker. He is a student of the place.

"The whole thing is sex," he says.

"White chicks come down for the express reason of having a black experience. Then along came these militants in African dress.

"But," he said sardonically, "they wouldn't be caught dead talking to any woman but a white girl. Some of them got nasty and mean and it's frightened a lot of white girls.

"Five years ago this was a beautiful place for meeting chicks," said Fletcher, who himself was militant enough to be a marshal at the Poor People encampment in Washington.

But in one way things are better, Fletcher thinks. "Five years ago if I was with a white chick I'd have to fight every two blocks, now no more."

The sociology major also was critical of many of the flamboyantly dressed youngsters who parade the MacDougal Street–Bleecker Street route. "Years back we dressed poor because those were the clothes we had. Now a chick puts on her Village clothes, or goes to her girl friend's house and rolls up her dress a couple of inches, unbuttons her blouse at the top and pulls up her bra.

"Then she comes down here and sees some cat wearing bell-bottoms and a floppy hat and says, 'Dig that hippy.' But that cat actually lives three blocks away from her in Queens."

One way that residents can distinguish themselves from tourists—who wear similarly unusual clothes and talk hip but live elsewhere—is with dogs. Obviously you can't take a shaggy Afghan down on the A train. In any case there are a lot of dogs, more big ones than small ones, more shaggy than sleek.

Some of the old ways are fading fast and the ghost of Joe Gould probably no longer stalks the street. But a sense of the bohemian live-and-let-live attitude that he represented and allegedly wrote about in his never-published "Oral History of Civilization" still persists. Bleecker Street is a place where the 10th Street Boys can play roller hockey against the Carmine Street team from two blocks away and the neighbors don't scream too much about the racket.

It is a place where the House of Oldies ("Turn back the hand of Time to your favorite year and listen to the records that were popular then, 1959, 1951, etc.," says a sign in the window) can coexist with Fiacco's pork and sausage store. A place where a store that sells light machines and environments can be called "A Bird Can Fly but a Fly Can't Bird." And where a man can paint a Rolls-Royce with multicolored serpentine swirls if he wants to.

Just such a car was parked the other day at the corner of Bleecker and Christopher Streets. A youngster passed it and turned to his companion. "Who the hell would do that to a Rolls-Royce?" he almost whined.

Two shopping ladies walked by craning their necks at the wildly patterned auto. "Why would anyone do that?" they asked each other.

The answers came a bit later from John Pucci, a 23-year-old artist. "I did it," he said.

Why?

"Because I'm getting married. Tonight I'm driving Pat Reilly to City Hall in this car I borrowed and we're getting married. Then we're driving up to Provincetown for a honeymoon and then the rain will come and wash away the paint."

PART FOUR

TENSIONS AS A SOURCE OF COMMUNITY CON-FLICTS AND INTE-GRATION

In medieval times, cities were walled enclosures designed to protect their inhabitants from attack, "rural" crime and banditry. Later, when they emerged from feudal or state control into self-government, civic associations or guilds of magistrates set up specialized police agencies to provide for the orderly conduct of civic life. As urban populations grew, especially by the influx of peasants, city life became more dangerous. Some personal protection was afforded by architecture: the private home was built like a fortress, frequently surrounded by a wall. Windows were shuttered and a central gateway was guarded by a concierge or doorman. The streets, however, were unsafe, and the upper classes often traveled in groups, with armed guards. Thus private police services were available. The development of municipal police forces in the middle of the 19th century came relatively late in the history of cities.

To a large extent, however, peace and order within the city were dependent on the civic pride and loyalty of its citizens. But this was always threatened by the influx of large numbers of outsiders, usually peasants and the rural disenfranchised. In the United States, over the years, every minority group that has settled in the cities has produced a high percentage of delinquents, criminals and other deviants, especially among the children of immigrants.

At present, the newcomers to American cities, as we have noted, are primarily blacks, chicanos and Puerto Ricans. Disturbed by the poverty, the dislocation, the "anomie" of the city, they respond in ways that parallel the response of earlier immigrant groups. Their problems are exacerbated by lack of economic opportunity—of unskilled and semiskilled jobs in a highly industrialized economy; by the general belief that a society should provide equality of opportunity for all its citizens; and by the fact that these groups have known intense discrimination and exploitation in their rural past.

Both political protest and individual acts of violence are intensified by the easy availability and low cost of mass-produced lethal hand weapons. This has once again made crime, "law and order" and "safety on the streets" an issue in city life, an issue particularly salient in black, white and Puerto Rican urban neighborhoods. It has developed at a time when police forces, while highly organized, appear to be inadequate to the task of providing protection for urban citizens. As a result, residents of many neighborhoods have organized to protest not only the inadequacy of the police but steps taken by welfare, correctional and social work agencies to bring into their neighborhoods prisoners and ex-prisoners, addicts and ex-addicts, welfare recipients and low-cost housing projects.

These protest movements have often led to the organization of nongovernmental civic associations, which in effect organize new communities out of mere population aggregates. At the same time, dogs, private policemen and doormen have been revived as instruments of self-protection, and new ingenious ways of locking and sealing residences have been devised (accounting for a boom in the lock industry). New patterns of architecture, housing and transportation are designed to promote safety and security—an interesting revival of the medieval city-as-fortress pattern.

Ethnic and class conflicts, however, go far beyond the issues of crime and safety. Whites in the slum and ghetto areas attempt to resist the expansion of the black, chicano and Puerto Rican ghettos, especially when it is the product of administrative action by municipal government. Particular resistance is focused upon the creation of low-cost housing projects in middle- and lower-middle-class neighborhoods. In suburbia, the problem expresses itself in resistance to changes in zoning regulations, which would permit working-class residents of all ethnic groups to enjoy the advantages of suburban life. When whole cities, such as Newark, become minority-group cities, there are conflicts over how much state aid for welfare, housing and schools is needed to overcome problems which, by virtue of the populations, are basically ethnic.

In other cities, a struggle occurs within various ethnic centers for the control of municipal institutions and agencies, especially those focused on the ghetto. Characteristically, city institutions have been dominated by older ethnic groups that have become acculturated to urban life. New arrivals thus feel left out in the face of municipal governments and institutions that are alien to their culture, their felt needs and their policy and patronage aspirations. In response, they demand community control of municipal institutions. These demands go far beyond the purely political; they are struggles over patronage, life-styles and the distribution of political and economic resources. Quite frequently, they activate the older ethnic groups and force them to organize political counter-communities to defend their established advantages. The effect of this activity is to intensify the conflict between old and new ethnic groups. But the ensuing struggles do not produce simple linear gains and losses for a particular group. Temporary and partial victories are often reversed, and defeats lead to intensified hostilities and a renewal of ethnic identities. Ethnic assertiveness is a permanent part of the urban scene, but it is only one of the forms of urban conflict.

Political conflict arises as the city develops because of the very nature of urban government and planning. As the city grows, municipal governments are forced to make vast and broad decisions affecting the way of life and the ethnic and class distribution of its populace. Thus the location of a subway, an apartment complex, an urban renewal project or the construction of a department store can all become the basis for conflict and for the political organization of a community.

The tendency to politicize urban communities is in part a result of a new activism based on social science. Groups previously unorganized and unaware of their opportunities for political action have discovered new possibilities. Youth has learned, at the level of local politics and government, the power inherent in their numbers. Whenever a group becomes concentrated ecologically, new potentialities for organization and activity are revealed.

In the past, traditional political machines organized these "minority" groups, but the machines were not mechanisms for the expression of minority-group claims and grievances. Today, a new awareness on the part of all groups has resulted in special-interest-group political machines organized by ethnic- or class-oriented politicians. This direct organization of specialized constituencies is a major innovation in American politics.

SUMMER'S URBAN VIOLENCE STIRS FEARS OF TERRORISM

by JOHN HERBERS

The United States has passed through another summer without massive urban riots, but group and political violence—from civil disorders to the ambushing of policemen—has become so widespread and persistent that some authorities find this more troubling than the concentrated upheavals of the nineteen-sixties.

Preliminary 1971 statistics and interviews with experts on the subject indicate that violence resulting from social unrest has remained at a high level in urban disorders, bombings of buildings, harassment of authorities and racial clashes. There have been declines in some categories but increases in others.

The chief law-enforcement concern now—aside from the steady rise in nonpolitical crimes such as homicide, rape and assault—is the prospect for a continued rise in terrorist groups that oppose the established order.

The National Commission on the Causes and Prevention of Violence, headed by Milton S. Eisenhower, disbanded at the end of 1969, but some of its members have kept up with developments on an informal basis. "We feel that in the various areas of violence we covered there has been little if any abatement," said Lloyd N. Cutler, a Washington lawyer who was executive director of the commission.

Although he noted an apparent decline in violence on college campuses, a trend he attributed to reforms and changes instituted locally and the winding down of the war in Vietnam, he said:

"We believe there has been a substantial rise in terrorism as seen in the polarization of young blacks, in the prison uprisings and in the ambush shooting of policemen, and terrorism is the most difficult form of violence to cope with.''

If present trends continued, Mr. Cutler said, ''I think we are going to make Belfast look like nothing in another decade.'' He was referring to the civil strife in Northern Ireland.

Group violence in the United States, which began on a large scale in the sixties, has followed a general pattern. It has moved from one battleground to the next—first in scattered areas of the South as white terrorists sought to put down the civil rights movement; then in the central cities nationwide with massive and destructive protests by blacks and other minorities; then on the college campuses in mostly peaceful but sometimes violent clashes involving the war, race and protests against the institutions involved; then in scattered bombings and other terrorist acts involving a variety of protests.

In each of these areas the violence has peaked after a time and declined as the battleground shifted elsewhere. But current statistics, although incomplete, suggest that a substantial residue of violence has remained in each area, adding up to a fabric of disorder.

For example, some radicals say they have given up bombings, but the police find high school students putting together bombs in their suburban homes; the Ku Klux Klan, which reached its peak about 1966, is now linked to the bombings of school buses in Pontiac, Michigan; four years after the big Detroit riot there is still burning and looting in some cities; though violence on the campus is declining, the president of Harvey Mudd College in California had his office fire-bombed.

Although the war and other issues have figured prominently in disputes leading to group violence, the grievances of blacks and other minorities are becoming predominant and represent the central issue while the battleground appears to be moving to the prisons.

The Justice Department, which for several years has been monitoring the trouble in the cities, counted, for the first eight months of 1971, 11 major civil disorders and 32 serious ones. This compares to 19 major and 49 serious disorders in 1970, in keeping with the pattern of decline since the major outbreak of riots in April, 1968.

Minor civil disorders showed an increase—133 through August of this year compared with 93 last year.

The Justice Department classifies a major disorder as one having all of the following elements: bombing; arson; use of outside policemen or troops; looting or gunfire; imposition of a curfew; more than 300 participants not counting the police; more than 12 hours' duration.

A serious disorder has any three of the "major" elements, lasts more than three hours and involves at least 150 participants.

A minor disorder contains one to four of the "major" elements, lasts up to three hours and involves at least eight, but not more than 150, people.

Riots of the kind that occurred this year have become so commonplace that they are not widely reported outside the communities in which they occur, with the exception of major upheavals such as those this year in Jacksonville, Florida, Chattanooga, and Albuquerque, New Mexico. Before the late sixties, observers believe, 176 civil disorders in American cities in an eight-month period would have drawn considerable attention.

What has emerged this year, according to Dr. John P. Spiegel, director of the Lemberg Center for the Study of Violence at Brandeis University, is "microviolence," scattered fragments of violence.

Two years ago, authorities in urban affairs expressed the belief that the day of the massive urban riots—on the scale of the ones in Newark and Detroit in 1967—was over, even though tensions and grievances in the central cities continued at a high level.

There were several reasons for this, including the following:

The riots did not bring massive response to alleviate slum conditions.

The police had developed better riot-control techniques.

The damage inflicted was largely in neighborhoods where the minorities involved would have to continue to live.

There was a new sense of purpose and direction in the central cities involving political power and community development rather than protest, which was moving into the hands of a small number of radicals who lacked a broad base of support.

The pattern was for the riots to spread to the smaller cities, where trends generally lagged a year or two behind those in the large urban centers. In few cities were there repeats of major riots.

According to this belief, then, the extent of unemployment, poverty or other grievances was no important indicator of the extent of disorders. This summer, the belief was put to a test as economic conditions, already severe in the central cities, worsened.

The National Urban Coalition established a commission, headed by Mayor Lindsay of New York and Senator Fred R. Harris of Oklahoma, to take a look at the cities and evaluate conditions as they had developed since the National Advisory Commission on Civil Disorders (the Kerner commission) issued its report in 1968.

"Our basic finding," the Lindsay-Harris commission said in a draft of a report to be published soon, "is that, despite the Kerner report's widely accepted findings that one major cause of the ghetto rebellions of the 1960's was the shameful conditions of life in the cities, most of the changes in those conditions since 1968 have been for the worse.

"Housing is still the national scandal it was then," the report continued. "Schools are more tedious and turbulent. The rates of crime and unemployment and disease and heroin addiction are higher. And with few exceptions, the relations between minority communities and the police are just as hostile.

"People are angry. Perhaps they are angrier, even, than they were four years ago.

"But their anger no longer seems to be the helpless kind that can express itself only by smashing and burning. We heard only a little talk of burning.

"The most striking point most of those we spoke with made was that they had no faith at all in 'the system'—the Government and the private wielders of power—as a protector or provider. This disenchantment has plunged many into cynicism or apathy or despair.

"But in others it has inspired a new tough pride, self-confidence and determination.

"Every place we visited we found at least a hardheaded cadre who knew that the people will have to rely upon themselves for most of whatever they get."

Some who have given up on the system—blacks and whites who have been radicalized—have given rise to terrorist groups which appear to be fragmented and scattered.

Since July 1970, the International Association of Chiefs of Police has compiled on the basis of national surveys the number and nature of police casualties and bombing incidents. There are no prior statistics to provide an accurate comparison of trends, but it is believed that the number of very destructive bombings has peaked while the number of incidents involving explosives has increased.

The number of policemen killed or wounded in ambush has increased.

From July 1, 1970, to June 1, 1971, the last period compiled, the association's bomb data center recorded 1,425 bombing incidents, resulting in 15 deaths and 155 injuries.

A spokesman for the association said, "It used to be that only the hardened elements set off bombs, but now it's gotten to be general. All kinds of people are fooling around with explosives."

In the 13-month period ending July 31, the association's police weapons center reported that 116 policemen, 462 suspects and six other persons were killed in violent clashes of various kinds. At the same time, 965 policemen, 457 suspects and 16 others were injured.

In January, at the end of the first six months of the study, it was concluded that unprovoked ambush attacks represented the largest single cause, 25 per cent, of police deaths, and that civil disorder and protests represented the largest single cause, 36 per cent, of police injuries.

A similar pattern has prevailed this year, according to the reports.

The ambush attacks do not show any signs of an organized campaign of terror but, rather, scattered alienation toward the police.

Statistics have not been compiled that would show the picture of violence on the college campuses and high schools for 1971. But some who are compiling the data say that, while there has been a general decline in the protests and demonstrations over-all, the last school year saw a rise in racial clashes in high schools, many of them involving violence, and it is feared that there may be more this year.

The rise in terrorism, according to Mr. Cutler, who directed the Eisenhower commission, stems from what he describes as the Government's failure, "perhaps our inability," to make reforms recommended by his commission and others and from continued incidents such as the recent one at the Attica Correctional Facility in New York.

"A few more Atticas and I am afraid that [terrorism] is really going to go off," Mr. Cutler said, explaining that such incidents cause a substantial portion of citizens to sympathize with those in revolt against government.

John Naisbett, president of the Urban Research Corporation in Chicago, suggested that prison conflict had become the "theater" for the central cities.

"Look at the list of demands made by the prisoners at Attica," he said. "Better education, narcotics treatment, legal assistance, better recreation, more black workers, the search for dignity. These are the demands of the ghetto."

YOUNG HOODLUMS PLAGUE SAN FRAN-CISCO'S CHINATOWN

by DOUGLAS E. KNEELAND

© 1971 by The New York Times Company. Reprinted by permission.

SAN FRANCISCO—The slender, middle-aged Chinese man stood quietly the other night a few feet from two towering policemen who were leaning on a patrol car talking to a friend inside.

As the crowds of tourists and Chinese shoppers whirled by on Jackson Street, just off Grant Avenue, in the center of Chinatown, the man kept casting nervous glances over his shoulder until he caught the eye of one of the policemen.

The policeman walked over to him, listened to a few whispered phrases, and then strode quickly into the Great Star Theater. The man, who vanished as fast as he had appeared, was the theater manager. And he was faced with his nightly problem, young Chinese toughs who bully their way into the theater without paying.

In a few minutes, a long-haired youngster dashed out of the theater and raced up the street as the policeman emerged leading two others.

A crowd that had gathered was respectful, not hostile, as the police went about their work, but some complained in Chinese that the young hoodlums would be back in the street in hours.

The theater manager is not the only merchant in Chinatown who has been plagued for the last three years by the marauding youth gangs. Restaurant owners tell of demands for free food and of youngsters walking out without paying large bills. And reports circulate widely in the district that merchants have been told to "donate" from $25 to $200 a month to "youth movements" or have their stores damaged or customers terrorized.

"There's a lot of so-called extortion here," said one of the officers of the Chinatown detail who asked not to be identified, "but we can't get any complainants because of threats against them. So far what we've got, though, we think there are about four adults in their thirties and forties behind these kids for extortion.''

While the police find it difficult to pin down the extortion reports, the Chinese community, as reflected in a dozen conversations, seems to be solidly behind their recent crackdown on the youth gangs.

The trouble started in the late nineteen-sixties as a wave of newcomers, mostly from Hong Kong, arrived in the already overcrowded district under relaxed immigration laws. Many of the young men, who could speak little if any English, dropped out of school in frustration or never attended at all.

They scorned the long hours and low-paying jobs that had been the lot of earlier immigrants. And with a severe language problem and little training they could not find other work. Many of them took to the streets and eventually drifted into outspoken youth groups like the Wah Ching, which openly defied the Establishment of Chinatown.

Steeped in the tradition that respect for one's elders, education and hard work are virtues, Chinatown was shocked. Three years ago community leaders held a meeting with the Wah Ching in an attempt to deal with the problem, as they have always dealt with the problems of their district. The Wah Ching demanded $4,000 immediately and continuing financial support. They warned that ''riots and greater violence'' might follow if they did not get their way.

The community leaders, incensed at what they considered an ultimatum, refused. And the harassment of merchants and tourists has continued.

This summer, at the request of worried merchants, the police have strengthened their patrols in Chinatown and have been arresting the youths whenever they get a complaint. But the charges have usually been misdemeanors and the youngsters, finding that they are quickly freed on their own recognizance, have apparently been little troubled by the arrests.

''They're not getting the idea,'' one policeman protested. ''When the police walk around in Chinatown, there's usually one of them a block in front and one a block in back, keeping an eye on us and warning their friends that we're coming.''

Meanwhile, according to the police, a new group called the Yo Le has achieved ascendancy over the Wah Ching.

''The ones that are causing all the trouble now are the Yo Le,'' a policeman said. ''The Wah Ching have lost all their power because one of their leaders is in jail for murder and the other went to Canada.''

The Chinese population of San Francisco, reputedly the largest outside of Asia, is estimated at 70,000, about double what it was a decade ago. The city's population is about 704,000.

The number of youths affiliated with the street gangs is a matter of speculation. Some community spokesmen have put the figure as high as 300, but others have said that the real hard core may not be much more than 20.

Whatever their numbers, they have aroused the wrath of much of Chinatown. Recently, one of the old tongs, whose wars in the early years of the century are legend, placed an ad in *The Chinese Times* warning of retribution if their members were troubled any more by the youth gangs.

But even that has apparently had little effect.

"The tongs used to control them," a woman merchant said sadly, "but they don't do anything any more. These old men over here in the tongs, they don't do anything any more."

FEAR IS STEADY COMPANION OF MANY HARLEM RESIDENTS

by CHARLAYNE HUNTER

There have been times when Mrs. Pauline Withers, a mother of five who lives in one of the worst crime areas in the city, has been so afraid walking home after dark that she has talked to herself.

"Once I ran into a neighbor," she recalled recently, "and I said, 'Miss Lewis, did you hear me talking to myself?' and she said, 'No, I was too busy talking to myself.' "

No one person is truly representative of any group, but Mrs. Withers perhaps can stand for many of the people living in central Harlem. Her fears and her attitudes toward the police are shared by a number of her neighbors, some of whom have set up patrols to help protect themselves.

Some of Mrs. Withers' former neighbors have fled to other boroughs, trying to escape before their children become a part of the rapidly growing addict population, or after they had been victims of crime in the area, attributed mostly to narcotics addicts.

But Mrs. Withers, a perky woman with a calm, Southern air about her, said that based on what friends had told her, it's just as bad and sometimes worse in other places.

"If you run away from it, you run into it," she said. So for the last 15 years, she has stayed in the small but comfortable three-bedroom apartment in a six-story building in the Abraham Lincoln Housing project near 135th Street and Fifth Avenue.

But staying has meant many moments of unease and constant vigilance for herself and her children, who range in age from six to 23. Once, for instance, while working as a beautician in a shop a few blocks away, Mrs. Withers got a call from a neighbor who told her that she had just rescued Mrs. Withers' 11-year-old daughter from a man who was pulling her onto the roof.

Since then, Mrs. Withers has made a practice of being "always positive that someone is here," even though she is working and is out a lot attending meetings of the Brandeis High School Parents Association, of which she is president, the Daughters of the Elks and the Square Deal Republican Club and a number of others.

The crimes reported in the 25th Police Precinct, where Mrs. Withers lives, show why she is concerned. So far this year there have been seven murders, nine rapes, 407 robberies, 117 assaults, 442 burglaries, 177 larcenies and 81 stolen cars reported, a total of 1,240 crimes.

In an area of similar population density—the 114th Precinct in the Astoria-Jackson Heights section of Queens, crime reports totaled 1,332, and 512 of these were motor vehicle thefts.

While figures from the Housing Authority indicate that crime is decreasing inside the Lincoln project, a series of crimes in the last few months led Lincoln residents to complain in public demonstrations and forums about a variety of problems, including the inadequacy of the housing police.

Mrs. Withers, for instance, complained, "They [policemen] are always hanging around people's apartments. You call sometimes and it takes them three or four hours."

A Housing Authority police spokesman said he "couldn't say that it's not happening. I just don't buy this as much as people complain." He said he encouraged residents to report such instances, giving the building and the time and the area.

In the absence of her husband, Mrs. Withers relies heavily on her 23-year-old son, Amar, who is home after running out of money to continue in college. They share the feeling that the residents themselves must be involved in taking care of their own problems.

Mrs. Withers is membership chairman of the Tenants League, which screens people entering five buildings in the evening. She also supports a youth patrol inside the project area instituted by the Harlem Youth Federation. Amar, who is more than six feet tall and well-built, is one of its members.

"We felt something physical had to be demonstrated," he said recently. The young men, who say they have been "hassled" somewhat by the housing police, but have the tacit approval of the precinct, move around in groups that have numbered as high as 12.

But activities are restricted to the weekends, they say, because they do not have enough equipment. They say the Housing Authority police failed to provide them with adequate equipment as they had previously promised. They walk a shift, they say, from 9 P.M. until at least 1 A.M. and have a few walkie-talkies, sticks, bats and pipes.

A spokesman for the housing police, who deny the young men have been harassed, said that at one point the patrol had been stopped from "interfering with an arrest."

Amar, who sometimes takes his eight-year-old brother, Roosevelt, along with him on patrol, says:

"We know where the shooting galleries are; which benches they use; what needs to be tightened up. Before the patrols, the younger sisters just moving into prostitution used the hallways; the male homosexuals, same places. We just tell them. 'Brother, move on!' Now the halls are clear."

Both mother and son feel that the police are often "insensitive." At present, 27 per cent of the 25th Precinct force is black or Puerto Rican.

"Take family static," said Amar. "These white cops come in here and they can't counsel—that's the thing about having our police live in the community. If he is an alien and a total stranger, his attitude is 'Niggers is raising trouble and I got to stop it.' That's a negative attitude.

"Then he doesn't understand the feeling between a black man and a black woman. He's got to show his woman that he's a man, so he strikes out at the policeman. And then . . ."

Mrs. Withers thinks maybe it would help if the police and firemen and other men in uniform were more visibly involved in setting up programs for the youngsters in the community.

She does not worry too much about her own children. In fact, they are her source of reassurance.

"One day, they might get me," she said of criminals in the neighborhood. "But I don't live in fear. Sometimes, I get a little frightened. But then I know they will always come and pick me up or stay up until I come in."

GOWANUS VS. ORGA-NIZED CRIME

by CHARLES GRUTZNER

Along Brooklyn's sprawling waterfront—where a few years ago the Mafia "button men," or common soldiers, of the Gallo Brothers gang waged a murderous but unsuccessful revolt against their bosses in the organized-crime family of the late Joseph Profaci—a new kind of button man is making the scene.

Some longshoremen have begun flaunting brown buttons lettered in red: "Fight Organized Crime."

A few shopkeepers on Columbia Street—a once-bright, lively shopping area for the Gowanus-Red Hook Italian community, but now pockmarked by boarded-up stores behind garbage-strewn curbstones—also are wearing the buttons.

The antiracket slogan appears more often on the jackets and shirts of teen-agers, antipoverty workers and residents who are groping for a way to combat narcotics, gambling, loan-sharking and other local evils that they attribute to underworld control of much of the waterfront activity.

Similar buttons have appeared recently in Newark, Rochester, Detroit, Chicago, Washington, Miami and Tampa. The seeding is the work of a Johnny Appleseed of the campaign against organized crime. He is Ralph Salerno, who until his retirement two years ago from the Police Department was supervisor of detectives in its anti-Mafia unit, the central intelligence division.

Mr. Salerno, now a consultant to the National Council on Crime and Delinquency, spent most of his waking hours in the Gowanus sections during the Mafia's "Gallo War," in which recorded casualties on both sides were nine dead and 16 wounded from 1961 to 1963.

Mr. Salerno believes that a successful citizen attack on underworld influences on the Brooklyn waterfront may inspire similar attacks in other parts of the country.

The Gowanus Canal, a foul industrial waterway knifing more than a mile inland from New York Harbor, connects the Gowanus district with the outer waterfront, which stretches for 10 miles from the old Navy Yard southward through Red Hook and South Brooklyn to Bay Ridge.

The Gowanus neighborhood, straddling the canal, has about 44,000 residents, of whom about 6,200 are blacks and 3,000 are Puerto Ricans. Most of the rest are Italians. Forty years ago it was all white and mostly Italian, with a substantial Irish minority.

Red Hook, which runs westward from Gowanus to the harbor, is a slightly smaller area. Its 41,000 residents include many descendants of old Norwegian, Italian and Irish families and since 1945 about 7,500 blacks and 8,200 Puerto Ricans.

The Gowanus waterway was not always the oil-covered, noisome sink of pollution it is now, nor were the lands beside it an industrial jungle and the haunt of racketeers and exploiters.

In the 17th century, Dutch settlers took oysters (sometimes a foot long, according to historians) from the clear waters of Gowanus Creek. Rich farms sloped down toward sailing vessels at their docks.

Without expecting a return to that idyll, some residents—including newcomers from Manhattan who have bought and refurbished old brownstones and red brick-fronts—are trying to root out some of the evils.

A civic group has sought to remove some of the stigma by devising a new name, Carroll Gardens, after tiny Carroll Park, for a section just west of the canal.

Real estate men have adopted the new name but to most of the old Italian families and the rest of the world Gowanus is still Gowanus—and the old-timers are against the effort to put the historic name into limbo.

The idea of the antiracket buttons came to Mr. Salerno three weeks ago as he was having coffee with three community workers, one of whom wore a button with the legend: "I'm an Effete Snob."

"There was a lot of joking about the inscription, but the button sure attracted a lot of attention," recalled Mr. Salerno a few days ago.

"That's what we need most in the fight against organized crime. We've got to bring it to everyone's attention that there is such a thing as organized crime and that it affects everyone of us in one way or another. Maybe you start with curiosity, go on to education and end up with personal involvement in breaking it up."

Mr. Salerno asked his companions what it would cost to have anticrime buttons made. Salvatore Scotto, Jr., a funeral director, guessed they would come to three or four cents apiece if ordered in quantity.

Mr. Salerno and Mr. Scotto—who is no relation to Anthony M. Scotto, a vice president of the International Longshoremen's Association—put up $50 apiece and bought 3,500 buttons. The central distribution point in Gowanus is a storefront office at 445 Court Street, a few blocks from the two fortresslike buildings at 49 and 51 President Street, known locally as the Gallo Barracks.

The rebellious Mafia brothers had housed their small army of captains and button men in the barracks, which during the Gallo War was as well stocked with guns, ammunition and food as a Western outpost of the United States Cavalry in the Indian wars.

The store on Court Street was used until recently as an office for an architect hired by the civic association to draw up plans for cleaning up the polluted Gowanus Canal and developing its shore areas. The plan is now before the City Planning Commission.

The store has been rented by Mr. Scotto as headquarters for neighborhood improvement projects and for his upcoming campaign for the Democratic nomination for representative in the 14th Congressional District. John J. Rooney, the Democratic incumbent since 1943, will seek re-election this year from the district.

"We were almost cleaned out of buttons in the first week," said Mr. Scotto. "Kids came in for them, but so did many grown-ups, including some longshoremen who said they're fed up with conditions on the piers and in the union.

"We give the kids buttons when they ask for them because we want high visibility for the slogan. It will make people think about organized crime and, we hope, do something about it."

Tom Chardavoyne, a volunteer helper to Mr. Scotto, quit his studies at Manhattan College to take a job with the South Brooklyn Community Anti-poverty Corporation. Mr. Chardavoyne, a 300-pounder, intends to return eventually to college for a degree.

"My father's a longshoreman," he said. "He took 200 buttons and gave them to guys on the docks. He doesn't know how it will come out. Even the numbers guys asked for them. They wear them as a big joke—they know they can't be touched now. But the time will come when they'll lose their immunity."

Besides gambling and loan-sharking, the open sale of narcotics is a serious local problem. The civic association operates a storefront social center at 482 Court Street for teen-age former addicts and also arranges for young users to enter shelters for cures.

Mr. Scotto said the fight against organized crime would require rank-and-file action by waterfront workers.

"We've got to get union members to help fight organized crime," he declared. "It's no easy task. Some people have advised me not to stick out my neck."

An interviewer recalled that Peter Panto, leader of a rank-and-file movement against corruption on the Brooklyn waterfront, disappeared in 1939 and that his remains were found six years later in a New Jersey lime pit used as a Mafia burial ground.

"My father conducted the funeral for what was left of Peter Panto," said Mr. Scotto, who was 17 years old at the time. "There was a strong rank-and-file movement then, but its hopes were buried in that lime pit with Peter Panto. Maybe they can be revived again."

AS THE BLACKS MOVE IN, THE ETHNICS MOVE OUT

by PAUL WILKES

The signs were there, all right. The little photography studio on the corner of Harvey and 116th Streets, where I had looked at the latest brides, their lips retouched deep red and eyebrows dark, was now a karate and judo school. A storefront church, Pilgrim Rest B.C., was on 93d Street near Dickens. Protective grates guarded the front of Rosenbluth's, our local clothing store, whose recorded Santa Claus laugh had scared the patched corduroy pants right off me as a youngster. A public housing project rose from the mud. And in the streets there was a stillness.

As I drove back through my old neighborhood on the East Side of Cleveland last month, there was so little noise. No horns. At 8 o'clock in the evening, there were few cars on the street. There must have been more people walking around, but I remember only a handful at well-lit intersections.

There had been no dinner served on the flight to Cleveland, and as I turned onto Forest Avenue I thought it was just as well. There would be a pot of beef soup bubbling on the stove and huge lengths of garlic-spiced *kolbasz,* the soul food of my ethnic group, the Slovaks. Over such food a son could talk more easily with his father. Over such food it would be more comfortable to talk about the crime that appears to be sweeping this, the peaceful and benign neighborhood where I spent my first 18 years. With hunks of rye bread in our hands and caraway seeds falling softly to the table, we could even talk about *them,* the new immigrants, the blacks who had broken the barrier and swept into this formerly homogeneous area of Cleveland. As the conversation began, though, it was embarrassing for me, always previously eager to shuck the ethnic business and a blue-collar background, to start asking questions about the family and the old neighborhood only because an idea had come to mind and an article had been assigned.

My father—his family name, Vilk, already Americanized to Wilkes—came to Cleveland with my mother and six brothers and sisters a year before I was born in 1938. They left an area that would soon stand for white poverty—Appalachia—and came to one where other Slovaks years before had found work in the factories that spread from the Cuyahoga River up the gentle slopes of streets like Kinsman, Union, Woodland and Buckeye.

They soon bought a house that "wasn't much," my father explained through a wad of Havana Blossom chewing tobacco that remains virtually a part of his anatomy. "There wasn't any sheeting beneath the siding, the floors were wavy, but to your mother it was a mansion." The purchase price was $4,000 and the monthly payments about $35, a third of my father's wages with the W.P.A.

Living on Forest Avenue after the war and through the first half of the nineteen-fifties surely fulfilled all the dreams of the Slovak and Hungarian immigrants and their offspring. There was regular work nearby, the brick streets were clean, lawns were mowed and—except for some home-grown hooligans who might beat you up—it was safe. Blacks? Sure, we knew about blacks. They were a growing mass of look-alikes who flooded in after the war to produce fantastic basketball teams at East Tech. They lived on the crumbling rim of the downtown area seemingly content to wallow in their poverty. They were at once out of mind and a dull pain that would surely trouble us more in days to come.

For the Slovaks, the center of life was St. Benedict's Church, just four blocks from my house, the place where education, religion and social life peacefully coexisted. When asked where I lived in Cleveland, the response was never the East Side, never the 29th Ward. I lived in St. Benedict's Parish.

In its neighborhood of modest older homes the new St. Benedict's Church, completed 17 years ago, is something of a shock. It is a Byzantine mammoth, built at a cost of a million dollars by a blue-collar congregation that raised more than its share of children. As I rang the bell at the parish-house door, I could hear the chimes within, a long, majestic carillon whose frequent use would drive any but those with a Higher Calling right up the wall.

The pastor, Father Michael Jasko, hasn't changed much over the years. He is 65 now, his hair still regally silver, his voice nasal and high. As he began to talk about his parish, it was obviously painful. The glory that was St. Benedict's, the optimism that had built a church with a seating capacity of 1,100, had faded.

"We had 2,000 families and 8,000 souls when you were here," he began. "Now it's 1,000 families and 3,000 souls, and most of them are pensioners. We stopped the Canteen [a weekly dance for teen-agers] 10 years ago and hoped to reopen it, but never did. We made $45,000 in a big year at the bazaar; last year we got $24,000. Novenas and other night-time services have been stopped. The old ladies of the church were getting beaten and robbed on their way to early mass, so we stopped those. Now the first mass is at 7 o'clock, except in the summer when we have the 5:30. Early this year, we're starting a drive to pay off the $95,000 owing on the church. If we don't do it now, we'll never be able to.

"We had a lot of trouble with school children being beaten, in fact the entire baseball team and their coaches were overrun by a gang of 30. I guess you heard about the eighth-grade girl who was raped by four boys from Audubon." I had, and Audubon, a public junior high school now almost entirely black though surrounded by a predominantly white neighborhood, was the reason given by many people for the old neighborhood's current state. "We stopped most of the problem by starting school a half hour before Audubon and letting out a half hour before them. The children can be safely home before they get out.

"The solution," the pastor said more than once, "is more police protection. My duty in these troubled times is to encourage the souls under my direction that we are in a changing world. I never mention 'black' from the pulpit, but I always talk about accepting *them*. No, we haven't visited the homes of these new people to ask them to join. They know about the church; they hear about it from their neighbors. We have a few blacks who attend." In a neighborhood that is 20 per cent black, with the percentage rising weekly, one Negro family is on the parish rolls.

A recent event had intensified the resentment in the neighborhood: the bludgeon slaying of Joe Toke, who was killed during a holdup at the service station he had run for more than 40 years. Had his murder been mentioned from the pulpit? "No, my own judgment tells me it was best not to mention him," and Father Michael hesitated before saying, with no hint of expression on his face, "I wouldn't want to pinpoint the problem."

St. Benedict's School, which I had attended through the eighth grade, seemed to have changed little—the walls were still painted bland and restful beige and green, and the Blessed Virgin, who had looked out over us from her second-floor pedestal, was still standing firmly on the writhing serpent, though both he and she had been chipped and gouged over the years. But the appearance was deceptive.

While the 1,100 of us in the student body had been stuffed 50 or 60 to a classroom, there were now only 350 students scattered loosely about the school, and precious space was allotted to an audio-visual room and a library.

The student body now includes 25 or 30 non-Catholics—I can't remember a single one in my day—and four blacks.

A lunchroom has been built because even those parents who live only a few blocks away won't allow their children to come home at noon. It is considered too dangerous. A thousand lunches are served free each month, and 400 more go at half price. The total price for those who can pay is 20 cents.

Joe Toke's Sunoco station at Buckeye and 111th is one you could easily pass by: nothing fancy, no spinning aluminum or Day-glow disks, no posters proclaiming free glasses or soda pop. But for the neighborhood people there was always Joe, eternally growing bald, a taciturn man whose stern look was a veneer over a heart of gold. His hydraulic lift could be used without charge, credit was extended without a raised eyebrow, kids' bicycle tires were cheerfully filled with free air. Joe had been warned that the neighborhood was changing, that five merchants or property owners had been killed during holdups in the last few years. His response was, "Who would want to hurt me? Anyhow, they can take the money, I'll earn some more."

That night two weeks earlier Marcella Toke had supper on the stove in the simple apartment, made uncomfortably warm by an oil burner in the middle of the living-room floor. She saw the lights going out in the gas station next door, but began to wonder what had happened when Joe didn't appear. She found her husband in a pool of blood in the station. His eyes were open, and Marcella Toke thought at first that he was looking at her. His tire gauge had deflected a bullet, but his skull had been crushed in a remorseless beating.

"To people around here, Joe was a fixture, the honest businessman who had made it by hard work," his widow said. "We all knew the neighborhood was changing, but then this. . . . I think of leaving the neighborhood now, but where would I go? Everything I know is here. I just want those killers found, and I want them to get their due."

Each month the parishioners at St. Benedict's receive a copy of *The Post,* a paper put out by the church's Catholic war veterans. Frank Stipkala, a 38-year-old bachelor, writes many of the stories and editorials, and he is proud to describe himself as a "super-hawk and ultraconservative." Campus protest marches, such pop singers as Janis Joplin, new liturgy and liberal senators of the Kennedy and Church sort have all drawn his stern rebukes. Frank's rhetoric is still hard to take, but his concern for his nationality group and his love for the neighborhood were far more significant in our conversation.

Frank is an efficient man; he had outlined some things he wanted to tell me. A telephone booth on the corner of his street had been damaged so often that it was removed. A mail box had been burglarized on the day Social Security checks were to come. A doctor had installed a peep hole in his door and had gone to irregular office hours to thwart robbers. A mentally retarded boy whose joy was a paper route had to give it up after his collections were stolen and his papers thrown into the street. Somody's Delicatessen closed between 2:30 and 4 each afternoon to avoid harassment from the Audubon students.

"In everything I've told you," he said, "I've not once mentioned race. It isn't race; it's law and order. We Slovaks are too trusting, too honest, too open. There was never trouble here just because blacks moved in. In Murray Hill, the Italians told the blacks they would kill any who dared to move in. In Sowinski Park, the Polish pointed shotguns at them. That is not our way of life, but look what we are reaping now. Many people thought this neighborhood was a fortress, that we would never have trouble, but how we kidded ourselves. The streets are empty because people are afraid to go out and those that must go out are prey.

"We didn't even know the Hungarians in our neighborhood, and we certainly weren't prejudiced against them. Slovaks come from a country that was a collection of small villages; there was no such a thing as national spirit. Here in America, the center was the church, and our people did everything within that church. The Slovaks have been occupied before, by Russians and Germans, by the Hungarians, and now we are being occupied by the robber, the rapist, the murderer. But this is by far harder to live with, the unknowingness of it all. I see two solutions to help the neighborhood; one is very short-term, the other long: Post a policeman every 150 feet to start. Then go to work on the sociological problems like giving these people a better education."

Frank's sister Ethel stopped by, as she often does. She lived on Manor, several blocks away, and had just sold her house at a $4,000 loss. She planned to move to the suburbs with her husband, a teacher, and their children. She flicked off her knitted cap, and—though she has a son ready to graduate from high school—looked like the lovely, shy, dark-haired girl she was 20 years ago. "One of the turning points for me was when I heard people were buying guns. I asked some of the women on the block and found three of them—just like that—who carry guns in their purses. Imagine, women who have never fired a gun in their lives carry one to go to the Pick 'n' Pay."

My next stop was at Bill's Grocery, the "corner store" for Forest Avenue and the most crowded store I have ever seen. Bill carried thread, dye, fruit, cough syrup, kits, canned goods, boiled ham, hand-dipped ice cream, socks, two brands of prophylactics (lubricated and plain—both good sellers, he admits) and now items required by his new clientele—canned okra and Jiffy corn-meal mix. He has had some call for chitterlings, but can't bring himself to stock them.

Bill Blissman never married, and it became obvious in our conversation that if he had something, someone to go to, he would close up.

Bill smiles a lot these days. He has been fitted with a good set of uppers and it's a good smile, but beneath all that, he is afraid: "I used to stay open until 8 or so, now I close at 6. I keep the door locked most of the day and look through the window to see if I want to let the person in. Three of them drove up in a car the other day, and I was happy I had the door locked." Bill can see out reasonably well, but seeing in through his window and the labyrinth of key chains, suckers, Kits candy, Dark Shadows Bubble Gum and novelties is impossible.

Bill's complaint was familiar. Things were bad before Mayor Stokes, a black, was elected, but since his election, the situation in the neighborhood had quickly become untenable. Stokes is responsible for encouraging blacks to come up from the South and get on Cleveland's welfare and crime rolls. Stokes has allowed a new permissiveness. The blacks are cocky because one of their own is downtown. It doesn't matter that crime has risen in cities with white mayors. In Cleveland, in the old neighborhood, it is largely Stokes's fault.

Bill and members of my own family had trouble remembering people my age who grew up in the neighborhood and were still there. Joe Kolenic, my buddy through St. Benedict's and Cathedral Latin School, had married and lived in the neighborhood until a few years ago, when like all of our contemporaries who stayed in Cleveland, he joined the migration to the suburbs. Joe and his wife, Shirley, chose a tri-level tract house in Euclid.

We were sitting in their recreation room, where the Kolenics spend most of their time. Its floor is covered with indoor-outdoor carpeting, and there is a huge color television set and black imitation-leather furniture. Joe has gotten just a little pudgy over the years, but as we talked I saw him as a lean and physically mature eighth grader on the St. Benedict's defensive line. He happily admits to being the stereotype young husband. He wants a safe home for his wife and children, one that he is buying, not renting; a steady job; a winning season for the Browns or Indians, and a good local golf course.

Joe, an accountant, was asked in 1967 to trade his white shirt for khaki and go down into the Hough area with his National Guard unit to quell the disturbance. "You remember our football games at Patrick Henry field; that was a nice neighborhood. And there we were with guns in our arms stepping over garbage in the streets, watching 6- and 7-year-old kids running around in the middle of the night. It was a horror show. Our city. I wasn't a racist then and I'm not one now. But that time in Hough leaves its impression. To be honest, I didn't want to face that possibility every day in the neighborhood, so I left.

But I'm not against the blacks. Hough taught me they need an education to help them help themselves. Back in the neighborhood, we thought they'd never get across 93d or in from Woodland Hills Park. The dam broke there; it can happen anyplace.''

William Ternansky has taught at my high school, Cathedral Latin, for 37 years. His remaining hair is now more gray than black, but otherwise he had changed little since I graduated from Latin in 1956. He still wore a nondescript suit, a V-neck sleeveless sweater beneath, and had a bunch of papers clutched to his chest. He smiled when I told him who I was and why I had come. He remembered me and he smiled—and for both I was immediately happy.

"The neighborhood lived by the Christian ethic of love thy neighbor," he began, "and that pales at the beginning of wrong-doing. The neighborhood is a new ghetto of fear. But for now it is a defensive fear, not an antagonistic fear that ethnic kids have, and that is what is so paralyzing. There is nothing to do but hide and shudder and withdraw with this kind of fear."

Rose Hrutkai is a strong-minded, strong-willed woman of Hungarian stock. She once discouraged a potential robber by going after a broom when he advanced toward her. When real estate agents call—they have been plaguing the neighborhood with panicky lines like "Sell while you can still get your money out"—Rose Hrutkai tells them off. Her house, down the street from mine, is in mint condition, a white double-decker with green trim that looks as though it goes through the weekly wash. Rose Hrutkai is boiling mad at what's happening, so angry she's going to stay in the neighborhood.

Rose sat in her living room in a shapeless cotton dress that didn't dare wrinkle. On her carpeted floor were a half-dozen smaller rugs that protected her larger one.

"My husband is a maintenance man, and we've scrimped through all these years, raised two daughters, sent them to Catholic schools and paid off the $15,500 the house cost," she said. "That's about all we could get out of it if we sold it, because we would have to give points so the new people could get the down-payment money. I love this neighborhood, my garden; everything I have is here. My husband will be retiring soon, and we can't take on house payments. And what could we get for $15,500? A tar-paper shack, maybe. Every day you hear about a lady having her purse snatched, a house being broken into. It's that rough stuff coming up from the South. They drive up in a fancy car and even steal bags of groceries out of women's hands. It's sad when women have to pin their key inside their dress and put their grocery money in their shoes."

Her daughter, Mrs. Gloria Town, joined the conversation. Girls Gloria's age—middle twenties—were once commonplace on Forest Avenue, living upstairs in their parents' homes. Now they are a rarity. "We just couldn't face $250 a month in house payments," Gloria said. "I didn't want to live here, but listen, my husband isn't a $15,000-a-year-man, not a $10,000-a-year man. I work, too. And we barely make the payments on our car and keep eating. We really wonder if we can ever afford kids. It's tough to just make ends meet, and then the neighborhood has to turn into a jungle. I hate to leave the house any more. But who wants to hear the complaints of the little American? The rich have power, the poor get attention. But we got nobody."

Her mother added, "I've got nothing against the colored that are moving in as long as they live the way we do. But so many of them are so lazy. The houses need paint, the lawns need cutting."

There had been peeling paint before and scrubby lawns. But in earlier years that was the extent of the neighborhood's blight—a few unkempt houses for a few years. Now the people of the neighborhood see it going downhill. These houses were built 50 to 75 years ago in the tradition of Middle Europe, with huge, sloping roofs for the mountain snowfalls that would never come to Cleveland. There were a few fine touches; porch columns might have a scroll on top and bottom or a worked portion in the middle. Leaded glass graced living-room windows. Not elegant homes, but big, substantial, ready to house families with many children. That was the appeal to people like my parents and those who had settled here directly from the "Old Country." What appeal do they have to the new immigrants, the people who were alternately received and cursed by the neighborhood?

"At our old place down on 81st and Kinsman, I'd get up in the morning and the smoke from the factories would just about make you sick; all I could see out my windows were chimneys and the filth in the air." Mrs. Mary Owing was talking in the simple gray house an uncle and aunt of mine had owned, diagonally across the street from my old home. "Here I walk out on the porch and the air is so fresh, the birds are chirping and I feel like I'm in paradise. They tell me that tree on the front lawn will blossom so pretty in the spring. I can't wait for that. At the old place, all we had to look forward to was the next rotten building being torn down."

For eight years Mary lived with her husband, a mechanic and competition driver of dune buggies, and their four children in a $50-a-month apartment. Rats and roaches were unwelcome but regular visitors. A husky, good-looking woman with a smoky voice and a warm smile, even though two front teeth are missing, Mary went to school in the Kinsman area, dropped out in the 10th grade and was married at 16. She is a neat housekeeper, but on Kinsman there was a constant battle with the black soot that invaded her house daily. On

Forest Avenue she enjoys cleaning the house because the environment doesn't despoil her work.

Her husband replanted some burned-out patches of grass late in the summer and nursed them along so carefully that they look better than the rest of the lawn. He wants to replant the entire lawn this spring. Contrary to what the whites on Forest say, Mary Owing doesn't want the black influx and white outflow to continue indefinitely; she wants a racially mixed neighborhood, and she plans to keep her house up. No neighbors have stopped by to welcome the Owings, but some have said "Hello" as they passed. Still others have stared icily at Mary, who enjoys sitting on a kitchen chair on the front porch. A woman a few doors away found her sidewalk cracked—the work of children with hammers—immediately called the police and told them it was the work of the Owing children. As it turned out, it was not, but the woman sold her house and moved in a few weeks. "I don't want them to move out," Mary says, "because most whites do keep up their houses better than blacks, but what can I do? Tell me and I'll do it."

Across the street from Mary Owing, two doors away from Rose Hrutkai, lives Mrs. Lorainne Gibson. She and her husband, a telephone-panel repairman, and their small daughter were the first blacks to move onto this part of Forest Avenue. They lived before on East 90th Street, off Euclid, where the neighborhood scenery included a house of prostitution across the street and flashily dressed pushers selling to shaky young addicts.

Lorainne was folding her baby's diapers in the living room, absent-mindedly watching an afternoon soap opera when I called. She opened the door readily after I introduced myself and told her what I was doing. (In white homes I was viewed with suspicion and forced to ask the first few questions through the pane of a storm door. When I was a boy, even the magazine salesmen were invited in to give their pitch before being turned down.) Lorainne was wearing a bright orange pants suit that seemed strange during the day in a Forest Avenue house; cotton dresses and aprons were the usual attire.

"If it does anything, renting down there makes you appreciate having your own home," she said. "I will never have roaches. I will never have rats here. I saw some roaches down at Bill's Grocery the other day, and I don't go there any more. I go up to Stevie's, a black-owned place; it's cleaner."

Her husband was able to secure a minimum-down-payment G.I. loan for their $18,000 two-family house, on which they pay $150 each month. The upstairs apartment brings $100 a month, and Lorainne supplements her husband's earnings by watching the two children of the woman upstairs, who works and receives child-care public assistance. "No two ways about it," Lorainne says, "we don't want this neighborhood all black; we have an investment to protect. But I'd like to see other young black couples, other white couples, move in because sometimes it gets a little boring around here for the housewife. The only thing wrong with the neighborhood is that there's a generation gap. Crime? The crime rate is going down. Mayor Stokes is doing a beautiful job.''

Her attitude was typical. Most of the blacks in the neighborhood have come from high-crime areas, and they see their new homes as relatively safe. The older white residents, who remember when a mugging in the neighborhood was unheard of, feel that the area is crime-riddled and dangerous.

"Mostly," Mrs. Gibson said, "the white neighbors have been nice. One lady brought over a pitcher and glasses as a gift. Mrs. Martin showed me how to plant in the backyard. Then the lady next door buried a piece of rail—you know, like from the railroad—in her lawn, which is right by our driveway. Maybe somebody's car from our driveway ran over the grass a couple of times, but I never even saw a tire print. Now some of our friends have done hundreds of dollars of damage to their cars on the rail. That rail would have never happened if a white family had moved in. Listen, I'm more against all the lazy blacks on welfare than you are. I lived with all that down on East 90th.''

I found Mrs. Ollie Slay, my father's next-door neighbor, at home on a Saturday morning. She works as a maid in a hotel during the week, and her husband is a carpenter and general handyman. In the Slays' backyard was a large German shepherd on a length of heavy chain. I can't forget his deep and menacing bark and the grating sound of the chain as it was pulled taut by his lunges.

"I didn't know much about this neighborhood, about all the ethnic business," Ollie said after she turned down the Wes Montgomery record on the stereo. "All I wanted was a place I could live and let live. Down at East 100th, where we lived, we were robbed three times. We bought the dog and started looking for a house. Originally I came from a farm in Louisiana: no electricity, no indoor plumbing. So this house, this neighborhood . . . well, I love it. I just love it.

"Everything we have, we worked for," she says. "Scraping together $1,500 for a down payment was the toughest thing we've ever done. So maybe blacks are the cause of crime in this area. But it isn't me out there bopping old ladies over the head. Talk about law and order—yes, sir, I'm for law and order. You can put me down as in love with the police.''

In the City Council elections last year, the people in my old neighborhood did a strange thing. They elected a Republican—a Republican of Scottish ancestry, at that. Jayne Muir ordinarily could never have been elected, regardless of her intent and qualifications. But, by marrying a Ukranian named Zborowsky, she gained a name as politically potent as Kennedy, Roosevelt or Taft. She is a former social worker whose constituency is distrustful of change and reform. Father Michael, for instance, says, "She's pushing the black movement too hard. She should listen more to the people."

In her storefront office on Buckeye Road, the usual complaints are handled by a group of New Frontier-like college students. The water inspector will be sent out on Friday to see why Mrs. Kovach's bill was so high. Mrs. Sterpka's petition for a new streetlight where an elderly woman fell and broke her hip will be forwarded with a properly irate letter to the illuminating company. But Councilwoman Zborowsky wants to do more than party pols and hacks have done in the past. One morning while puffing her way through a half pack of Benson and Hedges and self-consciously trying to rearrange an uncooperative head of hair, she talked about her area.

"The 29th Ward is a ward in transition. That means whites move out, blacks move in, businesses close and everybody forgets about it until it's a slum, then Model Cities is supposed to rejuvenate it. We have 40 per cent black, a lot of ethnics and a few WASP types on the upper edges, where we touch on Shaker Heights. We have people who are used to taking care of things by themselves and of living within their own world. My job is to bring them together for cooperation and to let them know at the same time they don't have to go inviting each other over for supper. They can still be private people with their own traditions, but divided like this, they'll be eaten alive. Crime is up 25 or 30 per cent, and there's no reason why it won't go higher. Blacks are suffering, too, but they are used to it. The press on the ethnics is so strong, they want to kid themselves it's going to be O.K. tomorrow. So they wait and hope. Useless!"

Realizing that one of the irreparable casualties of "transitional neighborhoods" is often the shopping area, Mrs. Zborowsky—in an effort to head off the problem in her district—has organized the Buckeye Area (Cleveland) Development Corporation. "Through it we hope to get foundation money, local, state, Federal money for development of the area that is beyond any businessman. There is no developer—as there would be for a suburban shopping center—ready to fly in here and be our angel." She found that of the 186 business locations in the Buckeye-East 116th Street area, there were only 11 vacancies, and she wants to be sure that the number won't grow quickly.

The development corporation may or may not get off the ground, and Mrs. Zborowsky knows it, so she continues to work on smaller projects. She compiled a list of the more than 30 real estate companies working in the area and hopes to coerce them into stopping their scare tactics. She has been instrumental in helping streets organize block organizations. Through her prodding, the abandoned house that was the scene of the gang rape has been torn down.

"I have to avoid the expedient, calling names, placing blame, merely getting more police in. That's what I'm pressured to do. Education is an overused word, but that's my job. The old residents of this ward have always relied on private institutions—their families, churches, clubs, lodges. Now they must be taught to report things to the police and not worry that they will in turn be prosecuted. This neighborhood has fantastic shops for ethnic baked goods, meats, renowned restaurants like Settlers Tavern and the Gypsy Cellar; there is something to be preserved. Right now I'm working to have an Outreach Station funded. It would be manned by an off-duty policeman and be a clearing house for complaints, a place where people could have problems taken care of. The reaction? Mixed. I get complaints like 'You mean I get mugged down on East Boulevard and I have to run up to the station on 116th Street to report it?' It's hard to get a new idea across.''

For every optimist like Jayne Muir Zborowsky in the neighborhood, there are 10 nay-sayers. There were nay-sayers when I was a boy, but then the problems were cosmic and removed—like a pigheaded haberdasher named Truman or a war in a strange nation called Korea—or local but containable—like an increase in tax assessments or the placement of a stop sign. Then "bitching and moaning" was a part of ethnic life, our variation on "Nobody Knows the Trouble I've Seen."

On my visit I found people in the neighborhood, knowing that they are the forgotten Americans and no longer relishing the fact, doing two things. First, they leave. This is difficult to watch, but who can blame young families who want both good schools and safe streets for their children? The other reaction is frightening. These second- and third-generation Slovaks and Hungarians are digging in, hardening their attitudes because they are tired of being oppressed.

Take, for instance, one of the young policemen in the old neighborhood. He would talk only after I assured him I would not use his name. He admitted he was a typical Cleveland cop, ethnic, bitter and not afraid to say he was afraid. He feels the old neighborhood is so unsafe that he has opted for the suburbs.

"I was off-duty the other day, and I walked into a bar on Buckeye and kiddingly—you know, like Dodge City or something—I said, 'O.K., you guys, all the hardware on the bar.' Ther're five guys in there. Four pulled out guns. I'm a bigot and I know it, but arming isn't the way. These people are going to get those guns rammed right up their own butts someday.

"Dope is the big problem beneath it all, and blacks who don't have or don't want work. In the old days, a black man couldn't even ride through the neighborhood without it being a big deal. Now they can move freely because blacks live here. The bad element has found a gold mine, and they're going to work it. The worst thing is that nobody's on the street any more. Those that have to go out are prey for the wolves. Half the crime would stop if more people would be out.''

The anxiety and fear in the neighborhood have forged one significant group, the Buckeye Neighborhood Nationalities Civic Association. I attended a B.N.N.C.A. meeting one evening at the First Hungarian Lutheran Church. There were 15 or 20 people there, but two of them dominated the proceedings. Ann Ganda, a woman with sharp features and a high, shrill voice talked about the proposed Outreach Center. ''Those two colored kids have Legal Aid after they attacked us [there had been a street assault on an unnamed person], and what do we have? I'm in city housing. They demand tile in the kitchens and they get it. Sliding doors and they get it. We have to demand. We don't want an Outreach Center; we're too kind already. We want more police.''

John Palasics, a scholarly-looking man with a graying tonsure, three-piece suit and a low, calm voice, took me to the back of the room to display a street map another member had drawn. ''This is our battle plan,'' he began slowly. ''We want to have each house with a code number so that our police can get to any house in minutes. The city police won't cover us, so we are willing to give of ourselves. Special Police, Inc., has many people who have taken courses at their own expense to learn crime prevention and first aid, and if we can get the support, we'll have them on the street next year.

''I know people are calling us vigilantes,'' he said, and it was as if a switch was thrown some place inside him. His eyes widened in their red rims, his right index finger jabbed at the air. ''Anything the blacks say against us is out of ignorance. This neighborhood should be preserved as a national historic monument to mark the contribution of the nationalities. Monuments are WASP or black, nothing for us. We don't want our neighborhood liberated as a slum. And we don't want blacks in our group; we are for the preservation of the nationality way of life.''

Words like ''liberated'' and ''slum'' came out of his mouth as if he had bitten down on some bitter fruit. ''Listen, we know things the F.B.I. doesn't even know yet. When the blacks control this area,'' he said, sweeping his hand, now trembling, over the map, ''they will put up roadblocks to keep the whites out of downtown. We know about all this. A black boy came up to me on the street the other day and said, 'We gonna keel you, whi' man, so get yo' ——— out N O W.' Let the Anglo-Saxons turn their houses over to them. We demand a right of self-determination.''

They are calling my neighborhood transitional, and it is not much fun to go home again. The old formula just doesn't seem to work any more, and there are few people left who want to move along positive lines. So the ethnics continue to abandon the neighborhood, each saying he hates to go and he'll hate to come back in five or ten years when, as many say, it will be another Hough. Most major cities must have neighborhoods like it, neighborhoods that are being left to new immigrants who want to believe they have moved to Nirvana.

On a Monday morning I prepared for the trip back to New York, feeling confused and depressed at what I had found. As I walked my dog along Forest Avenue, he did his duty on the lawn of the new black family next door. I moved on, deep in contemplation. A few minutes later, John Slay walked up and, after saying good morning, hesitated. I expected a final plea, a demonstration that the black man wanted to do right by the neighborhood.

All that John Slay asked was, please, and don't take offense, clean off the lawn.

NEWARK HELD AN ANGRY AND AN- GUISHED CITY

by FOX BUTTERFIELD

NEWARK—Newark has become an angry and anguished city as its black community gradually takes over the city's politics, schools and cultural life from an ever-decreasing white minority.

Almost every issue confronting the city, as in the struggle between the Newark Teachers Union and an alliance of black leaders and the black-Puerto Rican majority on the Board of Education tends to become a racial conflict.

With a black population that grew by nearly 25 per cent during the last decade and is now 60 per cent of the city's 380,000 people, Newark faces the possibility of becoming the first virtually all black major city in the country.

When the school board voted last week to reject a settlement to the 10-week-old strike, Jesse Jacobs, the tough, muscular president of the board implied that he hoped the lack of a contract would force white teachers to leave Newark.

"If this is to be the year of attrition, then let it be," he said. "In the words of the old Negro spiritual, 'Free at last, praise God almighty, free at last.' "

The predominantly black audience at the board meeting, which had continually heckled white speakers, roared its approval.

Although Mayor Kenneth A. Gibson, the first elected black mayor of a major Eastern city, spoke out strongly over the weekend condemning such racist talk, many white people in Newark wonder how long they can go on living here.

Steven Adubato, the chairman of the Democratic party in the predominantly Italian North Ward and a racial moderate who has been attacked as a "nigger-lover" by fellow Italians, is despondent.

"All the prophecy from whites about what would happen if we elected a black mayor seems to be coming true," he said bitterly. "The teachers union will be broken if the school board continues to refuse to pass a contract, and white teachers with any dignity will leave town. I don't know of any white people in Newark who feel comfortable living here now."

Many elegant houses in the few remaining exclusively white areas, such as the Vailsburg and Forest Hills sections, have "For Sale" signs posted on them.

A few whites remain philosophical about the gradual transformation of the city.

"These people are just going through what the Irish in Boston did under James Michael Curley," said a moderate white businessman who lives in the suburbs. "All they want is a share of the power."

The physical change in the city over the last 15 years is striking. Vast stretches of the city, which once housed Irish, Italian and Jewish families, are now totally black.

About 10 per cent of the city's population is made up of Cubans and Puerto Ricans who have remained politically passive. They play only a minor role in Newark's racial struggles.

Weequahic, formerly a Jewish neighborhood of substantial homes and tree-lined streets made famous by the fiction of Philip Roth, is now part of the black slums. Many houses are badly in need of a fresh coat of paint, and abandoned cars, their fenders smashed, line the streets.

Where once there were 15 Orthodox Jewish synagogues, now there are only transient storefront churches.

Newark has long suffered from a depressing catalogue of urban ills.

It has the highest incidence of per-capita crime in the nation, the greatest percentage of slum housing and the worst incidence of venereal disease and infant mortality. With one of three people on welfare, it has the highest percentage of welfare recipients.

The unemployment rate is 13 per cent for the city as a whole, and 30 per cent for black males between 16 and 25. Despite a property tax expected to be nearly $10 for each $100 of assessed valuation this year, the second highest in the nation, Newark faces a real prospect of bankruptcy.

"Whatever troubles American cities have," Mayor Gibson is fond of saying, "Newark will get there first."

Ironically, the mayor's own father was a victim of Newark's ills last week when he was badly beaten by five youths who attempted to rob him near his home.

Particularly since the riots of July, 1967, when 26 people were killed, everything in Newark seems permeated with a tense, racial quality.

Militant figures in both communities, such as the poet and playwright LeRoi

Jones and former City Councilman Anthony Imperiale, seldom go anywhere without a retinue of bodyguards, often numbering as many as 20.

Several meetings of both the City Council and the school board have had to be adjourned in chaos this year because of fights between white and black members of the audience.

The black community's first real assertion of power came last June with the election of Mayor Gibson after a heated, racially divisive campaign. In a runoff election, Mr. Gibson defeated Mayor Hugh J. Addonizio, a two-term incumbent, who was on trial on charges of extortion and income-tax evasion for which he was later convicted.

Shortly after taking office, Mayor Gibson, who was formerly a structural engineer, asserted that corruption in city government was deeper and more widespread than he had previously thought. However, he has moved slowly in naming new city officials and has been particularly cautious about naming blacks to city posts.

He named William Walls, a black municipal judge, as City Corporation Counsel, and he has appointed blacks to head Newark's antipoverty and Model Cities programs. But he has also appointed two white men to the critical jobs of Police Director and City Business Administrator.

The appointment of the police director, John L. Redden, has been vigorously opposed by Mr. Jones, who last week called Mr. Redden a "racist turkey" who has "trained his zombies to eat black flesh."

Mayor Gibson's two personal secretaries are black women, but to the surprise of many visitors to City Hall, four of his six staff aides are white. "A lot of people in the community ask me how come I've got all these white guys around," Mayor Gibson has said, "and I tell them that it's because they are the best people I can find."

How much political power the black community really wields is a subject of debate. There is no strong black political party organization, and despite the election of Mayor Gibson, only three of the nine city councilmen elected at the same time are black.

The City Council members are elected on the basis of one from each of Newark's five wards and four at large. Since three of the four elected at large are white, it suggests to some people here that there are still many blacks not registered to vote.

The one area of the city in which blacks have made almost no gains is the business community. As the banking and commercial center of New Jersey, Newark has powerful business interests, and they remain under the control of whites.

Although many of the major employers, such as the Prudential Insurance

Company, New Jersey Bell Telephone and the First National State Bank, have instituted minority job-training programs, the top management is dominated by whites.

Black business has made little more than a painful start. Imperial Mold, which made molds for lamps and with 80 workers was the largest black-owned business in Newark, was forced to close last October because of tax problems.

"The real problem with black business is lack of experience, not money," contends Al Cunningham, human relations coordinator for the Newark Chamber of Commerce. "We have black people now who can go out and borrow money, but they don't know how to run a business. When they really need an accountant, they hire a lawyer to run things.

"Some leaders in the black community like to pretend they can get along without white business, but Newark just wouldn't be viable as an all-black city."

The effort to pay greater attention to black culture in Newark has been led by Mr. Jones, who prefers to be called by his Swahili name, Imamu Amiri Baraka.

In person a small, slim bearded figure with a soft voice, Mr. Jones has tremendous appeal to many blacks because of his insistence on the need to create a separate black culture and identity. He has regularly criticized the Newark Museum and the Newark Public Library for their exhibitions of what he calls "white colonial art" and their failure to have art and books relevant to the black slums.

Mr. Jones, who lives in Spirit House, a three-story frame building painted red, green and black, the colors of the black nationalist flag, has also clashed with Henry Lewis, the conductor of the New Jersey Symphony and the first black musical director of an American orchestra. He has urged Mr. Lewis to play less European music and more African music.

One of Mr. Jones's most innovative programs is the African free school, a federally financed class in the Robert Treat elementary school that draws on Africa and Black America for its subject matter and tries to teach the students Swahili.

As in a physical training class he runs for young black boys called Simbas at the office of his Committee for a Unified Newark, there is a heavy stress on obedience, discipline and pride in being black.

A black aide to the mayor said recently that he thought that Mr. Jones and his group "probably could get 80 per cent of the vote in the black community if they campaigned on an issue." But the Reverend William E. Hedgebeth, pastor of the Mt. Olives Church of Christ's Disciples and a racial moderate, disagreed.

"LeRoi makes a lot of noise and he has a pack of bodyguards, but he doesn't represent one-fifth of 1 per cent of the black people in Newark," Mr. Hedgebeth said.

In Newark's bitter racial conflict, there has been little room for moderates.

John Cervase, a white member of the school board who thinks of himself as a progressive in racial matters after 10 years as a member of the local Urban League, was visibly shaken by the constant heckling he received at last week's school board meetings.

"They called me a honkie, a racist, and threatened me. My wife is scared silly about what they might do. I just don't know what it means," he said in an interview.

Although Newark does have a small, stable middle-class black section, most affluent blacks tend to follow whites to the calmer suburbs.

"I have to think about schools for my children," said a young black woman who works for a federally financed employment agency and lives in nearby West Orange. "Newark is so crazy, like a city that caught some sort of incurable disease, how could I really live here?"

POLITICAL CONFLICT

FOR WHITE AND BLACK, COMMUNITY CONTROL IS THE ISSUE

by NATHAN GLAZER

It may in the end turn out a tragedy that the issue of community control of schools was first raised on such a massive scale in New York City, where it inevitably became entangled in the escalating mutual distrust and dislike of Negroes and Jews, and in the increasingly fierce if ritualized conflicts that characterize labor-management relations between civil-service unions and government in New York City. We cannot wish away the reality that in New York City a public-school population with a majority of Negro and Puerto Rican children is now taught by a teaching staff with a majority of Jews; nor can we wish away the reality that New York City's teachers have followed in the path of transit workers, sanitation workers and social-service workers in militantly fighting for the defense and expansion of their salaries and privileges.

But both these special factors will have consequences far beyond the boundaries of New York City because New York is also the capital of the mass media and the seat and learning situation of many intellectuals—and they are likely to draw, indeed already have drawn, conclusions from the terrible teachers' strike that will not apply and should not apply to "community control" and "parental participation" in general, and not even in New York City.

The issue that has exploded in New York City—and increasingly we can expect it to come up all over the country—is one, we should be clear, of "community control," and not really one of "decentralization," even if that is the way most people refer to it. "Decentralization" means a pattern of organization in which decisions are made at the local level rather than centrally—but these decisions can be made by the agents of the central authority without the participation of the local community. "Community control" means a pattern of organization in which the local community has power over decisions. You can have decentralization without community control (though if you have decentralization the local community people will at least know where to go to complain or put on pressure); you cannot have community control without some substantial measure of decentralization. Nor does community control mean *total* community control. Local officials can be removed by the state. If the state will not act, and the suppression of rights is too blatant, the Federal Government may intervene (Little Rock). Thus community control is never and need not be total. Nor is it nor need it be a mandate for the teaching of race prejudice or the suppression of rights—though it has been used for these and other evil ends.

Many of us are beginning to forget that the fight for community control, and for the restriction and the breaking up of the powers of great bureaucracies, particularly where they affect the ordinary day-to-day life of people, has been under way for perhaps 15 years, and that it is not a product of the black revolution alone. Indeed, for 15 or 20 years, the middle class has shown a growing discontent with the bureaucracies that control the ordinary social services that affect citizens. It did this long before it was forced to be concerned with the problems of the urban black poor, and even in countries where the issue of race did not intertwine with and complicaate all other problems.

Fifteen years ago we were in the middle of the first burst of literature on the "suburbanization" of American life. At that time, suburbanites were not attacked for abandoning the central cities to their difficult problems of increasing crime, rising welfare loads, intractable educational problems and to their prospect of racial violence—while to some extent some of these were problems even then, none were anything like the major issues they have become since. At that time, if we recall, the suburbanites were criticized for depriving *themselves* and their children of the rich urban experience—varied ethnic groups, income groups of different levels, cultural opportunities, more interesting politics and the like. And the suburbanites' argument—where they had defenders, at any rate—was that they were exchanging a situation in which they were the object of distant and indifferent bureaucratic forces to one in which they had direct access to and direct influence over government.

Thus I recall an article by Harry Gersh in *Commentary* describing his move from Brooklyn to Westchester—and reporting with wonder that when the garbage was not collected there was someone to *call,* and he could expect a response. Here was a middle-class citizen who nevertheless found he exchanged powerlessness in the city for some power in the suburbs. Robert Wood, in his book *Suburbia,* did present a criticism of the suburbanite for leaving the arena of major political decisions and did warn that if the middle-class population moved off to local municipalities of a narrower class and ethnic range, it would be more difficult to deal with the great problems of the society, and in particular those of the society that became evident in central cities.

Yet to many the main effect of the book was to underline how much the suburbanite gained by living in a small community which, even if it was economically part of a larger metropolis, had a narrow range of citizens and problems. Here he gained direct access and some modicum of control. If he had a position on a public issue, his fellow citizens were likely to agree with him in larger numbers than in the city, because their interests were the same. And if he had a point of view on elementary education, on zoning, on snow removal, on library services, not only would he find that he could organize some of his neighbors who agreed with him, but also that it was possible to influence local officials to take account of that point of view; or if they did not, it was possible to replace them with his friends and neighbors. It was a heady sense of power for people long deprived of much capacity to influence government—and it was a powerful attraction to get out from under the swelling and impervious bureaucracies of the central city.

The middle class thus led the way to the discovery that the urban bureaucracies, made increasingly insensitive by the replacement of political bosses by municipal unions, could be got out from under—by moving. Let us recall, too, who were the first critics of public housing. They were the planners and the middle-class reformers, not the poor who lived in public housing, or those who spoke for them as their militant leaders. The critics were Lewis Mumford, Catherine Bauer Wurster, Elizabeth Wood, Paul and Percival Goodman.

These men and women in varying degrees knew the situation in public housing and spoke from experience as well as from a general theoretical opinion, but in attacking the massive public-housing projects that began to rise in New York City and elsewhere shortly after World War II, they combined esthetic with social criticism. They attacked the public-housing bureaucracies, in Washington and in New York City, which made it impossible, it appeared, to design more attractive and human-scaled projects. The middle class despaired of bureaucracy in housing first—not that of course it meant that much to the middle class, which in any case lived in other settings.

And we can make the same point about the critics of urban renewal and urban expressways. The most influential single book on urban renewal was perhaps Herbert Gans's *The Urban Villagers*, which told with controlled objectivity and yet with passion the story of the destruction, by urban renewal, of the West End of Boston, and in particular of its working-class, second-generation Italian community. The West End was not Greenwich Village, but it had an Italian community, cheap and small-scale housing, a pleasant site near downtown, the urban amenities of small stores and street life celebrated by

Jane Jacobs in *The Death and Life of Great American Cities*. The West Ender, as Gans described him, was certainly attached to his community and his housing—but he was incapable of fighting for it, for he had no well-developed political skills.

But a sociologist and intellectual like Herb Gans was able to arouse other people—sociologists, intellectuals and others—to the enormity of the crime against the West End, and when in New York the urban-renewal authorities tried to move into the West Village—a similar community, but with many more intellectuals and writers—the community fought back, bitterly. Jane Jacobs, Eric Wensberg and others were deeply involved in that fight, and it took several years, in the early sixties, to finally bring the project to a halt—almost.

I recall the bitterness felt by those involved in that fight at the power and the imperviousness of the urban-renewal authorities. These had full-time staffs of publicity men, planners, lawyers, administrators, Federal money—and plenty of time. The local residents had, in this case, writing and political skills, but they fought part-time against the full-timers. And it was at that time that there first developed and became prominent among younger, radical planners such ideas as the one that the community, like the large central bureaucracy, deserves to have its own full-time staff, its planners and advocates so it will not have to exhaust its energies and its money in fighting a public bureaucracy—formally its "servant." The feelings of the middle-class people who fought urban renewal in the West Village, and who fought the plan for the Lower Manhattan Expressway—where again, they faced a full-time bureaucracy well supported by public funds—are to my mind very similar to the feelings now expressed by the poor and the black in many parts of our big cities. And we will not properly understand or respond to these latter feelings—if we are middle class—unless we recall those earlier fights.

It was about the same time too—in 1961—that there was an explosion of anger against the Board of Education—and once again, it was not an explosion led by the poor and the slum dwellers. The Board of Education it turned out was incredibly incompetent in spending money to build new schools—schools needed by middle-class people moving to Queens and the Bronx, as well as by poor people living in older parts of the city. The Board of Education was replaced. A scandal—a minor scandal—helped, but the frustration of the middle classes of the city of New York at the imperviousness of the board and its agents to those who were technically its masters was undoubtedly the chief politically combustible material fueling the outburst and the subsequent change in the procedures for selecting the board—changes that, alas, seemed to accomplish nothing in making the board and the school system more responsive to people's demands.

I recall vividly—10 years ago—the horror stories that then circulated. Graduates from good schools who wanted to teach in the public schools could not get information on how to apply over the phone and would spend endless time getting information and forms from indifferent and ignorant clerks at headquarters; parents could not get information as to the zonal boundaries of various schools. Ideas for innovation—such as using parent aides in the schools, using the city's resources of writers and artists in the schools, even if not licensed—could not get a hearing. Parents were considered foreign persons in the school. They could not enter it without a permit. I recall I could not even take my 5-year-old daughter to her first class in a public school—because parents were not allowed in school. Quite mad explanations would be given— they might break a leg and the school would be responsible, etc.

The local community advisory boards for 25 new local school boards—a very meager and hardly successful attempt at some degree of decentralization and parent influence—were set up originally in 1961, not because of the pressure and urging of the poor and the black, who were then scarcely active in these matters, but at the demand of the middle classes. Martin Mayer's *The Schools,* in 1961, had a great deal of powerful material condemning the impervious bureaucracy of the New York City schools—and he spoke out of a concern for education that had at that time much less to do with the black and poor as such than with a concern for education in general, which he felt was being thwarted by an overcentralized bureaucracy, too remote from any pressure that an aroused community and concerned parents could exert on it.

In our involvement with the tragic details of what happened in Ocean Hill-Brownsville, with the grim reports of racist teaching in some of the community-controlled schools, and with the reduction of the rights and privileges built up by teachers in these schools (many of whom have served loyally in situations which would probably not be tolerated for a week by those who criticize them), we are in danger of forgetting that the demand for community control is based on far more than the experience of blacks and the poor. I have indicated that the experience of the middle classes of New York and other cities—their opposition to practices of urban renewal and highway construction in the central city, their frustration in their efforts to exercise some control over the content and character of teaching and the management of the school system in New York City, their unhappiness over city services that were not responsive to their needs—has led to their own style of community control; moving to towns where they have more power, or into projects which have their own police forces, or moving their children out of public schools and into private schools. Many of the children going to private schools in New York City, we should recall, are children of poorer middle-class and of working-class families. Those attending parochial schools and Jewish day schools far outnumber the children going to fashionable private schools. Of course, the issue here is not "community control" in any simple sense, for it could be argued that the parents of children in religious schools have less control, and this in one sense is true. But what they do have is the power to select an environment in which their children are educated, even if in some cases it is a more rigid and authoritarian one than that of the public schools.

But if we are to get some idea of the full force of black demands in this connection, we must look outside New York City, and outside the country, to discover how powerfully all kinds of ethnic groups are demanding substantial autonomy and even independence. The same issues are rising everywhere—indeed many might say the same irrationalities. But if everyone is becoming irrational in the same way, one cannot help feeling that we are in the grip of a movement against bureaucracy and centralization—particularly where ethnic and racial divisions are involved—that in some way has to be taken into account. Thus, the association of this movement in the United States with the black and the poor (not all the black and the poor, of course) may conceal to many of us its real power and seriousness.

The catalogue of growing ethnic passions around the world is by now familiar. What is perhaps less familiar is the virulence with which these passions are being expressed and the degree to which they are now divorced from any objective facts of repression or inferiority. Thus, the Flemings of Belgium have long felt themselves to be dominated culturally, economically and politically by the Walloons. In recent years, the French-speaking Walloon section of the country has been in economic decline, the Flemish part of the country has been economically rising. Politically it is now certainly dominant. But this has done nothing to reduce the sense of resentment of the Flemings. If anything, it seems to have increased it.

To the outsider, the demand that the partially French-speaking University of Louvain should no longer conduct any work in French—because it was situated in the Flemish part of the country—seemed the height of irrationality. But it was fought for with violence, and the university is to be separated into two parts, with the French-speaking section re-established at great cost beyond the linguistic frontier. If this can happen in Belgium, where Walloon domination of Flemings is scarcely to be compared to the historic oppression of blacks by whites in this country, is it possible to expect that we will not begin to see the division of universities or colleges in this country?

Quebec is engaged in a process which it seems must lead to equally unhappy results. Montreal is a city that lives in fear of separatist French violence. The English-speaking already fear laws that will restrict their right to educate their children in English. The desire for freedom, it seems, among those who have suffered from an inferior status, cannot be assuaged merely by the full right to conduct whatever cultural activities they wish, or by full political power, or even by economic concessions designed to raise them to the level of the formerly dominant groups. It moves on inexorably to the demand, at least among some extremists, for the full "purification" of the territory, so that just as French is seen to defile Flemish territory, English is seen to defile French territory.

One of the most striking examples of ethnic separatism is now to be found in the French-speaking section of the dominantly German-speaking canton of Bern in Switzerland. Switzerland has long seemed to many of us a remarkable model of the largest degree of community control and participatory democracy imaginable. The central government is almost without power, the name of the President is hardly known to the citizens, and even the cantons into which that small country is divided yield most of their powers to the smaller communities which make them up. These are dominated by the direct voting of citizens on every conceivable issue—in many cases by the face-to-face town meeting, which has control over a much wider range of governmental activities than the vestigial town meetings of New England. Yet full citizenship in the most decentralized of all states, with the greatest degree of popular participation in government, does not satisfy some of the French-speaking citizens of the canton of Bern. There have been bombings and the demand to establish a separate republic.

The people of Wales and Scotland, who have been the beneficiaries for decades of special programs to build up the economies of declining parts of Great Britain, also support at this point rapidly growing separatist movements, which have also engaged in some acts of violence. At present there is some concern over whether the investment of the Prince of Wales can be carried off without unpleasant incidents.

In all these cases—and in many more I could refer to—we find not only the demand for cultural opportunity, economic equality, political consideration in proportion to one's numbers in a unitary state but what to me is the irrational demand that the "foreigners," the "others," with whom one has been associated in an integrated state for centuries, be removed—a demand that, it is true, is held in many cases by only a few extremists but one that eventually becomes politically potent through the silencing, via public opinion, of the moderates who see no objection to the maintenance of a mixed society. Everywhere the liberal hope for mixed societies—mixed in ethnic and racial character—gives way before a demand, now coming from the ostensibly dominated rather than domineering groups, for the clearing out of the dominators, so that the formerly inferior group can conduct its own life, without involvement with others. And, of course, we see the same demand developing in black communities in this country. Undoubtedly this, too, is at present the demand of a minority. But the majority is confused, passionless—and for the most part, silent.

If one were to make a complete catalogue of the rising demand for participation, of the rising opposition to bureaucracies, even when these appear to be reasonably competent, selected by rational and objective standards, and considerate, this article would shortly be out of hand. But there is one other functional area in which black separatist demands can be matched around the world, and in situations where racial and ethnic division is not an issue—the demand for participation in university government. This has now been raised in almost every country in the world, except Russia (where perhaps it has been raised but we know nothing about it), Israel and Cuba. It has led to truly revolutionary changes. In France the universities have, for the first time since the age of Napoleon, changed their system of government to allow for elected bodies in which students will have substantial representation. There is no question that the ancient universities of Germany and Italy will undergo similar changes; the students have demonstrated that they can prevent them from operating and can even physically destroy them if they do not undergo these changes.

Thus, for a variety of reasons, we must separate the issues of community control and participation from the specific circumstances in which they have been raised in New York. These issues have been raised by the middle class as well as the poor, by whites as well as blacks, by groups that have not been oppressed—at least in recent times—as well as by groups that have been, in ethnically homogeneous societies as well as in ethnically heterogeneous ones. Clearly they reflect some worldwide movement of dissatisfaction with the modern state and its manner of operation. Even though this state itself—in all the countries I have discussed—a democratic state, in which representatives directly elected by the people govern, through agents selected by the democratically elected representatives, it is considered by many as oppressive as if it were a dictatorship. Certainly the agencies of the modern state, in the view of many people, have escaped from popular control.

I think those who denounce the modern bureaucratic state exaggerate enormously the degree to which the agents of the state have escaped from popular control. I think they further engage in the worst kind of intellectual brainwashing when they fail to take seriously the differences between states in which there are popular elections and those in which there are not (or in which the popular elections simply approve the choices of the ruling party), states in which there are functioning civil rights from those in which there are not, states in which there is an independent judiciary from states in which there is not.

Nevertheless, one key issue has already been settled—in a formally and actually democratic state, disaffected groups, whether blacks, or the poor, or students, can act as if the state were a dictatorship, can gain wide sympathy for their position, and can maintain the kind of disruption that makes it impossible for many institutions important for the society to operate. Thus, universities can be brought to a standstill. High schools and now even elementary schools can be disrupted. The police of a democratic state can be cast in the role of oppressors—to the point where intelligent and educated people can justify the murder of the policemen of a democratic state. More or less the same thing can be done with other agencies of the state, whether highway construction agencies or urban-renewal agencies, to the point indeed where they cannot operate.

Despite this, I think it is true that most people—in this country and in others—are more or less content with the operations of the bureaucracies of the democratic states; consider the votes in this country, or in France, or in Germany, or in Japan. I think it is true that most of the people who man the bureaucracies are men of goodwill, interested in doing as good a job as is commensurate with their training, their abilities and their salaries. I think the process of selection for the bureaucracies is carried out in the democratic states with increasing concern for fairness and for merit, and that replacement of political selection and personal influence by objective tests (which probably in many cases measure nothing relevant to the job), is nevertheless an advance for justice and equity.

But all this does not seem to matter. While to most people the bureaucracies, whatever the frustrations they suffer from them, are seen as *theirs* (they are after all *related* to the teachers, policemen, civil servants, party officials, etc.), for many others, for increasingly dissident and violent minorities, the bureaucracies are seen as foreign, and when seen as foreign, everything becomes justified. Teachers can be spit upon, social workers can be physically attacked, policemen can be killed, the physical premises of government and educational institutions can be destroyed—and there will be an audience looking on, a good part of which will be sympathetic and encouraging.

This is the situation we face in many of our cities—as I have suggested, it is a situation we face in a good part of the rest of the world too.

What courses lie open to us? If we believe—as I do—that what we have is an over-all democratic and rational system, open to change, we will be tempted to consider the repression of those who act irrationally toward it. I think in most cases this will not work. Particularly in settings in which respect for the agents of authority is required, it is scarcely possible that this respect can be re-created and reawakened through repression. The police do not, after all, operate through force. Hannah Arendt has argued effectively that the state is not based on violence, physical force, but on power, and when physical violence is necessary to maintain authority, then it means power has been lost.

Now this has happened to the police in black neighborhoods. They are very often torn between the impossible choice of using violence, physical violence, in making arrests to uphold the law, or of simply abandoning any effort to uphold the law. Power has been lost, violence is necessary now if authority is to be maintained—but in a democratic society the exercise of violence, to the degree necessary to re-establish authority, is scarcely to be considered. Thus we have the result; lawlessness prevails, tempered by occasional police violence, and the chief victims are those who dwell in black neighborhoods and the few whites who must work there (storekeepers, the police, teachers, social workers).

The same thing is happening in public schools in black areas—the process is perhaps most advanced in New York, but is seen in many other cities too. The exercise of the teacher's authority, which once required only a severe look, a word, an admonishing touch, sending the student to the principal, now requires in more and more cases physical violence—we can call it restraint—direct forceful battling with rebellious students, sometimes by the teachers, sometimes by the police.

We can find the same thing in the welfare offices, and in other government offices, and even, shocking as it is to those of us raised in a setting in which libraries were to be approached in silence and books treated with care, in public libraries, which also now increasingly need guards if they are to operate—at the university level, as well as at the local level.

When authority is lost—and I think it has been lost in schools in black neighborhoods, by police in black neighborhoods and by a good number of the officials who deal with black neighborhoods—the only way it can be restored is by a change in the actual distribution of political power. I myself am not convinced that big bureaucracies in democratic states, and even highly centralized ones, do not work—they work well enough when their authority is accepted. The centralized educational system of France seems to make all the people literate, and up until a few years ago seemed to select efficiently a higher civil service and other important groups of specialists to run the state.

The highly centralized educational system of Japan seems to work even more efficiently if we consider such tests as learning to read and write and do mathematics. And I would wonder really whether the educational system of New York City, which seemed to have such wide acceptance among the people of the city in the thirties, has changed for the worse since then—I doubt that it has become more bureaucratic, or less responsive to public pressure, since then. The police have become more professional, less violent, more honest, and other government activities too are more honest and more efficient. David Riesman has argued that the universities and colleges are much better than they were in the thirties.

So I do not rest my argument for basic changes on the ground of the growing inadequacy of these institutions. I would rest it on the fact that they cannot gain acceptance of their authority among substantial minorities who have the power to resist any possible good they can do. At that point, I think we have to consider new forms of organization, and it is on this basis that I look favorably on plans like the Bundy proposals for breaking up the school system of New York City, and the participation of parent-elected groups in the governing of the smaller districts.

I do not want to go into the details of appropriate systems of decentralization and of greater community control for various government functions. I think we should recognize that we already have a substantial measure of community control in the form of elected bodies for municipalities, states, and the Federal Government. We have some partially working models for an increased measure of community control that could be expanded. The three demonstration districts in the school system of New York City are to my mind such partially working models.

Rhody McCoy seems to find it in his interest to insist that community control in New York City has been ''destroyed'' because the district was forced to take back the union teachers it tried to exclude. But no rational assessment can accept this judgment. Most of the teachers who have been accepted back formally will probably leave fairly soon—the power of the local board, the unit administrator and his staff, and the loyal teachers and students to make life unpleasant for them has already been demonstrated in a hundred ways. The demonstration unit still survives, with just about all the teachers it hired. It is getting more money, from foundations and from special programs for the educationally underprivileged. In other words, partial decentralization and community control in New York City is already a reality, and there will be more.

But leaving aside the special case of the demonstration school districts of New York City, we see other examples of decentralization and community control establishing themselves—even without benefit of over-all schemes for revision of local government—along the lines of the Bundy proposal. Thus, the Community Action programs set up under the poverty programs are established now in more than 1,000 communities. Within defined poverty areas, there are often elections or some other process for getting a representative board. The boards have powers over a budget, over a planning process for various local programs, over some ongoing local programs. On occasion, their powers are expanded. For example, many of them now have some voice in allocating the substantial Federal funds now spent for the education of the poor under Title 1 of the Elementary and Secondary Education Act. As a result of the Green Amendment, these Community Action agencies can now only continue if the appropriate local government agrees to their continuance to administer antipoverty programs. At the end of 1968, 883 of 913 reporting local governments elected to continue the existing Community Action agencies.

Thus the Community Action agencies, which were born in conflict, and have lived through intense conflict, have turned into really effective examples of decentralization and community control. In most communities, the locally elected power-holders, the mayors and councilmen—who of course also reflect community control, but at a higher level—have agreed that the bodies that represent poor areas for antipoverty programs should continue.

As Daniel P. Moynihan wrote at the conclusion of his "Maximum Feasible Misunderstanding," ". . . community action . . . survived; a new institution of sorts had been added to the system of American local government." And the Republican Administration has now accepted it. In the nature of things, when an institution survives, one finds things for it to do—or it finds things for itself to do. Those of us who believed that the conflicts over relatively small programs of no impact would become so fierce that communities would be torn apart with no gain have for the most part been proved wrong. While the conflicts were indeed fierce in many cities, in the end the local Community Action agencies have become established, have been accepted by local city government, have proved useful—at least useful enough so that the overwhelming majority of city governments are not prepared to abolish them.

With the rise of ever more extreme forms of black militancy, in addition, the leadership of the Community Action agencies, which seemed militant enough in 1964 and 1965, now turns out, within the political spectrum of poor black areas, to be generally somewhere in the middle. The agencies have provided a training ground for large numbers of local black community leaders, many of whom have become militant, it is true, but many of whom are now on the first rungs of careers in electoral politics, and look forward to participating in the system as democratically elected representatives of citizens, rather than tearing it down.

The same process is now under way as we develop Model Cities agencies in many cities. These agencies will administer much larger funds, for a much greater range of city functions, than Community Action agencies. They must be set up with the approval of local elected bodies—which has somewhat muted the conflicts in their creation, for city governments now have less fear (than in the case of the Community Action agencies) that an alliance of radical Federal officials and radical local people will set up a government in opposition to them.

These agencies have a difficult task, but one no more difficult than the Community Action agencies had. They must represent the people of a local area; they must develop a complex program with many different parts (the legislation requires that their programs have elements that try to improve housing, public safety, health, education, employment and a good deal more in the poor areas); they have to get local approval of programs that often arouse the suspicion of the city agencies in these various fields; they must get coordinated funding of all these programs from a variety of Federal agencies, etc.

Once again, to this observer at least, it appears that in our penchant for attacking all problems simultaneously and in achieving a high level of participation we may have placed a burden on Model Cities agencies that they may not be able to fulfill. Yet, in some cases with which I am familiar, I am impressed with the high level of many of those involved in developing Model Cities programs, and with the political skill with which these varied obstacles are being overcome. And once again, we are giving opportunity to new leaders, many black, who are gaining valuable experience and valuable political skills, and who see their future as dependent on their ability to deliver services to people, rather than on their ability to arouse them to a destructive rage.

Thus in a variety of ways, in various areas of government, a greater degree of decentralization and community control is being established. Whether we should try to formalize this process in the way the Bundy proposals do or in a more elaborate effort that breaks up city government into local sub-areas, with elected boards and separate administrators, I am not sure. But I am impressed by the fact that in the two cities overseas that are perhaps most comparable to New York in size, London and Tokyo, there is a system of borough (London) or ward (Tokyo) government. The boroughs or wards are smaller than our boroughs in New York—there are about 30 in both cities. They have an average population of about 300,000 each. They have elected councils or legislatures. They have control over elementary education, over health and welfare services, over some local housing programs, over libraries and recreational services. In Tokyo, at least, these wards generally have large, substantial headquarters, in which there are meeting rooms for citizens as well as government offices, and these headquarters are landmarks in a distinguished, contemporary architecture. The history of local government in England, Japan and the United States, has very little in common, yet despite this there may be advantages to this way of organizing the government of a very large city that we should consider.

There are undoubtedly safeguards we will want to consider and build in as we move toward community control. In other countries the main limitation to community control is simple efficiency, and that is one limitation here. It will not be possible for local community governments of small scale to take effective measures to improve metropolitan transportation or to control air pollution, to run colleges (though some might—they do in London), or to manage the Social Security system. But in this country, we have other problems to contend with.

Since one of the main reasons for this drive is to increase the number of black jobholders and civil servants and to increase the control of blacks over branches of government that affect them, we cannot really fully guarantee the rights to seniority and to specific jobs of all civil servants, as one could in other countries. We will have to expect some kind of turnover as community control becomes stronger—and we need measures that cushion this transition for those hurt by it unless we are ready to go through more New York teachers' strikes. The municipal unions will also have to realize that the principle of merit alone will have to be supplemented with the principle of representativeness—as it already is perhaps in many cities outside New York, which have found it possible to recruit far more black schoolteachers, principals and administrators than New York has.

The argument is often made that the introduction of the principle of representativeness will mean that people recruited for public service will be less qualified or competent than those who are recruited on the principle of merit alone. A good deal depends on how we define "competence" or "qualification." If we define it only in terms of the tests that have been developed, this certainly is true. But the tests themselves are only one way of getting at competence and qualifications. Very often test-making begins to lead a life of its own, and tests are developed and used that are themselves rarely tested to find out if they really select better teachers or policemen or firemen. Other cities (for example, Philadelphia and Chicago) do seem to have much larger proportions of black principals and teachers—even taking into account their larger Negro populations—than New York does. Further, for many purposes we have to define race itself as a qualification. A Negro teacher or principal, all other things equal, will, we expect, have a better understanding of Negro pupils and parents, and will do a better job for that reason alone. We have to take this into account in making appointments.

One strong argument against a greater degree of community control for poor and black areas is that since the areas are poor, they will not be able to raise their own taxes on their own property tax base (as can suburban school districts and other governments), thus they will be dependent on the tax resources of the city, the state, and the Federal Government, and these will not be distributed to them in the measure required if these areas have a larger degree of independence. In other words, the argument is these areas need more money, not more local control, and more local control will mean less money.

I don't see the force of this argument. We have already accepted in this country—both in state-aid formulas and in Federal-aid formulas—the principle that resources should be distributed on the basis of need, not on the basis of a real contribution to tax revenue. This principle is often used to give more money to rural areas and Southern states, but in the Elementary and Secondary Education Act, and in other acts, we now see money flowing to poor areas of cities on the basis of need. There are also various cases working their way up through the court system that may lead to a greater measure of public money going to poor areas.

Community control as such does not carry a major threat to this process. What does is the possibility that we will see the rise to power in the new small governments of black militants who will teach race hatred and an illusory and false view of history and reality. This is real danger, and the fact is we cannot fully protect ourselves against it. We must hope that the good sense of black parents and citizens will on the whole prevail, but we must realize it has not been possible for the Federal Government to protect Negroes from local and state governments in the South that teach racial hatred and systematically prevent blacks from gaining access to equal education, equal justice, equal participation in government. We must try to prevent the systematic oppression of minorities,—it will be black minorities, again—in Northern local government, as we try to prevent this oppression in Southern local government. But in view of how long it has taken us to make even the progress we have in the South, we cannot be very optimistic, and I think we must expect that some of the governments that will be set up in the Northern cities may well be oppressive, corrupt, inefficient and irrational. Budgetary controls in the hands of cities and states may prevent the worst abuses, just as budgetary power in the hands of the Federal Government has helped move the South toward equal treatment.

In the end, I think the main redress of those who do not like the new governments that are established is the redress that is always available in a democracy—changing the government, whatever the degree of pressure or terror applied by it, or if that seems too hard, moving away. As long as these safeguards are available, we can move toward decentralization and local control.

SUBWAY IS THE ISSUE IN FOREST HILLS

by LINDA GREENHOUSE

To most New Yorkers, Forest Hills is the neighborhood in Queens where famous tennis players meet once a year to compete, where Tudor-style homes evoke a quiet past, and where new luxury apartment houses attest to an affluent present.

For its population, recently estimated by the Queens Chamber of Commerce to be nearly 105,000, Forest Hills offers such amenities as public schools reputed to be among the city's best, convenient shopping and a lingering air of elegance reflected in the exclusiveness of the West Side Tennis Club and the Forest Hills Inn.

Forest Hills, in short, appears to be anything but a hotbed of angry community-organizing. But in the last two months that is exactly what it has become, and all the energy and angry words have one target: the subway.

Since November, groups of Forest Hills residents in this Central Queens section have mapped out four separate battles against the Metropolitan Transportation Authority.

The first—a fight to reroute a new express subway line away from a residential section—they won. The second and third—two attempts by groups of private landowners to change the plans for a link between Manhattan and Kennedy International Airport—are uphill fights. And the fourth—a broad attack on Queens subway service in general—is likely to go on for a long time.

The residents of the Forest Hills section that is called Virginia Village, a few square blocks of privately owned, attached homes, still smile and shake their heads in wonder when they recall what happened at a meeting with M.T.A. officials on December 11.

At that meeting, organized by David Love, secretary of the Mayor's Urban Task Force, they learned that Route 131-B would be rerouted under a public street instead of cutting across and destroying two blocks of their houses.

Six weeks earlier, no one in Virginia Village had heard of Route 131-B, although it had been on the drawing boards since March, 1968, as part of the M.T.A.'s over-all subway expansion plan.

It is to be a single-track, rush-hour "express bypass," running alongside the Long Island Rail Road right of way from the Independent subway station at Continental Avenue in Forest Hills directly to the Queens Plaza station, skipping the heavy loading point at Jackson Heights and relieving the extreme congestion on the "E" and "F" trains.

The idea is simple, but new construction is needed to connect the tracks at the Continental Avenue Station to the L.I.R.R. roadbed. It wasn't until November 1, when the M.T.A. put the required notice with all the details in the newspapers, that residents of the block bounded by 68th Avenue, 67th Drive, Booth Street and Austin Street learned that the connection was to be made through their block.

"I was like an old firehorse. After all these years I started organizing again," recalls Bertram Seigeltuch, a lawyer and long-time resident of Virginia Village who is president of the long-dormant Forest Hills Taxpayers Association. His swift action led to the December 11 meeting, where within two minutes he learned that his fears were over.

"When I got home, the phone never stopped ringing with congratulations. People asked me how I did it. I just said I didn't know, but right does triumph sometimes," Mr. Seigeltuch said.

M.T.A. officials later explained that the plans for Route 131-B had been drawn before the agency came into existence, and had been quickly adopted by the M.T.A. without a close check of the details. After the newspaper notice, when complaints started to come in, the agency hurriedly ordered a new check and revised its plans.

The effects of the victory linger on in Virginia Village. "This used to be a real community," Mr. Seigeltuch said. "Recently people had drifted apart, but there was a time when you knew everyone. It's starting to come back to that again."

Another group that has been newly united are the residents of the Forest Park Crescent building, a 240-family, 21-story, five-year-old cooperative on Union Turnpike across from Forest Park.

The building is the only major structure to be built along the L.I.R.R.'s Rockaway Division right of way since those tracks were abandoned in the mid-nineteen-fifties. The building itself is 30 feet from the right of way; its playground is two feet away.

The cooperators, in fact, lease the right of way on a monthly basis and tore up the tracks to build a parking lot.

But now the tracks are about to be reactivated as part of the high-speed, nonstop, rail link between Pennsylvania Station and Kennedy Airport.

George Bruckman, a young lawyer and original tenant who has been acting as unofficial attorney for the building's residents, contends that the city never informed the cooperators that the tracks might be used again.

Mr. Bruckman says that Forest Park Crescent's future as an attractive place to live has been jeopardized by the plans.

"Since the project was announced, there has been panic," he said. "Twenty per cent of the tenants have moved out. Our waiting list has shrunk to nothing. And these are the people that the city has to keep, the kind of people that are going to keep the city stable."

The M.T.A. has agreed to pay $400,000 toward constructing an enclosure for the tracks, the roof of which could be used as a parking lot.

The agency contends that "the understanding has always been that the stretch of track would someday be in public use again."

Enclosing the tracks, however, would cost about $600,000, and the anger of the building's residents is not assuaged. They say that the rail link offers nothing to Queens and was designed for the convenience of Manhattan businessmen.

"We're second-class citizens, there's no doubt about it," Mr. Bruckman said.

Another group that expresses the same feeling is the Forest Hills Little League, which five years ago paid the city $55,000 for a triangular plot of land along the L.I.R.R. right of way at Alderton Street. The group turned the land into four baseball fields, the only soft-surface play area in the neighborhood, and now has year-round programs for about 2,000 children.

Little League members are afraid that two of the fields, smaller than the others because of the shape of the plot, will become unusuable once the tracks are reactivated for the Kennedy spur.

They would like the transportation authority to reroute the tracks or put them underground, two concessions that an M.T.A. spokesman says are highly unlikely.

"As a regional agency, we are constantly torn between recognizing local needs and responding to regional needs, the spokesman said. "Unfortunately, there is no such animal as a regional constituency."

The criticism that the Kennedy line will be of no use to Queens—a widespread feeling in the borough—is a troubling one to the M.T.A., which has agreed to make provisions for adding a local line at some unspecified later date. Basically, the agency says, the new line is vital to the future economic health of the airport, which, as Long Island's largest single employer is itself vital to the future of Queens.

Whatever bitterness remains after these battles are fought will undoubtedly spill over into the next chapter of the struggle between Forest Hills and its subways—a developing public protest against the quality of Queens subway service in general.

Anthony Atlas, the leader of a liberal Republican club in Forest Hills, summarized the complaints recently. "The worst problem is that the service is just plain rotten," he said.

Mr. Atlas's La Guardia Club and the nearby Adlai E. Stevenson Reform Democratic Club have joined forces in a subway study committee. Their conversation has recently turned to such tactics as picketing, mass refusals to leave disabled trains and fare boycotts, although they have promised for the time being to hold to a "moderate course."

Meanwhile, the spirit in Forest Hills is growing.

Everyone's getting to know their neighbors," Mr. Atlas said. "When people meet each other at meetings now, they say, 'Oh, I know you, I see you on the subway all the time.' "

ATLANTIC AVENUE RE-NEWAL STIRS DISPUTE IN BROOKLYN

by PAUL L. MONTGOMERY

An obscure bill for the rehabilitation of Atlantic Avenue that went through the State Senate last week with barely a ripple had residents and legislators from Brooklyn Heights and surrounding communities on the battlements yesterday.

The bill, sponsored by legislators from Bedford-Stuyvesant with technical help from Governor Rockefeller, seeks to create an Atlantic Avenue Development Authority under community control. Its main purpose, the sponsors say, is to attract mortgage investments for deteriorating housing in the area.

However, residents in the landmark areas at the western end of the avenue fear that the plan is a mask for building a cross-Brooklyn expressway through their homes. Community groups from Brooklyn Heights, Cobble Hill, Boerum Hill and Park Slope say they were not consulted about the plan, nor was the City Planning Commission or the Landmarks Preservation Commission.

As originally drafted, the bill would have created a 29-member authority having exclusive control over demolition, construction, rehabilitation and transportation access in a five-mile swath across Brooklyn from New York Harbor to the Interboro Parkway.

Among the authority's prerogatives as originally proposed were powers to condemn any building, purchase any property or relocate any public facility it desired in the designated area.

When community groups outside the Bedford-Stuyvesant, Crown Heights and Brownsville areas of the project learned of the bill after its passage by the State Senate on Tuesday, an immediate outcry arose.

To these groups, the proposed area of the authority looked suspiciously like a superhighway route. Many recalled the two-year battle with city and state officials over the proposed Cross-Brooklyn Expressway and Linear City from

Long Island to the Verrazano-Narrows Bridge. That plan was dropped last year in the face of widespread community opposition.

State Senator Waldaba Stewart, Democrat of Bedford-Stuyvesant, who sponsored the bill, said yesterday that its opponents were deliberately misunderstanding its terms. He said that the bill had been amended heavily since the original proposal, and that the proposed authority's extensive powers had been diluted considerably.

In view of the opposition at the western end of Atlantic Avenue, he said, he would introduce an amendment to his bill this week that would take the area from Flatbush Avenue to New York Harbor out of the control of the authority.

Mr. Stewart said the strip through Brooklyn Heights and Cobble Hill had been included in the first place "so that we could syncronize the traffic lights all along Atlantic Avenue."

Regarding any proposed road building, Mr. Stewart said the only projects contemplated in drafting the bill were to put the Long Island Rail Road tracks below ground between Howard and Bedford Avenues and to rebuild the Atlantic Avenue roadbed from Flatbush to Pennsylvania Avenue. "There never was any highway," he said.

"This project is simply an attempt to give black people some control over rehabilitation in their own areas," he said. "We thought that by having an independent authority we would be able to attract private investment because of the tax incentive involved. The authority would not get a dime of state money nor one dime of city money."

Asked if there were any racial elements in the dispute, Mr. Stewart said:

"I don't want to fight the issue on those grounds. But I will state that a lot of people in my community are starting to say, 'Now wait a minute, what's all these compunctions the power structure has when they find out black people are involved?' "

Yesterday, in fine demonstration weather, about 500 protesters paraded around the intersection of Atlantic and Flatbush Avenues chanting "Kill the bill" and waving placards declaring "No more 'Rocky' roads" and "Underhanded politics degrades democracy."

Most of the protesters, who stopped traffic on Atlantic Avenue for a half-hour, were drawn from the white middle-class families that have bought brownstones in the area in the last 10 years.

A delegation from the Syrian Young Men's Association also participated. Joseph Shamoun, the vice chairman of the group, wearing a "Hell, No" placard, explained that the proposed authority would have an effect on business in the many Syrian shops and restaurants at the western end of Atlantic Avenue.

"That bill was being railroaded through," said Mr. Shamoun. "Rockefeller should go back to Caracas, where he at least owns some property."

Stanley Steingut, the Democratic minority leader in the Assembly, and three Democratic assemblymen from the area—Gail Hellenbrand, Joseph J. Dowd and William J. Giordano—also attended. The three assemblymen led a rearguard action in Albany last Monday and Tuesday that kept the bill from passing the Assembly after it had sailed through the State Senate. It is to come up in the Assembly again on Wednesday.

Asked to comment on the bill, Mr. Steingut had this to say:

"Unless there is a resolution by all the communities affected, I will vote against the bill. Under the best set of circumstances, the people should have adequate time to study the bill and respond to it. It also seems incomprehensible to me that the city government was not consulted."

Mr. Steingut also said that "I deeply resent the exclusion of many legislators and community groups from the drafting of the bill, and the intransigence of presenting it without proper study."

Mrs. Hellenbrand, who was primarily responsible for alerting the Brooklyn Heights community groups to the bill, said it was "unconscionable, a travesty."

Mr. Dowd said there was a "suspicion of the pork barrel" about it. "Let's be frank about it," he said. "There's a lot of fellows down here who would benefit by the bill."

Senator Stewart, who sponsored the bill, said the proposed authority was no different from others, including the Battery Park Authority created by the Legislature in 1968.

"These questions were never raised in the history of authorities," he said, "but now that black people are involved, all of a sudden it's a pork barrel. People from the power structure are circulating all these misrepresentations to defeat the concept of community control."

As for the charges that legislators from outside Bedford-Stuyvesant were not consulted about the bill, he said:

"I'm telling you point-blank that's the lie of the year. They were consulted on every stage of the development of this bill."

Mrs. Hellenbrand then moved to keep the bill from consideration in the Assembly before it could be studied further. "Imagine," she said, "I guess they thought they were putting something over on a naive woman. Well, I learned my lesson."

Mrs. Hellenbrand has been in the Assembly since 1965. She says she will not run again this year.

A press spokesman for Governor Rockefeller said the drafters of the bill had asked for and obtained help from the Governor's legal staff in the preliminary stages. He said the Governor "liked the general approach of broad-based community action for rehabilitation" but "would have to see the bill in its final form before deciding whether to sign it."

The spokesman said the meeting referred to by Mrs. Hellenbrand had been requested by the other legislators to tell the Governor about the bill "and hopefully to enlist his support for it."

A press spokesman for Mayor Lindsay said that the Mayor had not yet taken a position on the bill but expected to this week. He said the City Planning Commission and the Housing and Development Administration opposed it.

Assemblyman Vincent A. Riccio, Republican-Conservative of Brooklyn, was at the protest yesterday and said, "I'm with these people 100 per cent." Two Republican-Conservative assemblymen from Queens, John T. Flack and Rosemary R. Gunning, have also indicated opposition to the bill.

MOST POLITICAL CLUBS IN CITY ARE LOSING THEIR POWER

by FRANK LYNN

The Murray Hill Democratic Club was meeting in its musty, second-floor headquarters at 229 Lexington Avenue, but at first glance the meeting was not much different from that of a civic organization or a stamp club.

There were only six men, and none were chewing on cigars. There were 21 women, one a nun and two who crocheted their way through the humdrum meeting.

Instead of pulsating debates and whispered deals, there was desultory discussion about the ill-fated state transportation-bond issue and the club's meager finances, which will receive a transfusion at a cocktail party Friday, featuring Representative Wilbur D. Mills, chairman of the House Ways and Means Committee. The Arkansas Democrat is a Presidential possibility, but more important to the club, he is a big draw for the fund-raising soiree.

The most spirited discussion at the meeting involved the selection of a nominating committee to pick club officers for next year.

The session pointed up the fact that political clubs have reached a low point in power and influence on the eve of a Presidential primary in this state. The primary will see all the state's Democratic National Convention delegates elected for the first time at the local level, rather than handpicked by state and county "bosses."

Any Presidential candidate looking for existing political clubs for help in the primary will find that many are weak and ineffectual and that they do not preside over vast amounts of money and manpower. In fact, some clubs, particularly in slum areas, are vitually nonexistent "paper" organizations that could be operated out of telephone booths and frequently are.

Like other institutions in an era of upheaval, the political clubs have been hurt by changing times.

Civil Service has eliminated thousands of patronage jobs that attracted party workers. Patronage still available is often unattractive in an affluent era. Party discipline and party organization have broken down in the face of a more independent and educated citizenry.

Shifting populations, particularly from city to suburbs, have broken neighborhood ties and identitites. Antipoverty organizations compete with the clubs as dispensers of civic largess and conduits to City Hall.

The disarray in the Democratic party and an unbroken series of defeats in City Hall and State House elections have also contributed to the decline of Democratic clubs, accustomed to entree at least at City Hall.

The conversion of Mayor Lindsay to the party has not helped the clubs, since he has promoted his own rival organizations—the John V. Lindsay Associations in the five boroughs.

The Murray Hill club is no exception to the general malaise that has enveloped most political clubs, both Reform and regular, in the city. Murray Hill, a Reform club, needs more than a telephone booth for its meetings—but at times not much more.

There are larger clubs, such as the Village Independent Democrats in Greenwich Village, the New Frontier Democratic Club in Forest Hills, Queens, or the Andrew Jackson Democratic Club in Flatbush, Brooklyn, but the problems of the Murray Hill club are typical of the 120-odd Democratic clubs in the city.

Encompassing the 62d Assembly District, Part D, the Murray Hill club includes the affluent Murray Hill and Tudor City areas, the largely commercial midtown 50's and seedy flophouse hotels off Times Square.

The club has only 125 members, mostly in the 35-to-50 age range, out of 5,564 enrolled Democrats in the district.

Even fewer than 125 actively participate in club affairs. The club voted to oppose the transportation bond issue, for example, by a vote of only 17 members at the regular monthly meeting.

Ten years ago, according to Charles M. Kinsolving, Jr., the club's district leader, as many as 200 members would attend a meeting at the height of the Reform challenges of Tammany Hall. But attendance and membership have dwindled as that political war has subsided. The Murray Hill club won undisputed control of the district.

Mr. Kinsolving, 44 years old, is an advertising executive and a student of politics who finds joy in compiling vast arrays of voting statistics and trying to plot political trends. He has been district leader since 1961. His wife, Coral, is a former president of the Murray Hill club.

The articulate Mr. Kinsolving, who easily laughs at the foibles of himself and other politicians, ran for the Assembly once, in 1954. He lost and learned that he would need money he didn't have to run for public office, as opposed to party offices.

He sees his present post as a means of serving his home community and influencing his party. Mr. Kinsolving has often been mentioned as a potential county leader who could possibly appeal to most of the factions in the Manhattan Democratic organization.

Among the club's members is the woman Democratic leader of the district, quick-talking and dynamic Arlene Hershman, who is 37 and was first elected district leader in 1969. A college graduate like Mr. Kinsolving, she is a senior editor of *Dun's Review,* a financial publication. She speaks frankly of running for the Assembly if the incumbent, Assemblyman Andrew Stein, moves on.

Miss Hershman and Mr. Kinsolving preside over a club that will operate this year on a budget of about $4,000, with about $1,250 coming from dues and the remainder from a fund-raising dinner, a raffle and three cocktail parties.

The budget includes $3,000 annually for rent and the rest for postage, a telephone and printing expenses. The club's bank balance at the moment is less than $300.

Campaign funds? Strictly pay-as-you-go. If the candidate pays for or provides the campaign literature, the club will distribute it. At a pre-election meeting of the club, a worker for Beatrice Shainswit, a successful Democratic candidate for Civil Court, arrived with a shopping bag overflowing with Shainswit campaign literature.

Mr. Kinsolving explained that the club could not raise large sums of money for itself and depended for campaign funds for literature, posters and telephones on money "trickling down from high-visibility candidates, such as governor or mayor, to local clubs." In some clubs, campaign money is also used for direct payments of from $15 to $25 to workers.

Mr. Kinsolving noted that the last Democratic gubernatorial candidate, Arthur J. Goldberg, had difficulty raising money and concentrated what money he had on television advertising. "There wasn't a dime for the clubs, and it created a horrendous morale problem," he added.

Are the clubs really necessary in campaigns? Mr. Kinsolving, who has been politicking for 20 years, thinks so. "We are the candidate's channel to the local community," he said, noting that the club members distributed literature, tried to get out the vote, manned the polls and provided forums for candidates.

Mr. Kinsolving and Miss Hershman are often involved in a traditional function of the political club—helping constituents find their way through the governmental labyrinth. But they sometimes have as much difficulty dealing with the bureaucracy as the constituent does.

Among other matters, they have been involved in obtaining bail for the son of a constituent arrested on a narcotics charge; helping a woman get city action on a noisy parking lot next to her home, although there was some delay even after their intervention; winning reversal of a dispossess notice for a woman on welfare, and trying, unsuccessfully so far, to get the aunt of a club member into a public-housing project.

The club is also often the target of supplicants, such as the postal worker looking for a promotion who, unsatisfied with efforts in his behalf, warned Mr. Kinsolving to "stop looking down your nose at this pore old-line Democrat."

Contrary to the widely held view of district leaders, Mr. Kinsolving and Miss Hershman haven't dispensed many jobs. Untypically the club has only two patronage jobholders at the moment, an assistant corporation counsel and a Board of Elections administrative officer. Other clubs have as many as 25 city and state jobholders.

"We've got plenty of people who would be glad to be a commissioner, but they are not interested in $8,000 clerk jobs," Mr. Kinsolving said, while conceding that his relatively affluent district might not be completely typical in this regard.

Why do people join political clubs? Both leaders mentioned ego satisfaction. "Ego-tripping," Miss Hershman called it. Mr. Kinsolving said that the club had recommended at least a half-dozen members for unpaid, but potentially influential, community planning-boards posts.

Other members are political buffs, or began in politics through interest in a particular candidate or cause.

Sister Constance Peck, possibly the only nun in a Democratic club in this city, said she joined the Murray Hill club last spring "to show that we are interested in helping the community." The nun is assigned to the Divine Providence Shelter for the children at 225 East 45th Street.

"There has been a swing away from the clubs," Mr. Kinsolving said. "Activists are either discouraged at the prospect of changing things or identify with one-issue organizations, like the antiwar or ecology groups."

Whatever the reason, political clubs have seen better days.

PART FIVE

NEW COMMUNITY FORMS

When we speak of "defensive and conflict communities," we mean more than simply concentrations of an ethnic population in a single neighborhood— more than the struggle for jobs and for control of the organizations and institutions that administer a given area. We mean communities whose struggles have brought about the development of a self-conscious organization of ethnic groups with specific ideologies, loyalties, political organizations and programs. These result in the creation and re-creation of ethnic identities and the construction of self-conscious ethnic communities which extend beyond any territorial base, but which are often organized on the basis of neighborhood or locality.

In some cases, the construction of an ethnic community in this nonterritorial sense precedes the development of neighborhood communities. Thus the civil-rights movement, black militancy and nationalism arose in response to Supreme Court decisions and national civil-rights legislation. Only later did it become localized, as blacks attempted to implement the specific rights ensuing from these decisions. Their demands for community control, for jobs and for the end of discrimination and exploitation produced resistance among white ethnic communities as well as in white-dominated social, economic and political institutions and agencies. This reaction and resistance forced blacks to further ideologize their claims and to organize themselves at the level of the community. Such community organization was assisted by programs of community control and was supported by private foundations (such as the Ford Foundation), by the Federal Government under the aegis of the Office of Economic Opportunity and by muncipal governments in a wide range of community action programs.

The development of black community action programs—together with fear of race riots, loss of control over governmental institutions, loss of jobs and the incursion of blacks into previously white ethnic territory—caused whites to organize new neighborhood action groups and other organizations not based on territory. In some cases, these organizations were entirely new to a given ethnic group. Thus, white ethnics have become militant in ways which are totally untypical of previous community organizations. In other cases, older ethnic organizations were given new vitality and interest. The Chinese, at least in San Francisco, have organized themselves to resist school busing in ways not essentially different from those of Caucasian resisters.

All groups appear to follow the strategy of the Jews, who were the first group to organize themselves self-consciously and militantly against discrimination and defamation, and who worked out detailed strategies and organizations to preserve an ethnic identity and culture. But the communities created from the sixties to the present are much more overtly political and militant than were the strategies and organizations of ethnic groups in earlier periods. In the past, ethnic groups used nonpolitical organizations to present their claims, or veiled their claims when they used political institutions. At present, ethnic and racial issues are nakedly politicized and result in direct ethnic confrontation.

The development of such political communities is not smooth or linear. The emergence of new ethnic communities frequently results in political struggles within the ethnic community—over ethnic or community policy and over control of the ethnic community itself. To the extent that the parties to these troubles lack political background and experience, the internal struggles may be divisive and violent, not unlike the internal struggles of new nations as they emerge from colonialism. The development of political communities thus depends on the emergence of a viable public opinion, trust in the new community leadership and institutions, self-restraint by the new leaders and ultimately the establishment of legitimacy of the new institutions in their own community. This is an ongoing process, but one which usually takes decades, if not longer, to accomplish.

While there is some tendency to think of communities as emerging naturally out of the growth of commerce and trade, some early cities were created by administrative fiat, with courts, military fortifications, religious and administration centers set up in a fixed locality. (This, of course, was also true of later cities—as, for example, Washington, D.C.) In addition, the location of administration centers in some neighborhoods of established cities gave these centers the characteristics of the populations that were attracted to them. Yet the new kinds of communities that emerged by legislation and administrative action in the Kennedy and Johnson administrations are quite different from these earlier ones. Here the attempt was made to organize political and administrative communities in areas of the black ghetto where the indigenous populations were politically and administratively unorganized. The Economic Opportunity Act of 1964 resulted in the creation of over 2,000 community action projects. Private philanthropy and private organizations have also helped to create neighborhood, and at times city-wide, planning organizations aimed at urban renewal, development and long-term planning. Municipal governments have created neighborhood planning advisory boards drawing from, and sometimes creating, a neighborhood leadership corps. In the Model Cities program also, local leadership was co-opted into centralized and decentralized governmental administrative bodies.

These programs have had multiple consequences, and the ultimate results are not yet clear. First of all, whole new populations have been drawn into the planning and government of localities. As a result, neighborhoods have become political jurisdictions quite different from established political practice in local urban politics. Traditional governmental jurisdiction, as well as old-style party machines, has frequently been bypassed. At times the new leaders have become independent of their administrative creators and have used their new positions to confront and combat their original sponsors. At other times, the apathy of the co-opted leadership has paralyzed the actions of the sponsoring agency. At still other times, conflicts within community groups, together with a lack of experience in political action, have splintered and fragmented the communities, preventing the functioning of traditional political machinery while not creating an effective substitute machinery. Much of the new leadership corps is self-selected within a certain neighborhood. Thus in some areas a new black leadership has emerged; in others, a new middle-class local leadership.

In addition, commitment to national politics and issues has had peculiar and unanticipated effects on the politics of local communities. "New style" political leaders like Adlai Stevenson, John and Robert Kennedy and Eugene McCarthy, among others, have drawn the youthful members of the middle- and upper-middle classes into politics. At different times, this group has focused on such issues as control of the atom bomb, the war on poverty, civil rights, the war in Vietnam, ecology and the quality of life. With the death, defeat or failure of candidates and the loss of salience of issues, the new political groups have often thrown themselves into local politics. They have participated in "reform" politics, and have entered planning and community boards. Quite often they have been at odds with, or have bypassed, established party and political machinery, frequently rendering that machinery inoperative. At the same time, this new "government by amateurs" has not always been able to organize itself into a coherent, all-embracing political machine. As a result, the new local politics has often emasculated the older machine politics without creating workable alternatives.

The over-all effect of this new participation has been to politicize communities and create new ones, especially in areas once dominated by political machines and governmental agencies where residents have been apathetic or where agencies were unable or unwilling to respond to changes in the local population. These new action and community groups are a significant development in the American city, and the full effect of their activities remains to be seen.

At a different level, ongoing social organizations and institutions have become the basis for new communities. In a metropolitan area, a single organization can be so large that its very operation creates a community. Some of these are total institutions whose members are isolated from the outside population, such as prisons, mental institutions, detention centers, drug rehabilitation centers and even monasteries. Other institutions, because of their size, cultural and administrative separateness, technological specialization and spatial separateness, can create a specialized type of community with a distinctive culture. These include hospitals, universities, cultural centers and central organizational headquarters. Finally, some formally organized institutions become centers for community action on the basis of their self-selected specialization. Thus a day-care center, a local cultural center or a community center can become the basis of an organized community.

On the other hand, counter-communities can develop from opposition to such institutions, especially to prisons, detention centers, hospitals, universities or religious organizations. A counter-community can be temporary, organized to resist the policy of a particular institution, or it can itself become institutionalized and a basis of community organization. The number of total, semi-total and counter-communities in this country is unknown and almost uncountable, and yet they remain one of the central organizing modes of urban life today. The values upon which they organize themselves are as diverse as the values upon which individuals base their lives.

Attachment to a value can become the basis of voluntary one-dimensional communities of an almost infinite variety. Their location is not important, but ease of transportation is. Examples offered by the articles in this section are communities based on age, religion, and love of nature, but there are many more. Regardless of their basis, these voluntary one-dimensional communities permit the urbanite to escape from the tyranny of residential space restrictions and provide a range of activity and liberation which enables him to make the most of the advantages of urban life. All forms of human expression are capable of being institutionalized and communalized in a metropolitan area where the population density is great enough to supply the requisite number of members.

STRUGGLE FOR IDENTITY: WHITE MINORITIES REVIVE HERITAGE

by BILL KOVACH

BOSTON—The lid is coming off America's "melting pot" and a bitter residue is being discovered inside.

In city after city across the northern half of the country, communities of white Americans of foreign birth or parentage are beginning to attach a new importance to cultural identities that they have apparently never been able to submerge entirely in what has been called "the American dream."

In Cleveland, acknowledging their debt to black activists' tactics, ethnic groups began to demand a voice on boards and commissions, especially on examining textbooks "to be sure an ethnic identity could be found in the history books our children study."

In Pittsburgh, the Pan Slavic Alliance, a long-dormant coalition of Slavic groups, was rekindled and has begun to agitate for a series of Government-sponsored research centers.

Italian-Americans throughout the country have begun to strike back at the media stereotype, much as the black man earlier rejected the same habit of the larger society of making him the butt of jokes.

"In short," says Professor Paul Mundy, a Loyola University sociologist, "the third generation remembers what the second generation would like to forget—his ethnic identity."

The renewed interest in ethnic Americans was underscored today when the Ford Foundation announced in New York a new program of fellowships to encourage scholarship in the field of ethnic studies. Initial awards of $288,052 will go to 87 doctoral candidates at 54 graduate schools for the writing of dissertations on subjects dealing with the experience and culture of ethnic minorities in the United States.

The new program is designed to help stimulate the development of a body of knowledge on the history and culture of the nation's ethnic minorities, which already is becoming a subject of intense interest to a new generation of American students, according to F. Champion Ward, the foundation's vice president for higher education and research.

For many ethnic groups, the American dream has dissolved into a fearful reality as the communities they fashioned have begun to cave in. New black neighbors are competing with them for housing and jobs and a new generation of young people, including many of their own children, are labeling them beer-bellied slobs, pigs, fascists, warmongers and right-wing reactionaries.

Perhaps because ethnicity was generally accepted as a "passing thing," ethnic Americans in Boston, New York, Baltimore, Cleveland, Pittsburgh, Detroit and elsewhere—nowadays mainly Italians and various groups of Slavs— have for the most part been overlooked by the moving forces of society.

They have been sentimentally praised by politicians as "the salt of the earth" for their habits of thrift and their devotion to America. And they have been bitterly denounced as hoodlums and bigots, sometimes by Anglo-Saxons who years ago removed themselves from the problems of the cities.

But it was not until the end of the nineteen-sixties, amid the social confusion that accompanied a decade of civil-rights agitation, that ethnicity was rediscovered as a phenomenon worthy of serious attention.

In a series of open confrontations with expanding black communities, as in New York's school strikes and the late Reverend Dr. Martin Luther King's forays into the Chicago area, the white ethnic communities, largely Jewish or Roman Catholic, turned to their national leadership for help.

What they found, to their indignation, was that many of their leaders seemed distracted by "The Movement" and unsympathetic, even critical. And when the ethnic leaders heeded the resulting cries of complaint and looked more closely at their own communities, what they found was a deep well of frustration.

"They are representative of at least 40 million Americans who haven't been able to express adequately what is bugging them and as a result they have become anti-Negro, anti-intellectual, anti-Government obstructionists," said Irving M. Levine, director of urban projects for the American Jewish Committee. "They have enough negative power to polarize American cities."

To help cope with their problems, the American Jewish Committee organized the first national "Consultation on Ethnic America" at Fordham University in June, 1968, and soon after the Catholic Church established a Task Force on Urban Problems within the National Council of Bishops.

The involvement of these organizations has begun to create a picture of the urban ethnic community, still hazy, like a photograph slowly resolving itself in developing fluid, but already clear enough in outline to be recognizable.

In most cases it is a picture of a neighborhood in ruin. All the economic and social institutions—fraternal societies and neighborhood lending institutions—faded away as those who could moved to the suburbs. Those who stayed behind could look for support to only one institution—the church. Now that institution, caught in the squeeze of a diminishing flock and resources in the city, seems to be abandoning them as parish after parish disappears in consolidation.

"They feel betrayed—and that's not too harsh a word either," said one Catholic priest in Minneapolis, where 10 ethnic parishes are being merged into one. "No longer will they be served by a Polish church or a Slavic church, but all will be in one church and the bitterness this has engendered takes many forms. Some priests marched in a civil-rights march—a quiet, orderly march—and three church trustees resigned. Community kids leafleting outside the church in opposition to the Vietnam war were bodily removed by church members."

The Reverend Gino Baroni—the son of an immigrant coal miner, long an activist in civil-rights work and now head of the Task Force on Urban Problems—describes the ethnic community as flotsam in society.

"They cut themselves off from their cultural roots, because that was how you became an American," he said. "Now all the rules of society are changing and they have nothing to hold onto that seems real. All the rules have changed: He wants to send his son to college but is afraid he will come back looking like Mark Rudd and denouncing him for a fool. He wants to own a house but inflation and taxes are eating him alive. His church and the history of his homeland made Communism the archenemy of his life and his own children denounce him for supporting a war his government has labeled an anti-Communist crusade."

This pro-war sentiment in ethnic communities is a direct result of the changing character of these neighborhoods. Most are populated now by post-World War II immigrants made up largely of the middle-class elements of the old country who fled the expansion of Soviet influence in Eastern Europe.

These new immigrants have changed the character of the community. Few quaint scenes of street dancers or bocce ball games remain. These were the entertainments of the rural immigrants, most of whom now live in the suburbs. The newer immigrants have formal dances and debutante balls, efforts to maintain the higher social status they enjoyed back home.

But in turning back on themselves in response to change and challenge many see dangerous possibilities of political exploitation. A basic conclusion of a Workshop on Urban Ethnic Community Development sponsored by a welter of Catholic organizations was:

"In the present vacuum of concern by government, the foundations, the universities and, yes, the church, the danger is terribly real that the demagogues of hate will prey on the anguish of their communities and will divide those who should be natural allies in reordering the priorities of our society in the interest of human needs."

But the conflict goes beyond one of politics or race. Perhaps because it has been less closely examined, it seems to reflect all of the ills of a radically changing society.

The Reverend Paul J. Asciolla, an Italian-American Catholic priest in Chicago, has studied the ethnic American at home probably as closely as anyone, and he paints a grim picture of an ethnic worker's day:

"He gets up before daylight in a home he can no longer control because the kids have a better education than he and they look down on him for it. He takes a dirty train or bus to work—and the fare has increased again, cutting deeper into his inflation-riddled pay check."

SAN FRANCISCO'S CHINESE RESIST SCHOOL BUSING

by DOUGLAS E. KNEELAND

SAN FRANCISCO—The old Sun Sing Theater on Grant Avenue, the gaily lighted, tourist-choked heart of Chinatown, was jammed. Its 800 seats had filled up early, mostly with serious-faced Chinese women and squirming youngsters. Scores of latecomers stood patiently in the aisles and along the walls.

They were not well-to-do, most of them, but they had paid $2.50 or $5 apiece for the benefit show they were watching. That's a lot of money to the working people of Chinatown, especially to see such familiar local acts as dances by the Flower Drum Club and the Heavenly Lion Club.

Still, they obviously thought it was worth it. The money will be used to help set up private classes unless the Chinese Parents Committee can find a way to block a Federal District Court integration order that would cause many of their elementary grade children to be bused to other parts of the city when schools reopen here September 13.

"If you're giving better education by this busing situation, I'm for it," declared Mrs. Bertha Chan, a diminutive woman in a black-and-white-checked suit who is chairman of the Parents Committee. "But if you can't, leave my children at home."

Mrs. Chan's tone left no doubt that she felt busing would not improve the quality of education.

"I think in every community everyone feels the same way," she continued. "They want their children in neighborhood schools."

The court-ordered plan would affect thousands of the 47,000 children in San Francisco's 102 elementary schools. And predominantly white groups have been loudly threatening a citywide boycott should it be implemented.

The Chinese, however, pleading a special need, have chosen, for the most part, to go it alone. But time is running out on them.

Over the weekend, United States Supreme Court Justice William O.

Douglas rejected their request for a stay of the court order. In their petition, they had argued that unless the stay were granted, "the cultural and educational life of the Chinese community in San Francisco will, as a practical matter, be destroyed."

Quentin Kopp, attorney for the Chinese Parents Committee, had sought the stay to give his clients a chance to intervene in a suit brought by the National Association for the Advancement of Colored People against the San Francisco School District. The Board of Education is appealing the District Court ruling but the Chinese contend that the board has not adequately represented their point of view.

"The Chinese children are being subjected to a so-called cure that they neither need nor want," Mr. Kopp said upon learning of the Douglas decision. "We'll consider seriously filing a new suit in District Court based on the Civil Rights Act."

He said that the Chinese were being assigned "purely on the basis of race. That is a violation of their constitutional rights," he added.

Meanwhile, according to the Parents Committee, more than 1,000 youngsters have already been signed up to attend the planned private schools. Classes will be held in the community's five Chinese schools, where the language and culture are already taught for two hours a day to about 2,000 children.

"We're anticipating a lot of empty buses," said Dr. Dennis Wong, a 37-year-old pharmacist who is a leading spokesman for the Chinese community.

Seldom has an issue so stirred the public passions of Chinatown.

"It reminds me of the lioness in the jungle," said Herb Chew, a member of the Parents Committee, as he surveyed the overflow crowd at the theater. "You know, how docile she is until you bother the cubs? That reminds me of how we are about this thing with our children."

"We have a saying," added Dr. Wong, "that it takes 10 years to plant a tree and it takes 100 years to cultivate a person."

People still talk like that in Chinatown, with gentle allusions to lionesses and trees. But Dr. Wong was making a point.

"From that you can see," he went on, "it's not an easy thing to solve these integration problems. You must earn the respect of yourself and of other persons.

"The Chinese have gone through that process. We have been discriminated against here. It's much documented how the Chinese have been subjugated in San Francisco and in the mining towns and railroad towns.

"We have been passive. Now we are in the process of integrating. You can see the Chinese living in all neighborhoods in San Francisco."

Actually, according to the best estimates in the community, about 50,000 of the 70,000 to 75,000 Chinese in the city live within the expanding borders of Chinatown. With a population that has nearly doubled since the easing of immigration restrictions in 1965, the Chinese have rapidly spilled over into such areas as North Beach, Russian Hill and Nob Hill.

The tide of immigration, mostly from Hong Kong, which is still estimated at more than 4,000 persons a year, has further complicated the problems of crowded Chinatown.

Along with the other arguments against the integration plan that are used by the Parents Committee, which include most of those heard in white neighborhoods, such as the physical dangers of busing, the Chinese are concerned about the language barrier for young immigrants.

"What happens to the child 5 or 8 years old," asked Henry Gee, another of the earnest young parents, "who can't speak English well enough to talk? What happens if he's lost? He can't speak English well enough to say he's lost. We're worried about these kids who've come over here and they want to ship them out there."

For many in Chinatown, as for Mr. Gee, anywhere else in the city is "out there."

"The main thing is, we have to be recognized as Chinese," Mr. Gee went on, "not as a minority to be used against another minority. We don't want to be called a minority. We want to be considered Chinese and I think we have been considered that."

Blacks are seldom mentioned in the polite language of Chinatown, except in occasional disclaimers, such as, "We have nothing against the colored," or "We have always gone to school with Negroes."

"We as Chinese are not against integration," Mr. Gee insisted. "We are against school busing."

But with the steady influx of Chinese from overseas into the already teeming neighborhood, rents and housing prices are high, preventing much integration of the area.

"One of the reasons we don't have a colored problem," Frank Wing, a youthful electrical contractor conceded, "is that it's too expensive for them. The prices of these houses are too high."

Noting that one of the reasons that the Chinese are caught in the integration fight is that many have remained in the city while large numbers of middle-class whites have fled to the suburbs Dr. Wong, the pharmacist, said determinedly:

"It's no good to run. Here we will make our stand. If you whites can't stop this thing, we Chinese will stop it."

SCHOOL CRISIS HELPS OCEAN HILL'S "SEARCH FOR A COMMUNITY"

by BILL KOVACH

The Ocean Hill-Brownsville district of Brooklyn is a small piece of New York City filled with people searching for something that the outside world has assumed they already had—a thing called community.

By almost any standard, the word "community"—implying a whole range of common interests and organizations—is misapplied to Ocean Hill-Brownsville.

The idea that there is an Ocean Hill-Brownsville "community"—an idea that comes easily to those outside—is an indication of the power of the issue of community control of schools.

The simplest test, that of a sense of place, brings the concept of community into immediate question. On a map, Ocean Hill-Brownsville looks like a piece taken from a jigsaw puzzle of Brooklyn.

Within its boundaries—roughly Hancock Street and East New York Avenue north and south, and Ralph Avenue and Van Sindern Avenue east and west— lie about 100 city blocks.

Within these lines are parts of two communities with long historical identities. One is the northern tip of Brownsville, an area frequently singled out as one of the fastest decaying residential areas of the city; the other is a portion of Bedford-Stuyvesant, a name now nearly synonymous with ghetto, that is called Ocean Hill.

Those living there don't know why it is called Ocean Hill.

"It was always just referred to as 'the hill' or 'no man's land,' " one resident said. "I don't know why it's called Ocean Hill."

Lying as it does partly in two communities—and at times claimed as part of either, both or neither—Ocean Hill-Brownsville does not fall completely within or without a police district, a court district or an Assembly district. Political lines cut the district so that neighbor may never meet neighbor at the polling booth or "community" functions.

Oddly enough it was this alienation as part of any community that began the drive toward the building of an Ocean Hill-Brownsville community.

In the spring of 1965 the City Board of Education created a new school district—District 17. In drawing the bounds of that district, the area called Ocean Hill—which had previously been part of a district in Bedford-Stuyvesant with one school board member—was put into the new district but had no representation on the new district board.

This action occurred as the concept of community control of the schools was spreading through the poorer areas of New York, and under the leadership of the Brownsville Community Council and church leaders, the parents of Ocean Hill began to discover one another as neighbors with a common interest.

Around the eight schools in Ocean Hill and part of Brownsville there began to grow a feeling of mutual need and interest.

The results of that common interest are now making daily headlines.

Walking through the district a visitor finds few physical signs of a community in the making. The transition from block to block is so abrupt it is hard to see a bond that would hold them together.

There are blocks of neat, well-maintained brownstones and massive highrise housing developments. Across the street there are blocks filled with trash and litter, looking more than anything like the blasted blocks of a war zone.

Statistics compiled in a Board of Education survey of the district show a highly fluid population (56 per cent have lived here less than 10 years) of Negroes (71 per cent), Puerto Ricans (24 per cent), whites (4 per cent) and Orientals (1 per cent).

These figures show too that 68 per cent of those living here did not finish high school and over half of them earn less than $5,000 a year.

If anything, the statistics indicate Ocean Hill-Brownsville is not the place one would pick to organize a community.

But, around two figures in the list of percentages and decimals, the concept of community is formed: 9,000 students attend the district's schools and their parents (nearly 40 per cent of them) see education as the No. 1 issue in their lives.

"The schools have brought these people closer together than they've ever been and the concept of community—community involvement, community control—is beginning to take shape."

That was how Mrs. Thelma Hamilton of the Brownsville Community Council, an antipoverty agency, described the emergence of Ocean Hill-Brownsville as more than a descriptive phrase. Mrs. Hamilton has worked closely with people in the district to organize the local governing board to run the schools there.

"More than anything else," she added, "what this school struggle has done is to give these people an understanding of how the city works and the necessity of unity—of responding as a community."

This feeling crops up in unexpected ways—with a policeman, for example. A Negro patrolman with 21 years in the 73d Precinct—which includes Ocean Hill-Brownsville—searched desperately for a way to "clear the community's name" on the crime problem. It was true, he agreed, that the 73d had one of the highest reported crime rates in the city. But, he added:

"We've got all kinds of crime, but you've got to remember that's controlled a lot by the moon. You sit in the station house and you'll see."

Sensing his listener's disbelief, he quickly added:

"I know. I had a lieutenant tell me that 10 years ago and I didn't believe him, but you watch. When there's a quarter moon things are pretty quiet, but let it come a full moon and the junkies and the burglars all go crazy. You just watch it now and see if it doesn't happen."

A little farther on, across the street from J.H.S. 271, the feeling of community is stronger. William Hilliard of 1134 Herkimer Street speaks of his home there as part of a community where people work together.

"We don't complain to the sanitation people about the streets here," he said. "We just all get together and move our cars and sweep the streets when they don't get it done on time."

He paused from polishing his car to call across the street to a young girl:

"What were you doing out so late last night? Did your mother know where you were?"

They live down the street, he said in explanation. "We sort of keep an eye out for each other—especially since this school thing started, we all sorta look out for the kids."

John Ragone, a white store-owner who was born in Brownsville and later moved out, maintains his business across from J.H.S. 271. He said he had seen the neighborhood change from about 50 per cent white to almost completely Negro and Puerto Rican. He added that it was still a good neighborhood in which to do business, although insurance has become difficult to get.

For older residents, the search for community is for something found and lost before by the two communities of which they are sometimes a part, sometimes not. Originally settled by Scots or Dutch, the communities of Brownsville and Bedford-Stuyvesant attracted Jewish people seeking to escape slums of the Lower East Side around the turn of the century. The over-all area—especially Brownsville—quickly became one of the world's largest and best-known Jewish settlements.

The early communities of farmers gave way to the community of Jews built around nearly 100 synagogues and dozens of neighborhood organizations. Again the pattern of change came after World War II when Negroes and Puerto Ricans poured in.

Sitting amid the ruins of what was once a main street—Prospect Place—three Negroes reminisced.

William Hayes, George Jones and James Battle have all lived here for at least 20 years. The weak rays of a late afternoon October sun had attracted them to the gaping doorway on a dead street where they sat and talked. Stretching away on either side of them was a whole block of vacant, crumbling buildings, marked for demolition. Faded signs told of earlier days—for some stores only five months ago—when this was a street of shops and stores.

"Used to be," said Mr. Battle, "that you could get anything you wanted here without ever going out of the neighborhood. But all the Jews who owned these stores are gone now."

They had moved out much as they moved in. As succeeding generations prospered they sought the open spaces farther out that had drawn their fathers and grandfathers to this place. And, as their population declined, their organizations and institutions moved out.

Mr. Hayes remembered, too: "Yeah," he said, pointing to holes that once were display windows across the street, "that used to be the best place to buy suits; and that was a butcher shop, and that, uh, that was a shoe store."

Mr. Jones interrupted: "No, that was the fish market. Remember?"

"It sure would be good to see the street alive again," said Mr. Hayes.

That hope is alive and repeated by many in Ocean Hill-Brownsville.

Perhaps they see the same spark Mrs. Hamilton sees.

"I don't think these people will ever go back to the old apathy that was there before the school thing started," she says. "You know, we got over 1,000 people to vote in the school board election—that's three times as many as usually vote in an election."

"They're beginning to have hope now. They're beginning to see how to work together. They're talking now about how to get the place cleaned up a little, how to get the streets repaired. They're beginning to think like a community."

Then, too, in their experiment for community control of the schools, Ocean Hill-Brownsville has held to an important aspect of community—tradition.

One guidebook to New York says the area known as Brownsville has always been hospitable to new social movements.

"From 1915 to 1921," says a guide done by the Works Progress Administration in the nineteen-thirties, "this district elected Socialists to the New York State Assembly. In 1936 an American Labor Party candidate was elected to the Assembly, only to lose his seat in 1938. In 1916 Margaret Sanger established on Amboy Street the first birth-control clinic in America."

URBAN RENEWAL GIVING THE POOR AN OPPORTUNITY TO INCREASE POWER

by DAVID K. SHIPLER

More and more slum residents, almost all of them black or Puerto Rican, are exercising a power they have not had for long: the ability to block an urban renewal project in their neighborhoods, or shape its direction, or get a project where there was none before.

There was a time not many years ago when no huge crowds from the city's poverty areas turned up at City Hall to attend Planning Commission hearings, and even if they had the Planning Commission would probably not have listened.

Since the final years of the Wagner administration, panels of local residents have attained the power to shape decisions about what kind of housing will go where, who will design and build and own it and how tenants will be relocated from the tenements to be demolished.

In the 53 urban renewal areas throughout the city, the influence of "the community," as these articulate and outspoken residents are known, flows from their own drive and the initiative of the Federal Government to involve them in the planning process. The city has implemented the Federal mandate.

Black pride and self-assurance have worked in combination with the Federal antipoverty program to produce a sophistication and a battery of neighborhood organizations that have enabled some slum dwellers to find the pressure points of city government.

They can stop projects when they want to, as they have hindered construction of the proposed state office building in Harlem.

At a recent meeting of the Planning Commission, the long, wooden benches, like church pews, were crammed with people, and crowds filled the aisles and spilled into the corridor outside.

There was a hush as the people strained to listen to a woman from Harlem who was facing a row of commissioners seated behind a curved dais.

She began in low, angry tones, letting her voice rise finally to a shout. "We need your help." She jabbed a finger toward the dais. "But we'll accept it not on your terms. We'll accept it on our terms!"

The crowd behind her exploded into cheers, whoops and whistles. They were fighting a city plan to tear down what they said were four good buildings in Harlem to expand a site for new housing. But perhaps more important, they were fighting the city's failure to consult their established organizations on the plan.

The Planning Commission, faced with such a wall of opposition, voted to let the buildings stand.

"They have become pretty sharp; they know what they want," remarked one city employe who works in the Brooklyn Model Cities program.

These influential ghetto residents have formed a new class of their own, above the desperately poor. Most of the members of this new class were once on welfare but are now employed full-time in antipoverty programs, and they have been criticized for bourgeois attitudes that have led one city official to describe them as "povertycrats."

The city bureaucracy is listening to the "povertycrats." Planners have moved from high floors in air-conditioned downtown offices to drafty storefronts within the slums, exposing themselves to the turbulent winds of politics among the local people.

One high city housing official, who asked to remain anonymous, said, "We want the community to be able to sock it to the city."

That is just what happened when the city wanted to demolish the four buildings in Harlem without following its usual procedure of first asking the established organizations there.

Consequently, the objective of the highest housing officials in the Lindsay administration has been to build antipoverty organizations, block associations and other community groups into bases of political support for projects.

"You can't do it any other way today," commented Jason R. Nathan, who is soon leaving his job as the city's Housing and Development Administrator. "The old Moses approach of condemning 700,000 units of housing and expecting everybody to sit still—those glorious unsophisticated days are gone."

Robert Moses, head of the Slum Clearance Committee in the nineteen-fifties, used what came to be known as the "bulldozer approach," and the technique made "urban renewal" a chilling term for slum residents.

Now, in the evenings throughout the city, hundreds of people pour into church basements or school auditoriums for New England-style town meetings. There, in the course of discussing housing, they also vie for power and influence within their neighborhoods, often splitting along ethnic, racial or economic lines.

But Mr. Nathan maintains that projects move more quickly with community participation than they would without. And there are other advantages.

"If you've planned it yourself, man, you're not going to burn it down," said a young man from Bedford-Stuyvesant.

"When you are part of a creation, then of course it's you, it's part of you," explained Mrs. Dorothea Merchant, a city employe who works as a liaison between East Harlem residents and the Housing and Development Administration.

"You've given yourself to it, and you think, 'It's mine.' " she said. "It's quite inspirational."

Some professional planners have resisted community influence as a trespass upon their own territory. But others, such as Peter Abeles, a consultant to the city, have found their perceptions sharpened by local residents.

"I tend to think in terms of 90 blocks," Mr. Abeles said. "They are sensitive to what's happening in a block down the street."

The city has retained final authority over decisions as it must when it uses Federal money. Washington mandates community participation, but warns against community control.

Stopping short of giving real control has created some suspicion, bitterness and frustration among residents.

"True community participation never existed, really," remarked an active resident of the South Bronx.

"When the community talks of participation, they view this as completely different from what politicians and agencies view it," said Horace Morancie, the Mayor's project director for the Central Brooklyn Model Cities area.

"The community views it as control," he said. "But to control something, you must control the funds. Unless you control the money, you don't have control."

The city uses the terms "participation" and "partnership" to describe what officials believe is the proper role of communities. But these are loose words, some community leaders say, and their vagueness has allowed the system of planning to remain highly centralized, despite the community influence.

"Everybody's got to talk to Don Elliott or Jay Nathan or Bob Hazen because nobody else has got any authority," said one official outside the city government. Donald H. Elliott is chairman of the City Planning Commission, and Robert G. Hazen is Commissioner of Development under Mr. Nathan.

This means that the community's role has no formal structure in most neighborhoods. It depends largely on the attitudes of the highest officials.

In the Coney Island urban renewal area, for example, the city officials listen more closely to a predominantly black organization—once an antipoverty group—than to a white group of businessmen.

In other areas where there is white resistance to low-income housing, the Lindsay administration has found it difficult to match its goal of community participation with its policy of improving housing for the poor.

There has been some movement toward structuring local power. The City Council enacted legislation several months ago requiring the Planning Commission to consult with local planning boards, which are appointed by the borough presidents, before acting on matters affecting their neighborhoods. The commission need not follow the local boards' advice, but it must listen.

Each of the three Model Cities neighborhoods—Central Brooklyn, Harlem-East Harlem and the South Bronx—makes its desires known to the city through an elected board, most of whose members are well-known names in antipoverty organizations, churches and businesses.

In the largely Puerto Rican South Bronx, the "povertycrats" from the Hunts Point Multi-Service Center hold eight of the 23 seats, including the chairmanship, of the elected Model Cities committee. The others are businessmen, clergymen and employes of other poverty programs.

This discrepancy between the slum residents who have the voice and those very poor for whom the programs are designed has distressed some community residents and helped breed their deep suspicion of government.

"The simple people aren't involved," said Reverend Louis R. Gigante, a member of the committee and pastor of St. Athanasius Roman Catholic Church.

One of the eight is Ramon S. Velez, the stout, $18,000-a-year director of the Multi-Service Center, who is duly regarded and envied as one of the most influential men in the South Bronx.

He has 275 employes and he plans to hire more for his $4 million-a-year program, which his enemies have likened to a political club. He holds membership in 20 other organizations.

"I have no power," Mr. Velez said recently, as he sat at his desk, flanked by American and Puerto Rican flags. "I don't plan to run for election, I am not going to run for political office."

Since the Model Cities committee decides which organizations are to get certain Federal funds, a conflict of interest question has been raised by the Department of Housing and Urban Development and the Lindsay administration.

In a letter, September 26, Wendell P. Levister, general counsel to the Mayor's Model Cities Policy Committee, said the administration had "serious concern" about so many Multi-Service Center employes having seats on the South Bronx committee.

"Such employes may not serve in a voting capacity," the letter concludes.

But even Father Gigante, who is said by Mr. Velez to be seeking to extend his own influence, believes excluding antipoverty officials altogether is unrealistic. The "povertycrats" are often the most articulate and sophisticated, he said.

Furthermore, Mr. Velez, who is 36, contends, "I'm still in my mind as poor as I was 15 years ago. Money is not what makes a middle-class person. It's his attitude."

John Edmonds, project director in Harlem, echoes this. The activists, he says, "basically have the same social experience" as the very poor. "They live in the same neighborhood, they live in the same houses, go to the same schools, their social contacts are the same."

They have disdain for able-bodied men who are on welfare, he said, but not for women who are receiving welfare aid for their children.

However, in a recent study of antipoverty programs in a dozen cities, Dr. Kenneth B. Clark, a black psychologist who heads the Metropolitan Applied Research Center, concluded, "The poor serve as pawns in a struggle in which their interests are not the primary concern.

"The leaders talk in the name of the poor, and extensive funds are appropriated and spent in their name without direct concern for, or serious attempts at, involvement of the poor."

In the South Bronx, the competition for power among groups resulted in death last August. During a fight one evening outside a meeting, a 20-year-old worker for the Hunts Point Community Corporation, Edwin Rivera, was allegedly pushed in front of a car.

Three employes of Mr. Velez's Multi-Service Center, which was trying to get a share of an allocation of funds intended for the Community Corporation, were arrested and charged with homicide.

"Everybody's at each other's throats," said Mr. Velez, who thinks that he was really the target, and that the plot to kill him backfired.

Fighting derives from the fact that "the money that's coming is crumbs," he said. "There's so little, it's going to create conflict."

But in a sense, friction is healthy, Mr. Velez observed. "To give people an opportunity to develop themselves through conflict, through struggles, the same way unions developed themselves—that's good.''

But this kind of infighting has led some government officials and experts outside of government to oppose community participation as practiced by the Lindsay administration.

''Community groups have gotten two very distinct ideas,'' said one well-known official outside the city who asked not to be identified. ''One is that there's money in this, that if you raise enough hell there's money in it.

''Second, the city has made very clear that until it is satisfied that a particular community group is representative and makes known what it wants, the city isn't going to do anything. I think it's wild.''

Roger Starr, executive director of the Citizens' Housing and Planning Council, echoed that sentiment. ''It's one thing to consult,'' he said. ''It's another to tell them they're going to have the final say.''

City officials contend that residents have never been told they would have the final say. But they believe the great gulf between the poor and the Establishment, the deep suspicions about government, are being overcome, slowly.

RESIDENTS AND ARCHITECTS PLAN LOCAL CENTER IN BROOKLYN

by JOHN DARNTON

During the Reign of Terror in the French Revolution, a wooden, two-wheeled cart known as a *charrette* lumbered through the streets of Paris carrying the condemned to the steps of the guillotine.

A century later, a wagon known by the same name made the rounds of garrets that housed architecture students and brought their final projects to the Beaux Arts for critique.

As might be expected, the plans were sometimes less than complete, and students would race alongside the cart to scribble last-minute revisions and corrections.

The practice gave rise to the altered word "charette" spelled with one R, which in the lexicon of architects means a project hastily designed, sometimes by a team, under deadline pressure.

Today, the term is used to describe a new technique of "total community planning." This technique calls for the bringing together of an area's residents for discussions on designing a facility, such as a school to serve as a multipurpose center of activity for their community. In this context, charette is often spelled with two R's.

In the East New York section of Brooklyn, a charette was set up in October, 1969, to design a high school and three intermediate schools in the heart of the poor neighborhood. The ideas that the group formulated have now reached the first stage—the interviewing of architects—in a long and uncertain road toward realization.

The group began with a budget of $50,000 from the central Board of Education and $20,000 from the Department of Health, Education and Welfare. The Government also sponsored similar groups in other cities, notably Baltimore, under a plan that has since been discontinued for lack of funds.

The East New York charette was the first here and grew to be one of the largest in the country. It included residents and representatives of community organizations, consulting architects and educators, students from Howard University and even neighborhood children.

"There was never anything like this before," said Leo Lillard, a local activist who works for East New York Housing Services. "Everyone was involved, from white gun clubs to Black Panthers."

"At first the term 'charette' sounded very strange," he said. "But only the process was imported. All the ideas came from us."

The participants were asked to submit sketches of what the complex should look like and suggestions on what it should include. After months of planning, in smaller groups that discussed everything from curriculum to narcotics addiction, the participants held 12-hour sessions five days a week during April and May in a vacant warehouse.

The outline that emerged was for a 12-block educational center, at a projected cost of around $70 million, that would also serve the social, cultural and recreational needs of the blighted area lying between a string of cemeteries and Jamaica Bay.

The plans called for a planetarium, a nuclear reactor, three theaters, a swimming pool, a museum for local art, a cafeteria that could be used as a neighborhood restaurant at night and a multimedia center with a film studio and broadcasting facilities for a local radio station.

There would be centers for day care, health and narcotics treatment, to be staffed by students in the social sciences who would receive credit for the work. There would even be housing for the families displaced by the project.

Instead of being divided among four separate schools, the estimated total of 10,000 students would be classed in "houses" of about 540. These houses would be roughly analogous to the semiautonomous houses at Harvard and Yale. Each house would be subdivided into four "clusters" and would have its own administration and library. But the houses would use central facilities for such needs as the science laboratory.

The ideas that the charette developed proved so innovative that they have astounded and excited a number of city-planning officials.

"It's a very interesting concept," said Douglas Thompson of the city-planning staff's Brooklyn office. "There was a strong functional and implied architectural relationship between the school and the community, a total breakdown of the usual rigid line between the two."

Others voiced enthusiasm about the fact that the planning had begun at the lowest level—among those who would actually use the buildings—and had worked its way up, a reversal of the usual procedure.

"There's no question that city schools have been a failure, and that something new has to emerge," said Leopold Berman, an architect who served as consultant to the charette. "What is proposed here came from the community, has the support of the community, and that's the only chance for success."

Almost everyone connected with the project sees a clash in the months ahead, when the time comes to select the final architects, agree on the blueprints and guide the plans for the project through a plethora of city agencies.

Participants in the struggle would include:

The central Board of Education, which set up the charette and still has a say in the planning because the complex includes a high school, which remains under the board's supervision.

Community School Board 19, elected in March, which has a conservative tone and might tend to favor a rapid and more traditional school-construction program.

The charette, which technically dissolved in July but whose members continue to meet informally.

The district superintendent, Mrs. Elizabeth C. O'Daly, whose main concern is to find "more empty seats." Over the last three years, the number of students on half-session has been reduced to 2,000 from 6,000, but the district is facing an invasion of housing cooperatives.

Among the board's nine members, there are two blacks and no Puerto Ricans, while of the 37,566 students in the district's 28 schools, 50 per cent are black and 36 per cent are Puerto Rican.

Of the board's seven whites, five come from a higher-income predominantly white section, roughly north of Atlantic Avenue, and one from an integrated area dotted with high-rise apartments south of Linden Boulevard. The majority are church-affiliated or Conservative party candidates.

The board is sensitive to the charge, raised repeatedly at a recent meeting, that it has too many whites. Blacks from the audience bitterly prefaced their remarks with such statements as: "All we have to do is look at you to see that we're not represented around here!"

When the community board took office in July, it asked for and received written confirmation from the central board that, in fact, the charette no longer existed. But the influence of the charette lingers, and a number of city officials appear to regard it as a representative voice.

At its zenith, the charette involved 180 people. It sent representatives to other cities to gather new ideas in education, and drew upon the services of such educators as Dr. Max Wolff, senior research sociologist for the Center for Urban Education.

"It was such an exciting experience," remarked the charette chairman,

Mrs. Priscilla Wooten, an educator, "that it changed the lives of everyone who came in contact with it."

The meetings were often stormy. At one point, officers of the United Community Centers, an organization representing a neighboring area, withdrew from the charette in a bitter dispute.

They charged that the charette had been taken over by intimidating and anti-Semitic black militants whose aim was segregationist. The charge was denied by former charette members and disputed by outside observers.

Although $1 million has been budgeted this year for planning the complex, construction is years away. The site, now fixed between New Lots and Sutter Avenues between Ashford and Berriman Streets, was approved at a joint hearing of the community and central boards in October. It is now being considered by the city's Site Selection Office.

WHAT DAY CARE MEANS TO THE CHILDREN, THE PARENTS, THE TEACHERS, THE COMMUNITY, THE PRESIDENT

by PATRICIA LYNDEN

The 4's are in their midmorning work period. Abife Sawyer, the chunky, middle-aged, black teacher, sits on a scaled-down child's chair in a corner of the big, bright room and keeps an eye on a fort-building project: "We don't kick blocks, George, because one might fly and hurt someone. Vincent, how can the trucks go through the gate when the trucks are larger than the gate?"

The shelves around the room are filled with books, toys and tools. The rest of the dozen children in the class, which is equally divided among blacks, Puerto Ricans and white Anglo-Saxon types, work in small groups at woodcraft or painting—whatever they choose—with Abife's assistant, a young man with sideburns, and the student teacher, a young woman from Mills College of Education. The supervision and curriculum of the class are calculated to provide just the right balance between permissiveness and control, yet to afford plenty of stimulation. There is a consulting psychiatrist, Dr. Stephen Bennett, 41, who wanders in for a few moments of observation. "This is a real picture-book day-care center," he says, and adds, "It's even integrated."

This is the Lexington Houses Day Care Center, situated in a dreary, middle-income housing project at East 98th Street and Park Avenue, on the fringes of Spanish Harlem. Because it is so close to the Silk-Stocking District, it also has some children from the Upper East Side. It is supported by the city's Department of Social Services, which dispenses a combination of Federal, state and city money to it and 112 other city centers.

To working parents, Lexington Houses center is a good place to leave their kids during the day for as little as $1 a week. To its trained teachers with their degrees in early-childhood education, it provides children with an important educational experience. To President Nixon it is a means of getting welfare mothers off the dole and into jobs. Last fall, in his message to Congress on the Administration's welfare package, the President asked an additional $368 million to increase day-care facilities across the nation, thus providing for 150,000 more preschool children and 300,000 more school-age children. These would be mainly children of mothers now on welfare. At present, because of limited facilities, only half a million children in the country get day care of any kind. In New York City only 10 per cent of the 150,000 children who need it get it.

The President's day-care legislation, now making its slow way through Congress, is the means by which Mr. Nixon "hopes to make a big dent in poverty," according to Jule Sugarman, former chief of Head Start and now head of the Office of Child Development (a division of the Department of Health, Education and Welfare) in Washington. "The Government would pay people family assistance, put them in training and/or employment," Sugarman explains, "and, if they need it, give them day care as well." Sugarman insists that the program, even though a welfare measure, would be educational as well as custodial. The Federal Government would make sure its centers were staffed by qualified people, he says, by contracting directly with individual agencies—settlement houses, local Head Start programs, qualified church groups, even competent private groups—instead of giving the money to the state to pass out through their own, sometimes inadequate, programs. Flexible teacher qualifications would allow for variations in the skills available from state to state. In New York, where, in Sugarman's words, day-care standards are "pretty high," the Nixon plan would not noticeably alter the quality of the program.

While the President's proposal is applauded by early-childhood educators, his motives are not. For day-care professionals, getting a mother off welfare is at the bottom of the list of reasons for accepting a child at a center. Mrs. Shirley Cowan, the small, earnest director of the Lexington Houses Center, admits that she, in fact, sometimes encourages a mother to stay on welfare. "We are not here just to get mothers off welfare," she says indignantly. "We are not providing a baby-sitting service. We will take a child for a variety of reasons—sibling problems at home, an emotionally unstable parent, a disturbed child who might benefit from a group experience. We will often take a child even though he comes from Park Avenue if we see he'll go crazy at home.'' And she adds, ''You know, sometimes we get a welfare mother who comes in here and asks us to take her child so she can go to work. If we feel this child is not ready for day care, we'll encourage her to continue on welfare until he is ready.''

One possible consequence of Mr. Nixon's plan, which would doubtlessly dismay the President, is that day-care centers could become a focus for political action as the city's public schools did last year. The issue would be the same—community control.

Across town from the Lexington Houses center is a community-controlled center. It is called the West 80th Street Community Day Care Center. For the last three and a half years it has muddled along on private donations and small grants from various government agencies while negotiating for permanent support by the city's Department of Social Services. Negotiations have been slow in part because the D.S.S. customarily retains some control over the agencies it finances and the West 80th street center is demanding complete autonomy. Dorothy Pitman, a striking young black mother with a remarkable political talent and intellectual sophistication that belies the gaps in her education, founded the West 80th Street operation when she couldn't get her two young daughters into a city-run center. Her major innovation is a governing board of directors composed entirely of parents. Usually, as at the Lexington Houses center, a day-care board consists of professionals and a smattering of prominent citizens. Many on Mrs. Pitman's board are mothers who have been or are now on welfare. And contrary to what Mr. Nixon might hope, they and the center's other parents have become politicized and militant now that they have the center to give them a political base and a focus for action.

One of their demands, for example, is that the D.S.S. fund their center without requiring the usual state accreditation for head teachers or the minimum two years of college for assistant teachers. The center, as the parents see it, can help to upgrade the community by giving jobs or on-the-job training to persons among the poor who want to work in day care. They would be people who the board feels are qualified and talented with children even though they do not necessarily meet the formal qualifications the D.S.S. requires. ''What does a credential or a degree tell you about how good a teacher is?'' snaps Mrs. Pitman. ''All they ever teach children is white, middle-class values that tell black children they are second-class and that stifle curiosity.''

The center, which will soon move to better quarters in a Chinese restaurant it has bought and is now renovating, has spent most of its life in the squalid Hotel Endicott, a hangout for drug addicts. In the center's two enormous and practically windowless rooms, seven adults—black and white, some of them trained teachers—care for and teach 37 children, most of them black, from the West Side's slums. Many of them are children from homes on welfare or formerly on welfare. Roaches abound—in the office file cabinets, behind the children's paintings on the walls, among the children's bedrolls. There are regular floods from the ceiling, caused by rains or showering tenants above, which destroy toys, books and other equipment.

Outside, in front of the hotel, as gusts of wind send swirls of filth along the sidewalks, junkies slouch in their peculiar S-shaped posture, nodding or just waiting. Money is always a problem, and at times the educational director has to dip into her own purse to pay for laundering the children's blankets. Still, the cook turns out a tasty hot meal every day, the children are taught the rudiments of knowledge just as they are at the well-ordered and well-financed Lexington Houses center across town, and somehow teachers and children manage a happy élan despite the roaches, the disorder and the crises.

Mrs. Shirley Cowan sits in her corner office just to the right of the front entrance of the Lexington Houses center, manning the buzzer that opens the front door. She is fluttery and talkative and could be a clubby, charity-bazaar worker except that she is a hard-working, dedicated professional who is both director of the center and a faculty member at Mills College of Education, which founded the center. Her husband is a well-to-do lawyer, so while servants tend her house she works long hours, as she says, "to bring richness and stimulation into the lives of children who, because of a lack of mobility, may not have been exposed to a lot of things."

Mrs. Cowan thinks day care should be made universal. "A child must learn that there are other caring people in the world whom he can trust," she says. "He must also learn that there are many kinds of people in the world. The children here are given a lot of stimulation. They begin to see themselves as children, as individuals, and when they start school, they are ready. In fact, sometimes the teachers complain because day-care children are advanced beyond other children when they get to first grade."

The children call her Shirley even though she is a grandmother and near 50. The teachers are called by their first names, too. Shirley doesn't know why. "It's always been like that in day care," she says, "probably something from Dewey's ideas." She tells me to wander about the rooms freely, that the children are used to having visitors and things are not run so tightly that an outsider would disrupt the order of the classrooms. "I like to keep things fluid and sort of free," she says.

In the classroom of the 3's, a new little girl in a brand-new coat and with red ribbons in her hair is leaving early—in tears. Her mother, a slim young Puerto Rican woman, leads the child by the hand, an exasperated expression on her face. Hilda Parrott, the head teacher, says in her soft, Virgin Islands accent, "I'll see you tomorrow, dear." She stands smiling at the sobbing child. Hilda is ageless except for her gray hair. On the walls around her hang children's art, about the only "work" the 3's do. "Now I want you to do everything she tells you, understand?" scolds the mother, bending over her daughter. The little girl sobs tragically. "She will be all right," Hilda says quietly. "It just takes a little time."

As they leave, another little girl comes out of the bathroom and stands before Hilda, an over-all strap thrust out to be buttoned. "Did you make pee-pee, dear?" Hilda inquires, buttoning the strap. The child nods. "Did you remember to flush?" The little girl nods again, then shakes her head no and skips off to flush. Does Hilda ever use the scientific words with the children? "Yes, I use the same words they use, because that's what they're used to, but I also use the proper words so they'll get to know them, too." I notice that the boys and girls use the same toilets together. "We don't separate them," Hilda replies. "The children get used to it right away and it is more natural."

The 5's are the oldest preschool group at the center. Next year they will start school, attending the other "plant," as Shirley calls it, in the afternoon. It is part of the Lexington Houses project but in another building. To get the 5's ready for the greater discipline of school, the teacher, mini-skirted, 24-year-old Kathy Dohn devotes the first morning hour to training in proper classroom deportment, which doesn't come easily. "Now remember, this is the period when we practice for the first grade," she says in the slow, distinct, slightly sing-songy manner favored by teachers of young children. She sits in a low chair facing the children, who sit cross-legged before her on the floor. "Manuel, that is not first-grade behavior," Kathy says with a frown as Manuel and Lawrence begin to wrestle.

She reaches for the large, visual-aid calendar and places it on her lap. "Now," she says peering over the top, "what day is today?" She points to "Wednesday" at the top of a column. "Wednesday," shouts Lawrence, falling over backwards giggling as Manuel clutches him by the neck. "Raise your hand, please. Manuel, I'm sorry. This is not first-grade behavior. I think you'd better go sit at the table by yourself until your behavior improves." There is no impatience or exasperation in her tone, just instruction. Manuel dives behind a white wooden structure that looks like a piece of picket fence. Kathy ignores him. "Danielle has her hand up. What day is today, Danielle?" "Wednesday," replies Danielle. "Very good," says Kathy.

As director, Shirley frequently stops by the classrooms to observe the teachers at work and see how they apply their training. She particularly keeps a sharp, critical eye on the younger ones whose immaturity and inexperience can be reflected in their work. On this day Shirley has picked up the center's school-age children herself from nearby P.S. 198, and walked them back to the day-care plant. Now, inside the classroom with the 6- and 7-year-olds, she stands at a distance and watches the two young women teachers.

She is rather annoyed with Jane, the assistant, a young, pretty blonde from a wealthy family who Shirley thinks is working at the center because her boyfriend is also on the staff. Jane is attempting too much control of the children too soon after a long school session. Shirley had suggested earlier that they be allowed to run free; her advice was not taken and now Jane has the children on chairs in a circle trying to plan the afternoon's activities with them. They are restless but Jane doesn't change her tack. "Who wants to go get lumber?" she asks, and for a few moments the group is stymied. Only one little boy understands that lumber means wood. Shirley comments with a touch of irritation, "She should have explained the word 'lumber' before she used it."

She will discuss this later with Jane, who has at last taken a group off to a lumberyard to buy wood. There is a faint look of exasperation on Shirley's face. "There is no one philosophy of teaching, no one way to teach," she says, walking back across the project grounds to her office. "All the educational philosophies have something to tell us. A skilled teacher knows what to do and when to do it."

Every other Tuesday, Dr. Bennett, the psychiatrist, hired by Mills College, comes to the center. A tall man with a wry expression, he has a crew cut and wears a dark suit. Today he is sitting in the faculty lounge having coffee and cookies with Shirley and saying that the need for day care goes beyond the President's plan to get mothers off welfare. "You know," he says, "this city is just filled with all kinds of spooky, borderline ladies, both white and black ladies, who raise a child in complete isolation without ever seeing anyone. These poor ladies, they just don't know how to mother. Living with them, the children are just completely overwhelmed. A lot of these white ladies are well educated and come from well-to-do families, but because of their emotional problems they wind up here," and he waves an arm at the window through which tenements are visible.

Shirley mentions a child, referred to the center by a hospital, who presumably had been on the way to a mental institution after a diagnosis of schizophrenia. Dr. Bennett agrees that the child's improvement since coming to the center has been nothing short of amazing. At first the newcomer spoke to no one, stepped on other children and toys alike if they happened to be in the way, rode a tricycle into a wall and then screamed in rage at the wall. The child now talks and plays with other children, though there was a brief setback during the summer after three weeks spent at home alone with the mother.

In Dr. Bennett's definition the mother is one of the "spooky white ladies," a daughter of parents from two rich and famous families. She was given the classic "poor little rich girl" treatment as a child—shuttled about among uncaring stepmothers, aunts and governesses. Now, in greatly reduced circumstances, she lives in a tenement alone with a small child nearly as emotionally sick as she is. Dr. Bennett shakes his head and says, "These issues go beyond Mr. Nixon's getting everyone back to work."

Shirley keeps in close touch with each child's family situation through informal meetings with the parents. The meetings often occur on Friday, the day mothers stop by Shirley's office to pay their children's fees, which range from $1 to $25.25 a week, depending on what they can afford. One Friday Shirley spends a long time with a tremulous, high-strung woman of 37 who finds being a mother to two young children overly burdensome. She has decided to give up her 7-year-old son to his father, from whom she is divorced, and in tears she tells Shirley of her decision. Shirley replies that it was the best possible solution, for the son will like to be with his father and now the 5-year-old daughter will be much happier with a less burdened mother. The mother brightens, wipes her eyes and smiles. Her face is an odd combination of haggard care and childish innocence. I ask her what the center has meant to her and breathlessly she replies, "Oh, I would really be lost without it. Mrs. Cowan is so understanding."

In a sense each child who is accepted into the center is a special case. The waiting list is so long that priority is given to those children with special needs. On this day, for example, one of the women who drops in to pay her $2 weekly fee is a lively, 48-year-old grandmother whose grandson of 9 lives with her and attends the center. "If I couldn't put him here, I would have had to give him up," she says, before leaving for her bookkeeping job. "His mother deserted him when he was 8 months old. I work all day and haven't been married for 11 years. His father is my son, and he lives with me, too, but he is just 26 and he can't raise the boy." After the grandmother leaves, Shirley adds that the child's father is also an alcoholic.

One mother who comes in to pay $3 for two preschool children is a pretty, young, black woman with straightened hair. She is recently up from the South and so inarticulate that she can respond to most questions only with a drawled "yes" or "no" or, more likely, a shrug. She earns $30 a week at a simple clerical job in a hotel accounting department. She is divorced and gets no financial help from her former husband, so "the welfare," as she calls it, gives her a biweekly supplement of $58.60. What would she do with her children if they didn't have the center to go to? She shrugs, then says, staring blankly, "I don't know. Maybe my cousin would keep them."

Then there is "fighting City Hall," something Shirley had to learn to do years ago. A black book in her desk is filled with phone numbers of obscure city agencies. She knows just which one to call when the street cleaners deposit their accumulations outside the center or the derelicts sleep in the empty building across the street, and she doesn't mind hearing herself described as "that weird lady" by voices at the other end of the line after she has telephoned every day for a month without results. Still, there are times when she even has to threaten a march on Gracie Mansion to get results.

On a Sunday morning at 10 about 100 parents and children are gathered outside for a long-planned Bear Mountain cookout. The buses were due half an hour ago and Shirley is frantic. She telephones the Mayor's Task Force, which agreed to send the buses, and is told by a Miss Cook that she is sorry but there is nothing that can be done. "Please," Shirley pleads, "tell the man at the bus company that I'll pay him anything, just get the buses here." Miss Cook agrees to try, but several phone calls later, at 11:15, there are still no results. Meanwhile, the parents and children are still patiently milling about outside. Shirley feels terrible because she says the poor always have to wait for things only to be disappointed. Today, she resolves, they won't be let down.

It is just weeks before the mayoral election. She calls Miss Cook again. "Would you mind giving me the Mayor's number," Shirley says sweetly. "You have the Mayor's number," Miss Cook replies. "No, I mean the Mayor's private number. We're going to have our picnic at Gracie Mansion, but I want to let the Mayor and Mrs. Lindsay know we're coming. It isn't polite to drop in without calling first."

There is silence at the other end of the line. "Oh, never mind," Shirley continues. "I'll call a friend of mine at the city desk at the Associated Press. They'll have the number." A few minutes later Miss Cook calls back to say that the man at the bus company is waking up his drivers and buses will be there by 12:20. At 12:15 two buses arrive.

Day care began in New York City during World War II. It was instituted to help mothers working in the war effort and was not intended to be a permanent city-financed service. In fact, Fiorello La Guardia, the then Mayor, believed that child care was not the proper function of the state. Nevertheless, after the war ended, mothers wanted the service to continue.

Mrs. Elinor Guggenheimer, the wealthy, civic-minded wife of a Wall Street lawyer, who only last June ran with Herman Badillo in the mayoralty primary as candidate for City Council president, led the effort in those postwar years to include day care in the city's welfare scheme. During the same period she also helped found, and for many years presided over, the Day Care Council of New York. The council, which now represents 113 city-funded centers, among them the Lexington Houses operation, was set up to guard day-care interests, particularly against the heavy-handed bureaucracy of the welfare department.

While the council is active in keeping day care moving with the times, it has not been notably enthusiastic about community control of day-care centers or about parents' boards. Mrs. Guggenheimer, however, is very much a supporter of community control and is an ardent supporter of the West 80th Street center's Dorothy Pitman. "I'll do everything I can to help her," Mrs. Guggenheimer says. Mrs. Pitman was recently elected head of a newly formed citywide committee of some 160 community-control groups, which want to open—or have already opened—day-care centers and which could become a rival to the more establishment-oriented Day Care Council. Like Mrs. Pitman's West 80th Street center, members of the new group will also demand D.S.S. funds completely on their own terms.

The Department of Social Services is the city's biggest agency, with 30,000 employes and an annual budget of $1.5 billion. Day care is only a small division within the D.S.S. Bureau of Child Welfare. Because the D.S.S. is large, it is also insensitive and inflexible. The peppery Mrs. Guggenheimer says, "It might just as well have retained the name Department of Welfare because it still doesn't see itself as providing a service."

The head of the department, Commissioner Jack R. Goldberg, a beleagured, gravel-voiced man, declares that he is sympathetic to community-control efforts and appreciates that, when such groups quarrel with the D.S.S. over standards, they are not trying to lower educational or safety standards but to raise them. "When it comes to puritan values about hard work and education, Dorothy Pitman is a hell of a lot more puritanical than you or I," Goldberg laughs.

But the Commissioner heads a bureaucratic monster that neither he nor anyone else can control. Slouched in the chair in his downtown office, he says, "What these community-control groups want boils down to a question of eggs and apples. They're both all right. There's enough need for more day care so that we ought to have as many as we can get." The $32,500-a-year Commissioner says he also favors Mrs. Pitman's all-parents board, though it was not until recently that the D.S.S. agreed to accept it.

The principle that such a board should be composed primarily of professionals in early-childhood education has always been justified on the grounds that parents cannot transcend their private role as parents in the greater interest of a center as a whole. Commissioner Goldberg believes this tradition is based on "a precious professional decision" and that there is no reason why parents can't run a center. Slowly he and Mrs. Pitman have worked out most of the issues that stand between West 80th Street and the D.S.S. money. One remaining issue is whether D.S.S. support should include the salary for Mrs. Pitman's position of Administrative Director, a post not directly involved in the educational program of the center.

Meantime, the D.S.S. has granted funds to the center through the end of this month. While negotiations have at times been hostile, they have always been peaceful. Mrs. Pitman, however, is ready to stage a noisy and dramatic confrontation any time that negotiations break down.

The West 80th Street Community center is, however, by no means alone in the world. Working full-time in its behalf is Bob Gangi, a young, white Columbia University graduate who took part in Robert Kennedy's Presidential campaign and describes himself as "a community worker and political activist." With the help of three white, college-educated volunteers in their twenties, Gangi runs the New York Action Corps, a small storefront operation up the street from the center. This organization grew out of the Kennedy Action Corps—Robert Kennedy's campaign workers assigned to deal with issues involving poor people. After the assassination, some Kennedy people wanted to keep the issues alive through community organizations and today there are other Action Corps in operation around the country.

The New York Action Corps' sole purpose at present is to help Mrs. Pitman's center obtain permanent D.S.S. money to get the Chinese restaurant successfully renovated as a suitable day-care center. With what he describes as considerable *chutzpa,* Gangi has approached some of the city's wealthier citizens known to have liberal political views and asked them to give money to the West 80th Street center. His efforts have brought the center over $300,000.

Because of Gangi's work, Mrs. Pitman has picked up a good deal of liberal political support or interest from influential politicians like State Senator Manfred Ohrenstein; Congressman William Ryan; Mrs. Ronnie Eldridge, newly appointed Special Assistant to the Mayor, and U. S. Senator Charles Goodell. Mrs. William Haddad, wife of the prominent liberal Democrat, and Mrs. John Lindsay, have visited the center. Gangi has also lined up an array of names from the liberal wing of the Beautiful People—many with fortunes behind them—who have shown interest, donated money or actively participated in helping the center, including actress Lauren Bacall, journalist Gloria Steinem, entertainer Phyllis Newman, City Councilman Carter Burden, former United Nations representative Marietta Tree and Kennedy brother-in-law Steve

Smith. Many of these came to a $100-a-head party in December given by Marietta Tree in her East Side town house to raise money for the new center. Violinist Isaac Stern—whose wife has donated the better part of the center's kitchen appliances—played at the party, which netted $8,000.

Like Dorothy Pitman, most community-control advocates among militant day-care groups are interested in "the total community." For a government agency which is financing such centers, whether it is a city government or a Federal agency, the results could be ironical. For the government agency could find itself in the position of paying for antiestablishment political activities. Commissioner Goldberg understands this very well, which is undoubtedly why he wants to exclude Mrs. Pitman from D.S.S. support. A shrewd student of politics, watching the day-care issue take shape from the sidelines, observes, "There is an aspect to this whole thing that has to do with issues beyond day care. These community-control leaders are interested in a whole community-organization effort, and they are really trying to build a power base. They have to have salaries, and many of them are looking for them in the Department of Social Service, or any government agency that will provide money. Their salaries would come out of the day-care center budgets. They want to legitimate their non-day-care activities, and also legitimate funds for themselves."

Mrs. Pitman, a tall, handsome Georgia-bred divorcee with an enormous mop of Afro hair, sits in the plainly furnished living room of her fifth-floor walk-up near the 80th Street center and tells why, for $150 a week gross and with two children to support, she works day and night organizing blacks and other poor people.

"I want to change the system so that Americans can have a chance to live," she says. "I don't feel all white Americans want to be killers of a dream. But racism is a way of life for most Americans." Her 9-year-old daughter comes into the room holding a puppy and sits down before the television set. She smiles at her daughter and continues. "I refuse to let it be a way of life for me any longer. I can't live without changing things for myself, for me and my kids."

She pauses to tell her daughter to take the puppy out for a walk. Then she says wryly, "You know, I think I can live without bureaucracy. I think most black people could, too. It is the real villain—bureaucracy is a way to exploit. I don't want my children to be stifled, to be the conformists that most schools turn out. I want them to be free. I'm just not going to let anyone govern my life or my kids. To hell with that."

THEY FOUND A "HOME" WHERE THE AGED DON'T FEEL AS IF THEY'VE BEEN "PUT AWAY"

by OLIVE EVANS

Donal McLaughlin is old: 95. He has a bright smile, moves quickly and has strong opinions about life and about growing old. When his wife died five years ago, he thought he could fend for himself. But his two sons were worried about him, and, he now admits, they were right.

"To tell the truth, after I cooked a meal, I didn't know what I'd had, how it tasted or anything. So I saw it this way: Sooner or later I will have to succumb to circumstances, and I will never have my home cooking again."

Mrs. Nancy Petty is old, too: 82. A serene and stately woman, she doesn't look her age. Some years ago she made the decision to plan for her later years. Her plans definitely did not include living with her family.

"I think grandmothers are lovely, but I don't think they should be a steady diet for anyone," she said.

Mr. McLaughlin and Mrs. Petty are among a minority—but a growing minority—of old people who have made an emotional adjustment to aging. Like more and more older people today, they planned with their families for the day when they would need help in coping with life.

Instead of the painful experience of being "put away," entering a "home" became a goal. They opted for a life-style that would keep them in the company of their contemporaries, in a loosely structured environment, institutional but affording some degree of privacy.

"More people are finding that this is a better answer than living by themselves or with their families," said William C. Fitch, executive director of the

National Council on Aging. "But the need is for more facilities that are not highly institutionalized, where people are treated as individuals."

Of equal importance, he said, is the need for facilities that people on reduced or retirement incomes can afford.

There are now more than 20 million people aged 65 and over in this country. Census Bureau projections put the figures at 23.5 million in 1970; 27.6 million in 1990, and close to 29 million in the year 2,000.

"Advances in medical care and services will increase the proportion of old people, and therefore there will be a growing need for a variety of facilities, some of which we haven't even invented yet," said Mrs. Rebecca Eckstein, the council's assistant director.

No one knows how many of the one million people now in the nation's 24,000 institutions for the aged are getting good care. Recurring testimony about conditions in many old-age and nursing homes has revealed callousness and cruelty to patients by employes, filthy conditions, poor food, understaffing and overcharging.

By comparison, conditions seem Utopian at the Isabella Geriatric Center, 501 West 190th Street in Manhattan.

"It's a stunning setting," said Mrs. Eckstein about the nonsectarian, voluntary and nonprofit complex of institutions housing the aged and the aged ill, and dealing with the problems of the aging.

A sentence on the blackboard of a lecture room contrasts sharply with the treatment in some other institutions described at recent hearings: "Nursing care must communicate to the patient his value as an individual, and his status as a family member and as a member of society."

Only occasionally, in the oldest of the buildings, is there a flavor of what was once called an "old folks' home." Today the term is "retirement residence." Several residents gathered recently in a pleasant, sunlit lounge that is used for television viewing.

At 75, Nicholas Bessaraboff Bodley is young by geriatric yardsticks. He's a White Russian with a patriarchal beard—a frail and gentle man. He is proud of the engineering degree he received in 1915 from the St. Petersburg Polytechnic Institute in Imperial Russia.

Two years ago Mr. Bodley's health failed, and the decision was made to enter a "home." A man of some reserve, he has taken rather well, it seems, to the community style of living at Isabella. His article "Who is Bodley?" appears in the current issue of "Chatterbox," a newsletter "by the residents for the residents."

In it, he writes about his beard, ". . . I am not a rabbi nor a Russian Orthodox priest, but a professional man who had to shave about 50 years every day. After retiring, I decided not to shave any more. Oh, what a blessed relief!''

Mr. Bodley has translated esoteric philosophical works from the Russian, produced a compendium of information on ancient European musical instruments for the Museum of Fine Arts in Boston, and for the American Journal of Archaeology wrote an article on the auloi, a clarinet-like instrument of ancient Greece and Egypt.

Asked if he would like to return to Russia, Mr. Bodley said with a grin, ''If I would go back . . .'' And he finished the sentence with a quick, incisive gesture, as though cutting off his head at the neck.

Like most of the residents, Mr. Bodley has his own room. Costs at Isabella House, the residence for the more self-sufficient, range from $376.15 a month for a single room to $522 for one, or $708 for two, in a suite. Residents there do light housekeeping and prepare their own breakfasts; the two other meals are served in the dining room.

At Isabella Home, which is for residents needing more attention, costs for an individual are $647 a month. In the infirmary, where 24-hour-a-day nursing care is available, the individual rate is $1,431 a month.

The need for privacy, a recurring theme among these elderly people, was expressed when Mr. Bodley described what he liked most about being at Isabella: ''I have a key,'' he said in his soft Russian accent, ''and for the nighttime, I am closing up.''

What Mr. Bodley did not say was that should he feel ill during the night, he has only to ring the bell at his bedside to bring assistance. It is this availability of care, if needed, that motivates many of those who seek admission to retirement homes.

''Being here makes your children feel safe for you,'' said Mrs. Nancy Petty. ''My daughter told me, 'It's so wonderful to know that if you push a button you have a nurse.' ''

A widow for 38 years, Mrs. Petty used to be housemother at a boys' school in New England. A woman of independence, when the time came to retire, there was no question in her mind.

''I have a wonderful daughter and a wonderful son, and they both wanted me to live with them. But it's hard to mix up so many ages of people. I think you're so apt to infringe on your grandchildren's liberties. After all, I know a good deal more than they do,'' she added with a wink. ''Being apart keeps a love alive that might not have survived the test.''

Mrs. Petty thus highlighted today's changed life-style. Although it is not uncommon for four generations of a family to be alive at the same time, no longer do they live under the same roof.

"The three-generation family is gone, socially, financially and physically. The trend is toward nonfamily existence, so we have to do something about old people. The question is what," said Dr. Michael Dacso, who is dean of the Institute of Health Sciences at Hunter College and professor of rehabilitation and community medicine at Mt. Sinai School of Medicine. He is also a specialist in geriatrics.

"I love old people and I hate to see them in 'zoos' or on 'reservations,' " he said. He strongly favors keeping the aged in the community, so that they are not "isolated."

Mrs. Bertha Greenberg, however, finds herself not at all isolated at the Isabella Center. "It's been a year and a half of sheer bliss," she said.

After a lifetime as mistress of her own home and 12 years in a career, she went to live with her daughter and son-in-law. "I was dying of loneliness. I was happy as far as my daughter and her family were concerned, but it was being alone so much. I crocheted, read or played solitaire, but it was no good." Mrs. Greenberg arranged to enter the Isabella Home. Now she meets a variety of people her own age.

"I couldn't go back to the other life," she said. "There is a certain freedom here. . . . I can't explain it."

"My family was worried so they put me in a home," Bella Breger, 89, said in a voice firm and matter-of-fact, implying that she, too, thought it was a pretty good idea. Miss Breger was a social worker, a colleague of Jane Addams and Lillian Wald, pioneers in the field, so she understands well the problems of aging.

"It's not a bad life," she said from the wheelchair in which she spends much of her time.

Why did Dr. John Hastings enter?

"I was 90 years old," he said. And that, it seemed, was reason enough for the former City College professor of geography.

Mrs. Joseph Jablonower, a former teacher, had good things to say about her volunteer work as a tutor at the center, where residents help out in the infirmary or tutor staff members who may need some educational brushing-up.

Miss Arpie Shelton, director of this program, discussed its value as part of the total purpose of a geriatric center.

"You feel safe and you have something useful to do with the rest of your life," she said. "The system has set a time when you are old—65—and is wholly artificial."

No matter how benign the environment, entering a "home" is a radical change at a time of life when change is least easy to accept. Adjustment to the change is a measure of the individual's total emotional health.

As Mr. McLaughlin put it, ''Self-pity is the biggest disease we have here. Everybody tells you what a beautiful home he had. . . . You have to fight it.''

THE TERRIFYING HOMOSEXUAL WORLD OF THE JAIL SYSTEM

by LINDA CHARLTON

"It's definitely a homosexual world," said a man whose years as a prison inmate qualify him to speak with authority.

He was speaking about correctional institutions in New York State, but it could have been anywhere. Homosexual assault was among the many miseries prisoners in several New York City institutions said made their lives unbearable when they rebelled last year against the conditions of their confinement.

It is a problem that is persisting. William vanden Heuvel, chairman of the New York City Board of Correction, said after a recent visit to the city's adolescent remand shelter that "the younger prisoners expressed concern" about the dangers of sexual assault. The board is a citizens' group reactivated last year to serve as a voice of public conscience.

One of the board's 51 recommendations for improving the city's "correctional institutions"—most of which are in theory short-term detention centers but in practice places of confinement for many weeks and months—was that the State Legislature pass pending legislation that would allow a "furlough policy" for both those awaiting trial, who make up the bulk of the city's inmates, and for sentenced prisoners.

Such a policy would mean that prisoners would be allowed weekends at home. Mr. vanden Heuvel, among others, believes this would "help in the whole problem of administering prisons," both because it would permit the relief of the "sexual tensions of prison life," in Mr. vanden Heuvel's words, and allow a man in prison to retain something of his normal relationship with his family, with the world to which he must return sooner or later.

Many former inmates and criminologists find this indirect effect of the distorted sexuality of prison life even more disturbing than the immediate brutality of rape in shadowed corners of stairways and shower rooms. Quite simply, the distorted sexuality serves to widen the distance between prison society and the world outside. Some prisoners, particularly those young people who spent their preadolescent and adolescent years in such a society, may have their sexual definition affected for life.

But homosexuality, some believe, is endemic to any prison in which men and women are segregated by sex.

"Even the best wardens in the best prisons cannot cope with this problem," wrote Clyde B. Vedder and Patricia G. King in *Problems of Homosexuality in Corrections*. The authors asserted, "It cannot be eliminated in such unwholesome surroundings."

The "problem" is not that of homosexuality for those who chose it. Known homosexuals are segregated in all detention centers and prisons. The problem, rather, is the routine of sexual assault, of the stronger preying on the weaker, that horrified many readers of Jean Genet, the French novelist, and shocked theatergoers when it was detailed in a 1967 off-Broadway play, *Fortune and Men's Eyes*.

The situation in prisons has been well-publicized, but quickly forgotten, in real life, too. Andrea Dworkin, 18 years old in 1965, was a Bennington College student who spent five days in the Women's House of Detention, in Greenwich Village, after her arrest during a peace demonstration outside the United Nations headquarters building. She said:

"The homosexuality was rampant and pretty hard to take. It was orgies all the time and the sex play was constant. There were hands all over me all the time."

A 1968 report on sexual assaults in the Philadelphia prison system estimated that about 2,000 occurred during a two-year period—and that almost every young man of less than husky build was approached sexually within hours of his arrival.

"He comes in there, he's small, he's frail, he's cute, and after you're in prison awhile, you know, boys start looking much cuter," said a 30-year-old man who spent many of his first 20 years in correctional institutions.

It is "these young kids," he said, who are victimized, forced into homosexual acts at first by threats or violence or promises of small benefits. "Me and another fellow got the guy in the dormitory that night and propositioned him, which was no problem since by this time he liked what he was doing," he said.

From several other ex-prisoners interviewed came similar stories: mock "weddings" between two inmates, with a third serving as "parson"; sexual rivalries flaring up murderously; guards accepting bribes to ignore secret meetings or becoming participants themselves—a world in which, said one former inmate, "the abnormal things you get to accept as normal."

From these conversations there also emerged the feeling that many prisoners were even more disturbed by the potential destructiveness, in a less tangible form than that of physical abuse, of what one prisoner called this "warped environment." It was a feeling that the pervasively homosexual atmosphere only served to increase a prisoner's alienation from the world to which, in theory, he was being prepared to return.

To Gilbert L. Geis, a criminologist, this is "what makes it [homosexuality] a problem"—it is one of many factors in the prison environment that makes the environment an infantile one, in which "the individual is deprived of any kind of indication that he is strong, masculine (or feminine), worthwhile. . . ."

For Dr. Geis, "probably the most devastating aspect of the entire correctional system" is that, again in theory, it tries "to put an individual back into society, where the essence of his success is his ability to make reasonable choices, but his training [in prison] is bereft of the opportunity to make choices."

A prison, says Dr. Geis—and the ex-inmates agreed—"ought to, as much as possible, duplicate the real world." And in the real world, there is a range of sexual choice. In prison, however, there is officially only a denial of sexuality, including, in most institutions, regulations against masturbation, which Dr. Geis sees as typifying "the broader denial of humanity."

In addition, "to the extent that anybody's an involuntary victim," the prison-homosexuality pattern "is harmful in that it establishes an ethic of force . . . [and] creates within the prison an atmosphere of differentiation between the values of the custody staff and the inmates," said Dr. Geis, a professor of sociology at the California State College in Los Angeles.

But what is to be done to change the situation? The system of "conjugal visits"—allowing prisoners to spend a few hours alone with their wives, explicitly for sexual purposes, is in force in only one institution in this country, the Parchman Prison Farm in Mississippi.

And it is a concept that all the ex-prisoners interviewed found distasteful. "I think that's the reverse answer," said one, "because there you're dehumanizing the wife along with the husband or vice versa."

More appealing to them is the concept of allowing prisoners weekend passes for visits with their wives, now being tried experimentally at two institutions in California.

In Dr. Geis's words, the conjugal-visit system is "just too blatant" for most people to accept. "I think weekend leaves are much more the answer. The stuff we've got out of Norway [where such a system has been in effect for some time] is that they all come back. Still Norway is not New York City. . . ."

The present "solution" is largely a matter of policing the jails to prevent sexual assaults, placing three men in a cell instead of two. New institutions are being designed so that guards keep as close a watch on prisoners as possible, particularly at night.

As for the experiments in allowing prisoners leaves, Al Castro, spokesman for the city's Correction Department, commented, "I would say that in the future we will have this."

But for the present, he said, all prison systems are "caught" in the complexities of the problem.

Since prison homosexuality is so much a product of the prison system, from the concept of deprivation to the actual physical design of prisons, many experts regard as unlikely that the situation will change until the system does.

"FAMILY" OF 270 FOR-SAKES COAST FOR A TENNESSEE HOLLOW

by GEORGE VECSEY

PEGRAM, TENNESSEE—This quiet hollow in middle Tennessee is a long way from the windy hills of San Francisco, both in mileage and in style. But a "family" of 270 persons has traveled here from San Francisco with the hope of "slowing things down, getting back to the land," according to its leader.

More than 60 brightly painted buses and campers are parked on a farm here, with long-haired men and their women scurrying about, building bridges, planting seeds, removing debris.

Led by Stephen Gaskin, a former college teacher and now the "spiritual adviser," the group is living together for the first time after being scattered all over the San Francisco area. They hope to pursue their vegetarian, nonpolitical and "religious" movement permanently in this area and believe they are setting an example for others.

"We traveled all over the country, from October to February, and when we got back to San Francisco we realized that time was over," said Lawrence (last names are not used by the family). "We remembered how much we liked Tennessee and we wanted to settle here."

The people of the area have apparently accepted their new neighbors. Public officials have offered their services. Sheriff Dorris Wakely has labeled them "a fine bunch of people." The Methodist Women's Club has requested a talk on four-person marriages. And old-timers continually visit to offer farming tips.

"It's a groove," said Stephen, tall and slender, with hair hanging down below his shoulders. "We feel all kinds of positive juices here. Everybody is cool. We feel we've got a lot in common with the fundamental religious people here. They don't believe in vanity and neither do we. That's why we don't cut our hair."

A constant parade of friendly curiosity seekers led the family to close off its property except for Sundays. But some visitors are still welcome. A middle-aged worker named Davidson drove his pick-up truck all the way from Mobile, Alabama, yesterday "because I've thought a lot about it and this might be a thing of the future."

After chatting amiably with Lawrence for an hour, Mr. Davidson turned around and drove back to Mobile, saying he had "learned a lot."

The family is living on a 590-acre farm owned by Gene Campbell, owner of a Nashville construction company. But after putting down a $2,000 deposit, with 30 days to make the $50,000 down payment on the $150,000 farm, Stephen and his advisers realized that there were only 38 acres of tillable land instead of the 250 Mr. Campbell had promised. So the group did not expect to purchase the Campbell farm but would continue to look in this area.

"We've already made friends with the sheriff in Ashland City," Stephen explained.

Members of the family, many of them former professionals and most of them college-educated, have pooled their resources—$40 here, $900 there, all apparently given freely—and come up with an estimated total of $50,000. More money comes from the sale of a book, *Monday Night Classes,* which has sold 18,000 copies, according to Stephen, and is in a third printing of 25,000 copies.

The book is an outgrowth of lectures given by Stephen in the late nineteen-sixties while he was evolving from English teacher at San Francisco State to his preaching, leadership role with the family. He used to draw up to 2,000 listeners at rock auditoriums on Monday nights.

"It's not a new religion," said Arax, another member. "All religions have basically the same ideas. Love your neighbor. As you sow, so you shall reap. But when Stephen talks, a white light flows in the room. I've seen it myself."

The lecture series had to move when the rock ballrooms began dying several years ago.

"We outlived rock and roll," said Stephen. "We're really not into music any more. A few of our people play their guitars, but we're not plugged into mass music. It's all a-hype. It's commercial."

With the small communes scattered all over the Bay Area, Stephen had thought of his disciples as "a village that met once a week." But late last year, he set up a caravan to explore the mood of the country.

"One sheriff in Oregon checked us out for dope," Stephen said. "He felt we were clean and he felt our vibrations and he called ahead and said, 'These folks are all right. Don't hassle them.' After that we never got hassled."

They returned to San Francisco in February, expecting to settle down again.

"We drove down Montgomery Street—that's the stock-market area—in our buses and nobody seemed to notice us," Stephen said. "We realized that most of the United States wasn't like San Francisco—with its old Barbary Coast tradition, nudie movies, 750,000 people packed into 36 square miles. Then two oil tankers collided in the harbor and the sea gulls started dying on the beaches. We stayed there two weeks and we split."

Now the family is in Tennessee, growing all the time. Ten children have been born since October, with the help of a Mexican *Rural Midwives Handbook* and the skill of Margaret, who forms a four-person marriage with Stephen, Michael and Ina May.

There are 14 such marriages in the group, as Ina May explained to the Methodist Women's Club, whose members she has found to be "friendly and interested" and even intuitive into the possibilities of larger marriages. Family members talk enthusiastically of the sharing of problems and the greater stability in a four-way relationship.

The 42 children, who range from 2½ weeks to 12 years old, know their individual parents but responsibility is shared, as it was the other day when the women taught the children to make bread while the men cleared rocks and built a wood bridge over a rushing stream.

Most members are from the East and West Coast cities, but a few have farm backgrounds, while others have picked up knowledge of camping and farming. There is no medical experience except for Margaret's midwifing, but members say they are in excellent health because they eat vegetables and nuts and avoid meat.

"This is how we want to live," Stephen said. "We are not dropouts. We are a community. We practice a kind of householding yogi. Our daily life is our spiritual practice. We feel we have something special—and we feel we have a lot to share with people. The vibrations are good in Tennessee."

SUGGESTED READING

ON OVER-ALL TRENDS

Joseph Bensman and Arthur J. Vidich, *The New American Society*, Chicago, Quadrangle, 1971.

Constance McLaughlin Green, *The Secret City: A History of Race Relations in the Nation's Capital*, Princeton, Princeton University Press, 1967 (paperback).

Oscar Handlin, *The Uprooted*, New York, Grosset & Dunlap, 1951 (paperback).

August Meier and Elliott Rudwick, *From Plantation to Ghetto*, New York, Hill and Wang, 1970 (paperback).

Lewis Mumford, *The Culture of Cities*, New York, Harcourt, Brace, Jovanovich, 1966 (paperback).

Gilbert Osofsky, *Harlem: The Making of a Ghetto*, New York, Harper and Row, 1971 (paperback).

Robert E. Park and Ernest W. Burgess, *The City*, Chicago, University of Chicago Press, 1967 (paperback).

Henri Pirenne, *Medieval Cities: Their Origins and the Revival of Trade*, Princeton, Princeton University Press, 1925.

Arthur Meier Schlesinger, *The Rise of the City*, Chicago, Quadrangle, 1933 (paperback).

Richard Sennett, *Classic Essays on the Culture of Cities*, New York, Appleton-Century-Crofts, 1970 (paperback).

Gideon Sjoberg, *The Pre-Industrial Society*, New York, Free Press, 1960.

Maurice Stein, *The Eclipse of Community*, revised ed., Princeton, Princeton University Press, 1971 (paperback).

Arthur J. Vidich and Joseph Bensman, *Small Town in Mass Society*, Princeton, Princeton University Press, 1968.

Max Weber, *The City*, Glencoe, Illinois, Free Press, 1958 (paperback).

Lee J. Cary, ed., *Community Development as a Process*, Columbia, University of Missouri Press, 1972.

John J. Palen and Karl H. Flaming, eds., *Urban America: Conflict and Change*, New York, Holt, Rinehart, and Winston, 1972 (paperback).

John Walton and Donald E. Carns, *Cities in Change: Studies on the Urban Condition*, Boston, Allyn and Bacon, 1973.

James F. Short, Jr., ed., *The Social Fabric of the Metropolis: Contributions of the Chicago School of Urban Sociology,* Chicago, University of Chicago Press, 1972.

Max Birnbaum and John Mogey, eds., *Social Change in Urban America,* New York, Harper and Row, 1972.

Sandor Halebsky, *The Sociology of the City,* New York, Scribner's, 1972.

T. Chandler and G. Fox, *3000 Years of Urban Growth,* New York, Seminar Press, 1973.

ON METROPOLITAN SUB-COMMUNITIES AND CULTURES

Cleveland Amory, *The Proper Bostonians,* New York, Dutton, 1947 (paperback).

E. Digby Baltzell, *Philadelphia Gentlemen: The Making of a National Upper Class,* New York, Free Press, 1958 (paperback).

Bennett Berger, *Working Class Suburb,* Berkeley and Los Angeles, University of California Press, 1969 (paperback).

Nathaniel Burt, *The Perennial Philadelphians,* Boston, Little, Brown, 1963.

Saul Feldman and Gerald Thielbar, eds. *Life Styles: Diversity in American Society,* Boston, Little, Brown, 1972.

E. Franklin Frazier, *Black Bourgeoisie,* New York, Free Press, 1957 (paperback).

Herbert Gans, *The Levittowners,* New York, Random House, 1967 (paperback).

Cesar Grana, *Bohemian Versus Bourgeois,* New York, Basic Books, 1964.

Ulf Hannerz, *Soulside: Inquiries into Ghetto Culture and Community,* New York, Columbia University Press, 1969 (paperback).

Elliot Liebow, *Tally's Corner: A Study of Negro Street Corner Men,* Boston, Little, Brown, 1967 (paperback).

Ferdinand Lundberg, *The Rich and the Superrich,* New York, Bantam, 1969 (paperback).

Robert S. Lynd and Helen M. Lynd, *Middletown in Transition,* New York, Harcourt, Brace & World, 1937 (paperback).

C. Wright Mills, *White Collar: The American Middle Classes,* New York, Oxford University Press, 1951 (paperback).

John R. Seeley, Alexander Sim, and Elizabeth W. Loosely, *Crestwood Heights,* New York, Basic Books, 1956 (paperback).

Arthur Shostak, *Blue Collar Life,* New York, Random House, 1969 (paperback).

A. C. Spectorsky, *The Ex-Urbanites,* Philadelphia, Lippincott, 1955 (paperback).

Caroline F. Ware, *Greenwich Village 1920–1930,* New York, Harper and Row, 1965 (paperback).

William H. Whyte, *The Organization Man,* New York, Doubleday, 1957 (paperback).

Tom Wolfe, *Radical Chic and Mau-Mauing the Flak Catchers,* New York, Bantam, 1971 (paperback).

Harvey Zorbaugh, *The Gold Coast and the Slum,* Chicago, University of Chicago Press, 1929.

Dennis P. Sobin, *The Future of the American Suburbs: Survival or Extinction,* Port Washington, New York, Kennikat Press, 1972.

Nathan Kantrowitz, *Ethnic and Racial Segregation Patterns in the New York Metropolis,* New York, Praeger, 1972.

Howard M. Bahr and Theodore Caplow, *Old Men Drunk and Sober,* New York, New York University Press, 1973.

David Dawley, *A Nation of Lords,* New York, Doubleday Anchor, 1973 (paperback).

John Kramer, ed., *North American Suburbs: Politics, Diversity, and Change,* Berkeley, The Glendessary Press, 1973.

ON ETHNIC COMMUNITIES

St. Clair Drake and Horace B. Cayton, *Black Metropolis: A Study of Negro Life in a Northern City,* New York, Harcourt, Brace & World, 1970 (paperback).

Nathan Glazer and Daniel P. Moynihan, *Beyond the Melting Pot,* second ed., Cambridge, Mass., M.I.T. Press, 1970 (paperback).

William Moore, Jr., *The Vertical Ghetto,* New York, Random House, 1969 (paperback).

Elena Padilla, *Up from Puerto Rico,* New York, Columbia University Press, 1958.

Solomon Poll, *The Hasidic Community of Williamsburg,* New York, Free Press, 1962 (paperback).

Gerald D. Suttles, *The Social Order of the Slum: Ethnic Territory in the Inner City,* Chicago, University of Chicago Press, 1968 (paperback).

Dan Wakefield, *Island in the City: Puerto Ricans in New York,* New York, Corinth Books, 1960 (paperback).

William F. Whyte, *Street Corner Society,* Chicago, University of Chicago Press, 1961 (paperback).

Humbert S. Nelli, *The Italians in Chicago, 1880–1930: A Study in Mobility,* New York, Oxford University Press, 1973.

Jack O. Waddell and O. Michael Watson, *The American Indian in Urban Society,* Boston, Little, Brown, 1972.

ON TENSIONS AS A SOURCE OF COMMUNITY CONFLICT AND INTEGRATION

Nicholas Alex, *Black in Blue: A Study of the Negro Policeman,* New York, Appleton-Century-Crofts, 1969 (paperback).

Edward C. Banfield, *The Unheavenly City,* Boston, Little, Brown, 1968 (paperback).

Robert Bendiner, *The Politics of Schools,* New York, New American Library, 1969 (paperback).

Paul Bullock, ed., *The Aftermath: By the People of Watts,* New York, Grove Press, 1970.

Kenneth B. Clark, *Dark Ghetto,* New York, Harper, 1965 (paperback).

Otto Kerner (chairman), *Report of the National Advisory Commission on Civil Disorders,* Bantam, 1968 (paperback).

Gerald Levy, *Ghetto School,* New York, Pegasus, 1970 (paperback).

David Rogers, *110 Livingstone Street: Politics and Bureaucracy in the New York City School System,* New York, Random House, 1969.

Jerome H. Skolnick, *The Politics of Protest,* New York, Ballantine Books, 1969 (paperback).

Lewis Yablonski, *The Violent Gang,* Baltimore, Penguin, 1970 (paperback).

Herman R. Lantz, *A Community in Search of Itself,* Carbondale, Southern Illinois University Press, 1973.

Leonard Gordon, *A City in Racial Crisis: The Case of Detroit Pre- and Post- the 1967 Riot,* Dubuque, William C. Brown Co., (paperback).

Rubin, Lillian, *Busing and Backlash: White Against White in an Urban School District,* Berkeley, University of California Press, 1972.

Joyce E. Williams, *Black Community Control: A Study of Transition in a Texas Ghetto,* New York, Praeger, 1973.

ON NEW COMMUNITY FORMS

Edward C. Banfield and Martin Meyerson, *Politics, Planning and the Public Interest,* New York, Free Press, 1955 (paperback).

Joseph Bensman, *Dollars and Sense,* New York, Macmillan, 1967.

Lewis S. Feuer, *The Conflict of Generations,* New York, Basic Books, 1969.

Irving Coffman, *Asylums,* New York, Doubleday, 1961 (paperback).

Rosabeth M. Kantor, *Commitment and Community: Utopias and Communes in*

Sociological Perspective, Cambridge, Mass., Harvard University Press, 1972.

Steven Kelman, *Push Comes to Shove: The Escalation of Student Protest,* Boston, Houghton Mifflin, 1970.

Albert Parry, *Garrets and Pretenders: A History of Bohemians in America,* New York, Dover, 1960 (paperback).

Bernard Rosenberg and Norris Fliegal, *The Vanguard Artist,* Chicago, Quadrangle, 1965.

Marvin B. Scott, *The Racing Game,* Chicago, Aldine, 1968.

Charles E. Silberman, *Crisis in Black and White,* New York, Random House, 1964 (paperback).

Gresham Sykes, *The Society of Captives,* Princeton, Princeton University Press, 1964.

Carol A. B. Warren, *Identity and Community in the Gay World,* New York, Wiley-Interscience, 1974.

INDEX